LAND
AND THE
ENVIRONMENT
PLANNING IN
CALIFORNIA
TODAY

Prepared by
    SEDWAY/COOKE
    Urban and Environmental Planners and Designers
    San Francisco, California

Research Consultants:
    I. Michael Heyman
    Richard J. Fink

Other Contributors:
    Donald Gralnek
    Donald McBride
    Susan Pflueger
    Richard Recht

Planning and Conservation Foundation:
    Bill Press, *Executive Director*

LAND

AND THE ENVIRONMENT

PLANNING IN CALIFORNIA TODAY

Prepared for the Planning and Conservation Foundation
by SEDWAY/COOKE

Published 1975 by
William Kaufmann, Inc.

Library of Congress Cataloging in Publication Data

Sedway/Cooke (Firm)
  Land and the environment.

      A companion volume, by the California Land-Use Task
Force, was published simultaneously under title: The
California land.
  Includes index.
  1. Regional planning—Law and legislation—California.
I. Planning and Conservation Foundation. II. Title.
KFC810.S4   346′.794′045   75-19409
ISBN 0-913232-21-1

Printed in the United States of America by Banta West.
Composition by Holmes Composition Service.
Cover by Gabriele von Rabenau.
Design by John Beyer.

CONTENTS

INTRODUCTION

The assumption of many California planners and government officials is no longer whether the state's land use planning framework should be overhauled, but when and how the changes will be made. That assumption is accompanied by a deep frustration about the way things are done in the planning and allocation of land.

These attitudes are both salutary and hazardous. They are healthy in heralding change, although the nature of such change is unclear. Whatever the nature of the "new mood" in California about land use, the restructuring of state planning law, processes and institutions has yet to find suitable legislative expression. And therein lies the danger: a frustration which is hazardous because too many planners, elected officials and concerned citizens appear too receptive to a quick and easy transformation of California's planning law, institutions and intergovernmental relationships. Too many facile recipes abound, based upon superficial and fragmentary information and upon the confusion of effect with cause or basic malfunctions.

The process by which change is introduced can be as important as the nature of the information and critical insights needed for making informed judgements about the state's land use planning laws, processes and institutions. It seeks to convey a significant portion of the knowledge needed to provide the basis for a systematic process of change.

Four premises pervade this study. The first is that the concerned citizen of California needs to know enough about the state's land use related planning laws, processes and institutions to recognize their relative strengths and inadequacies. To do this, a straightforward, non-legalistic format is used which hopefully neither patronizes nor oversimplifies. The second premise is that some determinants of land use and environmental quality in California realistically must be seen as givens and viewed as a whole, crossing artificial state, regional and local distinctions. The third premise is that the current state of performance in planning at state, regional and local levels needs a hard, critical and open assessment. Given radical disparities between the planning law and actual planning practice, these assessments are essential. There is, however, a difference between being critical and being negative. The authors are both optimistic and critical because they believe that the most powerful change agent is information. The fourth premise is that change is overdue. Accordingly, alternate models for planning institutions and processes are presented as points of departure for constructive action.

This report makes no claim for total comprehensiveness. Land use planning influences almost every facet of public and private activity; conversely, literally hundreds of state laws and agencies have some effect on land use planning and decision-making. This report surveys and comments on those planning aspects which are most pervasive, direct in their influence or in need of change. In cases where emphasis had to be given, state-wide planning programs were accorded prominence over regional or local concerns.

The report does not attempt to cover laws or agencies which are not pertinent to the planning processes in the state, such as agencies engaged solely in development, land management, etc. Additionally, the performance of some agencies was not assessed where there were no firm conclusions which could be drawn, where a new agency had no "track record", or where the descriptive material was self-explanatory. Research was completed in January 1975.

The organization of this report has been determined so that the reader may first gain an understanding of the major forces at work which have influenced, and many of which may be expected to continue to influence, land use patterns and change. The report then covers the multitude of crucial laws and agencies operative in the field of land use and environmental planning in the state. The concluding section conveys summary findings and some generalized options for change. Because of the more technical and detailed nature of the material in Chapter Two on planning law and performance, that section includes detailed footnotes as a useful reference for the reader interested in further technical amplification.

An inclusive report inevitably reflects the efforts and insights of many persons as well as contributions from many sources. The statutory analysis and planning process assessment of Chapter Two reflects the efforts of several contributors. Until his appointment as Vice Chancellor of the University of California at Berkeley, Professor I. Michael Heyman was in charge of the legal research and was assisted by Catherine Silak, research assistant. Subsequent research was undertaken by Richard J. Fink, instructor at Boalt Hall Law School, University of California at Berkeley, and John Weld, Walter Rask and William So, of Sedway/Cooke. The overview of factors influencing land use decision-making in California in Chapter One is based in part upon papers submitted by Richard Recht of McDonald & Smart, Inc., Susan Pflueger, Donald Gralnek, and Donald McBride, as well as Allan Lind of Sedway/Cooke.

In addition, the input of many others is gratefully acknowledged. Bill Press, Executive Director of the Planning and Conservation Foundation, and his staff provided invaluable administrative help. Many representatives of public agencies gave graciously of their time, perspective and keen insights about planning process and performance. Their frank appraisals of the performance of other, and indeed of their own, agencies were most illuminating. Members of the California Land Use Task Force provided useful input both in terms of content clarification and emphasis. Richard Wilson, Planning and Conservation Foundation President and Chairman of the Task Force was most supportive throughout this study.

Paul H. Sedway
Sedway/Cooke
San Francisco, California

Chapter One

CALIFORNIA PLANNING:

BACKGROUND AND INFLUENCES

Of all the pressing environmental problems, those associated with land use patterns seem most intractable. Air, water, noise, and visual pollution control goals appear achievable within a reasonable span of years given adequate determination, resources and modification of lifestyles. However, unwise and outmoded land use patterns, represent a wholly different kind of problem for human and natural environments. As a practical matter, the environmental effects of existing land uses are seldom reversible because of irreparable damage to the land itself or the staggering financial, social and governmental problems involved with revitalizing existing urban areas and infrastructure. At best, the achievement of quality goals for the use and reuse of land in central city, suburban and rural environments is a long term strategy.

If current population forecasts prove accurate, California's population will double within 45 years—resulting in far more than a doubling of already very serious and unresolved land use problems and conflicts. And if that future seems unimaginable, it is made more ominous by the absence of credible policies for renewing and reusing the built environment or for channeling inexorable development forces into viable growth centers. Unfortunately, there is no coherent comprehensive planning process in California, and certainly not one capable of forthrightly addressing the economic, social, governmental, environmental and political tradeoffs to be made. The purpose of this section, then, is to overview some of the facts and figures, and the governmental, economic and social factors which influence land use decision-making in California.

A. THE CALIFORNIA SETTING

The most distinctive feature of California's changing environment until recently was its continuing population growth. The most distinctive feature today is its urban character.

California already has one of the most urbanized populations of any state in the nation. Of a population of over 20 million, more than 80 percent live in and around the major cities, in what the Bureau of the Census calls "urbanized areas." Fully 92 percent of the state's population (according to the 1970 Census) is located within the 16 standard metropolitan statistical areas. (These statistical areas, or SMSAs, follow county boundaries and so include a good deal of rural land.) In addition, the bulk of the population, as well as the lion's share of the growth, have been located in five SMSAs of Southern California. Income and housing opportunities will determine the extent to which current patterns of urbanization continue. Modernization of state planning processes and institutions will determine the modifiability of these trends.

The term "urbanization" suggests high density central city areas, overrun with highrise buildings, ceaseless traffic and hordes of people. Because of this misleading terminology, it would be more accurate to characterize the state's population as being "suburbanized," because suburbanization has been the dominant form of land development in the post-World War II era. This development has consisted primarily of subdivisions of single-family detached homes on the fringes of the existing urban areas.

The impacts of urban growth have been fairly well documented at the national level by a number of studies. Increased population, westward migration patterns and, until fairly recently, increasing incomes have combined to create the familiar pattern of urban sprawl and have been blamed for the physical decay and social disruption of the central cities. Unfortunately, however, similar documentation is virtually non-existent for California alone. Even straightforward demographic analyses are difficult to locate, generally sketchy and always rapidly dated. (The development of adequate data bases and analyses should be a primary concern of future state planning). Nevertheless, near universal perception of staggering environmental problems in the state has already generated substantial popular support for protection of coastal, open space and natural resources. However, the relationship between generally rural, endangered land with significant environmental values and evolving urban patterns is not widely appreciated.

When speaking of the environmental and land use problems in California, attention usually focuses on the state's vast and incomparable coastline, mountains, open space and prime agricultural lands. The high esteem in which they are held only intensifies reaction to their indiscriminate commercial exploitation. But even this reaction is diminished by the true magnitude of the loss of these valuable resources. During the past two decades, California has lost approximately 15–20,000 acres of "highly productive agricultural land" per year to urban uses. By 1985, 620,000 acres of currently cultivated prime agricultural land will be urbanized, with an additional 446,000 acres of potential prime agricultural land similarly lost to development. The situation is even more critical in certain rapidly urbanizing areas such as the Santa Clara Valley where almost one-half of the agricultural land may be converted to urban uses by 1985. Similarly, subdivision for recreational purposes (sometimes for "pie in the sky" investment schemes) has gobbled up over half a million acres of the state's open space. Even open space contained in government reserves (such as national forests) is not immune to practices which destroy the natural resource values that are supposedly being protected. Voracious logging practices destroy wildlife habitats, causing excessive soil erosion and stream pollution, and frequently make the land unsuitable for subsequent economic forestation. Logging on private lands may also seriously degrade public lands, as has occurred in the vicinity of the Redwood National Park.

Not only are prime agricultural and recreation lands being lost to economic exploitation, but other open space values are threatened as well. These include the utility of open space as watershed and aquifer recharge areas, pollution cleaning airsheds and flood control lands. The conversion of open space to urban uses invites landslides, forest fires and land subsidence from excessive ground water withdrawal. The latter is especially critical, because once land has subsided, the capacity of the aquifer has been permanently reduced, thus prohibiting any restoration of a valuable resource.

Of greater significance than the facts and figures of open space losses is the attitude of California's concerned citizens toward growth and development issues. Many California metropolitan regions are now actively questioning the traditional "growth and progress" ethic. Most importantly, land use regulatory powers are being employed to control residential development in the interest of more compact and environmentally sensitive land use patterns. Similar citizen concern can be found throughout California, including the "Save the Bay" movement (which resulted in the San Francisco Bay Conservation and Development Commission) and the Proposition 20-initiated Coastal Zone Conservation Act.

The various encroachments on open space and agricultural lands, however, are symptomatic of land exploitation pressures arising with the state's population growth and economic development. The operative function here is the process of urbanization. Urban expansion itself exploits the land, but what it represents—more economic production and consumption—extends its influence far beyond the boundaries of California's metropolitan areas. The importance of urban areas from a planning standpoint needs to be emphasized, because the consequences of economic and social decisions are considerably more permanent and irrevocable for cities than for non-developed areas. The artifacts of the urban landscape are buildings, roads and other infrastructure. These structures represent huge investments of scarce resources and nearly immutable commitments to certain types of human environments, commitments which are as a practical matter not reversible except at extreme costs.

The state's urbanized areas can be viewed environmentally both as pollution sources and pollution sinks. As noted above, the process of urbanization represents the primary assault on valuable open space and agricultural and other natural resources. But more importantly, activities in urban areas generate most of the air, visual, noise and water pollution and solid waste to be found in the state. Thus, except where pollutants can be transported outside their area of generation (as, for example, sewage in the Tahoe Basin or garbage in a number of cities), the pollution source area is also the pollution sink. Accordingly, California's metropolitan areas are the location of the most treacherous environmental problems because the dense urban populations are subject to very significant pollutant exposures. Furthermore, the trends discussed below suggest that the social and economic groups least able to compensate for a polluted environment are the ones most burdened by urban pollution.

Recent growth and development in California have taken the familiar form of suburbanization—the creation of extensive low-density housing subdivisions, industrial parks, commercial centers and miles and miles of streets and highways. Though suburbanization usually connotes "flight-from-the-city," vacant land on the fringes of already built-up areas is the only land that can accommodate the state's population growth. Studies indicate that the majority of the residents of the state's suburbs

were born out-of-state or in other suburban-type areas. Nonetheless, the "flight-to-the-suburbs" theory does validly suggest the social and economic segregation that has characterized the recent development of the state's cities and towns. While minority groups have not come to predominate in major California cities as has happened in the East, the state's metropolitan areas have followed the common national pattern indicated by the decline of white, middle-class households as major components of the central city population. The result has been that the demand for public services in the central cities has increased, while the ability of the population to pay for them has fallen. In Los Angeles between 1960 and 1970 for instance, the nonwhite proportion of the population grew from 27 percent to 41 percent, with the proportion in poverty reaching as high as 21 percent for some groups.

Associated with these trends has been the deterioration of the "physical plant" of the cities (e.g., 60 percent of the housing in San Francisco's Chinatown is substandard) the decline of central business districts, the loss of employment (especially blue collar) from high unemployment areas to the suburbs, the decline of schools and services, and the segregation of housing and public facilities. Moreover, inner city residents find themselves adversely affected by the activities and decisions of non-city residents against whom they have no force. Air and noise pollution caused by commuter traffic falls heavily upon the inner city environment.

Another constraint on the ability of the inner city residents to improve the quality of their lives is the housing market. Zoning and other exclusionary devices have combined to prevent the expansion of locational opportunities for minorities and the poor.

In addition, the economics of the new housing market prohibits the construction of low, moderate and sometimes middle income housing without subsidies. The resulting concentration of minorities and the poor in the older, inner cities has generated overcrowding, neighborhood disinvestment, and a general inaccessibility to employment, educational, health and recreational opportunities. Concerning overcrowding, 26 percent of San Francisco Chinatown's population, for example, lives in overcrowded units, while in Oakland, fully 13 percent of all households (20 percent of the poverty families) were in overcrowded conditions in 1966. But the areal scale of Los Angeles' inner city neighborhood, employment, accessibility and educational problems is larger than the entire city of San Francisco.

There is some question whether suburban communities are substantially better off from a large scale, long term point of view. (It would be hard to controvert the evidence that individual welfare is greater in the newer, lower density environments.) The harmful effects of expansive residential development on other land resources has already been discussed; what replaces the open space and farms is frequently not all that it could be. The aesthetics of suburbanization are inadequate (except perhaps at the microscale of the individual home), while inefficient land use patterns burden today's homeowners and workers as well as tomorrow's tax-payers. Whether suburban land use patterns are viable in light of skyrocketing energy costs is uncertain.

Thus, it emerges that urbanization and economic development have adversely affected and continue to affect open space and other natural land resources. In addition, the current pattern of urban land development—suburbanization—is undermining the social and economic welfare of residents of older cities. Ultimately, it is population growth that affects all aspects of the state's environment. Growth is planning's challenge and stumbling block.

B. FACTORS INFLUENCING LAND USE PLANNING

a. Governmental Factors

The decision-making processes of California governments have tended to avoid recognizing land as a scarce economic resource which, once allocated and developed, can be stripped for all time of irreplaceable environmental values and amenities. The processes which pervaded the state until fairly recently proceeded upon an implicit, and therefore not readily debatable, assumption that land was an atypical economic good—a commodity in endless supply whose allocations and uses should be principally determined by private markets. The role of state and local government was and still remains (with some notable exceptions) essentially that of accommodating and facilitating the land development process, even though that basic assumption is now recognized to be erroneous.

The accommodationist ethics of the state's government came to display three salient characteristics during the post-World War II land booms in Southern and Northern California. In the first place, state and local governments somehow managed to avoid seriously questioning the premises of California's then very profitable development process. Residential, economic and urban growth were held to be good—if not because of the American ethic of upward socioeconomic advancement, then because of the "need" for more single-family detached houses in more suburban subdivisions or because more residential development was believed (often erroneously) to "pay its way" through net increases in local economic and tax bases. It took the environmental movement of the late 1960's to inform developers and lending institutions what most economists knew all along—that land, like virtually all other economic goods, is a scarce resource. If it is not being allocated in socially optimal ways, then there may be informational or structural problems with the operation of California's land markets.

Moreover, because the state and local governments were wedded to market values, the decision-making posture of the public sector tended to be passive and reactive. Chiefly through their planning and plan implementation processes, California's governments continue to be overwhelmingly control and regulation oriented. They respond primarily to the land use development initiatives of the private sector, except for those well-circumscribed areas reserved for public development such as highway, water and urban renewal projects. Hence, the relevant public decision-making processes are generally activated only after the private land use decision has been made. Private land use rights and expectations are actually negated only by the exercise of eminent domain or by denial of development permits in critical environmental areas. Although private land use decisions take place within frameworks of public controls and sanctions, the predominant and entrenched attitude of many California governments has been to regulate, control and plan as little as possible—unless new development is perceived as injurious to community schools and services, economic and tax bases, or social homogeneity.

A third characteristic has been the pervasive tendency to rely upon piecemeal, short term and individualistic approaches to land use decision-making. The tendency for the state and many local governments throughout California has been to avoid making comprehensive, long range and effective land use decisions, as well as to avoid asking basic questions as to the nature, location, timing and net benefits of indiscriminate growth. If a land use problem can be avoided by shifting the burden or cost to another local government or the environment or future generations, then all the better. Here, too, public decision-making has tended to imitate the worst features of private economic decisions by seeking to externalize land use problems, policies, costs and responsibility onto someone else. Unfortunately, the public decision-making process seldom took the next step to inquire whether private development decisions sometimes reflected market failures that undervalued or underpriced the state's land, air, water and human resources.

Many activities of local planning agencies and commissions, accordingly, have been subject to considerable private and public pressure, especially regarding zoning, subdivision and environmental regulations. Naturally, it is their day-to-day actions which in large part determine how the local lands of taxpayers are to be used (or re-used), how profits and benefits are gained, how the tax base and social values are protected, and whether the local environment is preserved. In too many instances, the local planning law and processes have been simply too weak to withstand the pressures of developers, the accommodationist (and full employment) policies of local boards and councils and the internal maneuvering of local agencies and departments. In short, the local planning process in California has so far failed to develop a professional perspective and countervailing constituency necessary to resist inevitable pressures for ad hoc, short term economic, political and administrative decision-making. It is also an ironic legacy of the "good government" movement of the 1920's which espoused that planning should be detached and aloof from the real world of local politics. Planning has remained highly political, but with the trappings of detachment and complete objectivity.

Thus, land use planning decisions—especially those of local legislative bodies and planning commissions—tend frequently not to be explicitly grounded in the jurisdiction's general plan or adopted development policies. Sometimes such plans and policies either do not exist, are qualitatively lacking, or are too rigid or innocuous for effectively guiding multi-million dollar decisions involving complex public and private trade-offs. However, even superb local general plans have not been truly binding upon the city councils or boards of supervisors, as shall be documented in the study. An additional disincentive to good local planning has been a public decision-making process which can sometimes quietly settle zoning, subdivision and other land use matters without adequate regard for the niceties of due process, the burdens of public review or the imperatives of explicit statutory requirements.

In addition, major land use problems arise because of the internal and external fragmentation of decision-making responsibility in state and local governments. Internally, a land use matter may run the gamut of the planning department, public works departments, planning commission, zoning board of appeals, city council or board of supervisors. Externally, state and local governments can influence new development patterns by their interpretation and compliance with state and federal law as well as by their capital improvement programs and public works projects. Many public development projects, such as freeways, airports, utilities and water and sewer facilities, can create significant regional spillover effects due to a lack of effective coordination of intergovernmental, community and citizen inputs. Even where state, regional and local agencies agree to coordinate, their agreements typically receive uncritical public acceptance, but contain escape clauses for the more powerful agencies.

Public investments and public work projects, coordinated or not, can be growth inducing and thus integral to the success of large private developments such as suburban subdivisions, shopping centers and recreational housing. The availability or confident expectation of such public improvements and services increases the potential use and market value of land. The results in urban areas are conflicts among incompatible land uses, as for example residential development and preservation of prime agricultural and open space lands. Thus, the extension of government infrastructure and services to undeveloped areas is typically interpreted as a signal for the incursion of private development, which often tends to be low density, scattered and necessarily automobile dependent. The initial provision of infrastructure and services can generate self-stimulating effects in which the initial supply of infrastructure and services is then met by unanticipated demand and the need to supply even more infrastructure and services. Such self-stimulating patterns tend to be exacerbated if the private benefits, for example, of new freeways and public services, tend to be over-valued without regard for their environmental and societal costs.

The cumulative effects of governmental decision-making based on uncoordinated and supply-inducing-demand policies are reflected in prevailing land use patterns across the state. While due in part to autonomous decision-making processes at state and local levels, other contributory factors include functional mismatches among governmental scale, powers and planning capabilities and the private sector's expectations for public services and infrastructure.

The most obvious example of this occurs where the geographic scale of local government is too small for it to respond comprehensively to land use problems and pressures, so that unresolved problems spill over into other jurisdictions and the larger region. The land use planning and control powers of local governments extend only as far as their boundaries, and because many local boundaries were historically arbitrary, local jurisdictions tend to function at inadequate or improper scale, to fragment interlocal and regional perspectives, and thereby to elicit coordinative proposals—few of which are implemented. Matters such as zoning and subdivision controls; control of air, water and noise pollution; designation of transportation corridors; development of low and moderate income housing; and planning for balanced growth increasingly are well beyond the present capabilities of local government.

In addition, it increasingly appears that state agencies with land use impacting powers tend to avoid directly addressing critical land use issues, allowing them instead, to fall upon local governments having neither the scale nor powers for effective resolution and decision-making. The regional councils of governments in California were created in response to federal requirements, are not legally recognized in state law and consequently enjoy no clear role definition or planning powers.

Where land use powers are either inadequately bestowed in the first place or are widely diffused among different levels of government, the end result would necessarily tend to create strong and systematic disincentives for comprehensive local decision-making and planning. It is in such an institutional environment that preexisting tendencies to ignore and to externalize land use problems are allowed to thrive.

b. Economic Factors

The private economic decision-making process is the overwhelming determinant for initiating land use development and change in California. Major profit oriented institutions in the state's economy—land owners, developers and financial institutions—are major determiners of how land is to be allocated and used. Their decision-making is based generally upon seeking to optimize profits by maximizing revenues generated by a land resource, while concurrently attempting to minimize (or to shift and externalize) the costs associated with resource development and conservation use. The consideration of alternative uses of land and other resources and the timing of development are related factors in many private development strategies.

The economic forces affecting rural land in California are illustrative. Farmers, ranchers, and lumber and mining firms use significant portions of the state's rural land, but at present receive a smaller rate of return for their land investment than do owners of land more accessible to urban, suburban and recreational home development. As a result, many rural landowners become speculators if the market and tax value of their land reflect potential future conversions for residential or urban development. An increase in its market value will be reflected in increased tax assessments, because California assessors overwhelmingly appraise land for its "highest and best" economic use, not upon the value of current use and/or zoning. (Williamson Act lands are the exception.) Banks and other financial institutions frequently mortgage property on the assumption that agricultural land eventually will be converted to "higher" residential or urban uses. Market pressures to convert agricultural land are additionally compounded by a reluctance to make the capital investments which would make current uses more efficient and profitable.

Nonresident investors, chiefly from Eastern financial markets, have speculated heavily in California's rural lands, anticipating their conversion to more intensive uses and waiting for market values to appreciate. Ownership is held by individual investors as well as by corporations, banks and real estate syndicates; in the latter, professional real estate brokers in California sometimes serve as general partners or "fronts" for a real estate syndicate. Private land banking also is common where developers acquire land well in advance of anticipated demand and release it subsequently to meet actual demand.

However, it is the developers who occupy center stage in development decision-making. They sustain financial rewards or losses depending, in large part, on their ability to coordinate a highly intricate stream of land use, governmental, financial, construction, labor, political and marketing decisions. Although there are many types of developers, two are especially relevant: traditional developers and large corporate developers.

The traditional developer typically operates with more modest financial resources and thus is limited in the number and scale of projects he can undertake. He must carefully manage the development to shepherd his limited capital.

Corporate developers, on the other hand, more recently have entered the California land development scene with significantly larger corporate capital resources and management capabilities. Private land development corporations were joined in California in the 1960's by conglomerates which added (and sometimes later dropped) smaller development firms to their corporate structure.

Although corporate involvement favors large scale development projects, such activity has mixed consequences. The peripheral addition of real estate to a corporate balance sheet may affect the corporation's tax status and ability to secure bank credit. The traditional structure of corporate management tends to promote conservative financial perspectives which limit risk taking in land development, thus providing insufficient stimulus for social and environmental improvements. For example, new towns are not being built in part because corporate decision-making favors "tried and true" marketing policies and thus, lower risk "cookie-cutter" subdivisions.

The very large capital requirements for development and need to secure significant financial long term commitments establishes a significant role for banks, savings and loan associations, and other lending institutions in real estate development. Banks and savings and loan associations supply most construction loan and mortgage monies for primary homes. Insurance companies invest heavily in funding for office, industrial and commercial structures. Pension and trust funds have a similar role, providing some degree of specialization in mortgage and equity investment.

These financial institutions markedly influence land development by establishing the price at which funds are borrowed and by making funds available primarily for projects sufficiently profitable and with secure market prospects. Socially desirable developments such as new towns and low and moderate income housing typically need grant subsidies and/or loan guarantees, available only from the public sector, to meet their long term, higher risk financing requirements. Moreover, established conventional land developers are almost always favored by lending institutions (and some closely related federal agencies) over smaller, community based housing development corporations inclined to experiment with non-traditional development projects. However, all development slows as financing becomes scarce and is reflected in increased interest rates for long term projects. In such a funding squeeze, the less profitable but socially and environmentally beneficial projects inevitably fall by the wayside unless special governmental actions are taken.

The spatial arrangement of developed and undeveloped areas in California is largely determined by the combined market decisions and values of developers, landowners, financial institutions and individual consumers. Housing developers of single family units, for example, prefer sites with inexpensive, level land, good accessibility to employment and commercial centers, and highly marketable images and amenities. Heavy industrial uses require close and cheap accessibility to major transportation systems and proximity to labor pools. Developers of office buildings need high accessibility to urban commercial, communication and service centers.

A too narrow focus on locational values by private developers can result in untoward consequences. A suburban subdivision can convert prime agricultural and open space land as well as overburden municipal services, reinforce conventional marketing and finance policies, and contribute to additional socioeconomic segregation. Labor intensive (blue collar) firms and industries leave the inner city for cheaper suburban land and improved accessibility to suppliers or customers. Their outward migration, however, further undercuts the income and employment bases needed to maintain inner city homes, neighborhoods and public services. Retail firms with market clout frequently outbid local governments for land needed for parks, recreation and open space, or bid up acquisition cost.

Of special concern to local governments are urban fringe developments which necessitate extension of services and infrastructure and sometimes result in "leapfrog'' or ''checkerboard'' development patterns inter-mixed with agricultural land uses. Conversely, since local governments rely heavily upon property taxes, public decision-making has tended to promote intensive development promoting policies. Thus, industrial, commercial and upper income housing projects are fa-vored for their more lucrative tax base over low and moderate income housing. In some areas, land is over-zoned for industrial and commercial development while notably under-zoned (or non-zoned) for housing which can be afforded by low and moderate income families. In other areas, anticipated tax benefits from urban re-newal projects result in land redevelopment favoring large commercial firms and facilities, thereby hastening the demise of smaller firms and neighborhood retail cen-ters.

Because some governments have succeeded in de-veloping substantial tax bases, they provide a level and quality of services unthinkable in poorer jurisdictions. Radical disparities can be found within metropolitan areas in the availability of educational, housing, employment and recreational opportunities.

c. Social Factors

The decision-making processes which determine the use and reuse of land have critical social consequences, some of which are only vaguely understood. Control of land use is a potent power. The ways in which this power is exercised, by whom and for what purposes, will be reflected in resulting land use policies and pat-terns. These policies and patterns may be relatively explicit attempts to reject the poor and minorities by exclusionary zoning, or they may operate indirectly through ''fiscal zoning,'' and tax and growth limitation measures. Their effect may be short run, by refusing to issue water and sewer permits, or long run, by failing to support open space, parkland, low income housing and socially-oriented urban renewal projects and pro-grams.

Of all the factors relevant to land use decision-making, social objectives are the most elusive and most ambiguous, and typically seem to have the lowest prior-ity in public policy making. Land use controls are best understood as ''tools'' which can aggravate or amelior-ate social problems and conflict, depending upon their application and underlying motivation. For example, the factors underlying a local government's large lot zoning ordinance may incorporate legitimate desires for open space conservation, maintenance of viable public ser-vices, and preservation of community stability from mass culture and excessive rates of change.

Many communities perceive their social survival as being jeopardized by the economic forces of uncontrol-led growth (or decline) and the homogenization of mass urban culture and mass population. According to one observer, ''People should not have to abandon econom-ically productive and personally satisfying ways of life, simply in the name of a higher and better use of land.'' On the other hand, the interests in community viability and stability may simply be masks for racism and prej-udice, the maintenance of existing social and political power structures and the desire to avoid change by di-recting growth forces elsewhere.

In the broader arena of cultural values and expecta-tions, the definition and exercise of what are perceived as ''social rights'' can exert powerful influences upon land use decision-making. Widespread belief in a ''so-cial right'' to use and dispose of private property to maximize narrowly individual benefits has led to ir-reparable losses to coastal, bay, mountain, open space and public land resources. The ''right'' to personal mo-bility yielded an automobile-dependent lifestyle of wide ranging advantages and disadvantages. Similarly, the ''right'' to participate in a once gloried ''way of life'' included idealization of the single family detached house on the quarter acre lot in the suburbs with good (and homogeneous) schools and neighborhoods. While each of these ''social rights'' unquestionably yielded considerable near-term personal and group advantages, they also left legacies whose cumulative social in-equities and long term effects are rapidly surfacing to-day.

State and local government arenas constitute a separate but closely related set of influences with pro-nounced land related social effects. State fiscal policies, such as regressive taxes, hurt the poor and reinforce economic disparities among various socioeconomic groups. Failure to establish state housing finance and development programs as a practical matter means that the poor and minorities will continue to live in sub-standard housing, frequently concentrated in ghettoes, barrios and little Tokyos. State-level failure effectively to stimulate central city renewal means that the social and economic bases of inner cities will continue to languish, thereby reinforcing the flight of affluent whites to the suburbs. Service disparities among local governments in providing quality schools, health care, day care and rec-reation, result in radical differences in opportunities and quality of life within a single region. Geographic dysfunctions such as poor accessibility to freeways and employment centers and the "reverse commuting" necessary for inner city workers to reach suburban jobs, can significantly influence inner city economic opportunities and thus the personal and household income needed to maintain properties, neighborhoods and adequate public services.

In addition, there is the structure and workings of the governmental decision-making process itself. At every level, legislative body and administrative department, a decision affecting land use represents the translation of social values into policies, programs, plans or regulations. Similarly, avoidance of making a land use decision is a decision not to decide and thereby not to disturb the status quo with regard to land and impliedly to the distribution of social, economic and political power.

Community involvement and citizen participation in land use decision-making are policies frequently better observed in their breach than in meaningful recognition. The frequency, time, location, notice and conduct of public hearings has much to do with what voices are heard and how. Citizen advisory boards composed only of volunteers who have ample free time do not typically represent the full spectrum of community interest and opinion.

Statutory and administrative provisions which only vaguely provide for citizen advisory boards frequently create the illusion of citizen participation without troubling the bureaucratic waters. The nature of community involvement is not well understood by government officials uncomfortable with having their values, assumptions, procedures and products actively questioned, especially by different ethnic and socioeconomic groups. Community involvement, moreover, can prove frustrating for officials who see it, sometimes understandably, only in terms of reaction and negative criticism of their plans and proposals. Yet, as one observer views, "if specific development plans, as they emerge, reflect a working consensus among all groups legitimately concerned with the outcome, then the likelihood of actual implementation is considerably greater than if such groups are consulted after the fact."

d. Environmental Factors

Environmental factors influencing land use include conditions created by the natural environment, the man-made environment and their interactions. The environment basically functions as an intricate, complex but whole system. In comparison to social, economic or governmental factors which tend to impel certain decisions, environmental factors are more likely to constrain. Based on environmental indicators, options for use are often eliminated while others are occasionally enhanced.

However, environmental factors may indicate distinct advantages for certain types of land uses. Level ground, rich, well drained soils, available water, ample sunlight and clear air are excellent conditions for agriculture, for example. Unfortunately, they are also excellent conditions for residential development. The same land traversed by an active earthquake fault, subject to periodic flooding or vulnerable to fire hazards, should constrain a decision to erect habitable structures. Potentially hazardous natural conditions which abound in California and should influence land use decisions include seismic occurrences, landslides, land subsidence, floods and fires. Even though these conditions have been recognized and documented, development in California has not necessarily been rejected, although measures such as structural reinforcement, flood channels, or fire breaks have been used to mitigate adverse effects. Although these and other hazardous conditions occur naturally, they can be also precipitated or aggravated by actions of man, particularly by unwise land use decisions. For instance, the scarcity of essential resources restricts land use in other areas such as barren deserts, high altitudes, steep slopes, unstable soils, areas of salt water intrusion and excessively high water tables. Often, action to rectify these conditions, such as transporting the missing resource, only serve to alter ecological relationships.

Thus, whether by scarcity or hazard, the natural environment should constrain land development or at least types or certain intensity of use. Similar limits also are suggested by the presence of environmental opportunities and areas of public importance, such as a coastline, wilderness, rivers, prime agricultural soils and wildlife preserves. In some ways the natural environment is a very "demanding" influence on land use in that the proper use of resources, particularly unique and irreplaceable ones, is prerequisite for their continued existence, benefiting present and future generations.

The basic dilemma is that only rarely do natural resources in unmodified states provide maximum contributions to society, except in terms of passive recreational values such as open space enjoyment, solitude and visual pleasure. Because some use of land may often be essential, if only for access, the capacity of natural resources to serve human needs can be greatly increased through a balancing of human and natural requirements. Those resources which have alternative uses and thus create a range of opportunities are usually the least effective in directing land-use decisions; they are compatible with various land uses. Despite the fact that less than optimum land uses often exploit these resources, there is usually no outward "retaliation" by the natural environment, at least in the short term, to indicate that misuse or damage of resource is in progress. Even when such land resources as agricultural lands and scenic areas are completely consumed or contaminated, development still takes place, because human expediency in land use often exercises a stronger hold than environmental preservation.

Like the natural environment, the man-made or built environment creates opportunities and constraints to development, and is recognized as a major factor primarily when it approaches conditions of extreme decay or potential growth. Where the built environment has a high capability for public services, government decision-making tends to encourage land use allocations for development. Where blight exists and infrastructure is poor, local government may be led to other strategies of land allocation, such as urban renewal or decentralization. However, these environmental influences rarely occur independently of other forces. Thus, the overall influence of the natural and man-made environments,

is an amorphous factor in the governmental decision-making process. They create a context within which decisions take place and are safeguarded somewhat by legal requirements that must precede decision-making, such as environmental impact reviews.

The actual weight placed on natural environmental values at the time of decision-making is attributable to the influence, or the compromised influence, of interest groups having a stake in environmental quality and conservation. Groups arguing to protect the remaining agricultural soils for productive purposes or fighting to preserve the sensitive area of a wildlife habitat, put "the environment" into the limelight and provide the opportunity for informed, sometimes animated consideration of land use questions.

Natural and man-made environmental conditions can be viewed as assets or liabilities in terms of a proposed land use—such as easing the way for some uses or obstructing others. The existence of public infrastructure for highways, sewers and water may point to further suburban subdivisions. But the presence in the same area of forests, mineral resources and unpolluted air requires another assessment of the logic of development. Depending on the attitudes and goals of the decision-making process, these environmental factors may be seen as either opportunities or constraints on development.

Chapter Two

CALIFORNIA PLANNING:

LAW AND PERFORMANCE

Historically, the major determinors of the location, intensities and types of land uses and structures have been private and public developers. Their decisions have often been reciprocally dependent and have only been affected tangentially by public planners. The latter have operated primarily at the local governmental level.

In the past decade, however, the influence of public urban and environmental planners has become greater. This is a product of greater public sensitivity to the problems created by unrestrained private and sometimes public development as well as ineffective public planning.

This section contains synopses of a number of California statutes and governmental processes relating to land use, environmental and urban planning. They exemplify planning programs, institutions and processes at the three levels of government in the state: state/substate, regional and local.

As modern land use planning has begun to mean something, it has become apparent that local institutions alone cannot create and implement plans which are sensible from a statewide and areawide perspective. This statement is premised on a number of points. Three seem quite prominent. First, few if any counties or cities can control a number of key variables which determine development patterns. For instance, freeways and other state public improvements (e.g., the California Water Project) create development pressures which are almost impossible to contain. Similarly, some problems transcend county and municipal boundaries and can only be solved if they are addressed on a geographical basis commensurate with the problems. Filling and alteration of the shoreline of San Francisco Bay is a good example. No local government, even if well motivated, likely would bar fill of portions of the Bay within its jurisdiction unless assured that all other similarly situated local governments would follow suit. Likewise, no single local government can deal adequately with problems of intraregional transportation, especially mass transit alternatives to the automobile.

Secondly, as planning controls also have begun to mean something—at least their potential is appreciated—it has become apparent that some local decisions either to control development or forgo exercising such powers make little sense from a statewide or areawide perspective, even though such decisions might appear quite rational from a local perspective. For example, lack of effective local control on coastal development in a number of counties might be sensible from a local economic viewpoint, but the sum result would be to preempt much of the coast from use by a majority of the state's residents. Similarly, strict growth control by some municipalities might be sensible when viewed locally, but highly destructive to mobility and social justice if viewed regionally.

Thirdly, the past five years have witnessed enormous efforts at federal and state levels to deal with air and water pollution. Such environmental problems transcend municipal boundaries and their effective solution requires extra-local governmental action. We are only now beginning to witness the interaction between pollution control strategies and land use planning. As the interactions become more evident we will have to find adequate means to relate what has heretofore been local comprehensive land use planning and state/substate air and water quality planning.

Many problems also abound at the state level. Chief among them is the absence of an authoritative mechanism to develop comprehensive policy and to integrate the planning activities of state agencies which have obvious land use implications. Often state programs are in conflict. Highway planning conflicts with air quality planning, energy facility planning conflicts with water quality planning, and the like. Even in the absence of blatant conflict, state agencies often ignore the land use implications of their programs and thereby choose in effect to pursue an implicit policy of critical omissions. Suburban development was, after all, largely due to the particular type of transportation facilities and locations determined primarily by state and federal highway authorities. This constituted de facto state planning whether or not the resultant development patterns were intended.

Consensus seems to be developing that regional (areawide) and state land use planning are both inevitable and desirable. The substate transportation, air quality and water quality planning programs are fairly well-established, and there is increasing acceptance and planning capability of the federally supported Councils of Governments in the state's major metropolitan areas (also known as the critical air basins). At the state level, it is clearly apparent that several planning processes emphasizing transportation development and environmental constraints separately and collectively can determine local land uses and growth patterns—and thus assume de facto land use planning functions. The question is not whether land use planning should transcend local government, but when and how existing statutory and institutional configurations at the state/substate, regional and local levels are to be rationalized and integrated. The time is ripe for change. The statutory descriptions and planning process assessments that follow help lay a basis for identifying the ingredients for sensible change and potential points of leverage for such change.

A. STATE PLANNING LAWS AND AGENCIES

Because there is no overt land use planning and policy at the state level in California, there are at least two ways of looking at the myriad planning activities of various, separate state agencies as they affect land use development and related growth patterns. One way would be to attempt to rationalize these essentially incremental and disjointed activities according to substantive planning categories: comprehensive, development, environmental quality, energy and natural resources. This approach is used in this section of the report, chiefly because it is readily comprehensible. A second way, however, could be built around the types and efficacy of the planning-related powers bestowed upon the state agencies: weak (e.g., comprehensive and housing), development (e.g., transportation), constraint (e.g., environmental and energy) and managerial (e.g., natural resources). Although the second classification might be useful at the outset to establish procedures, the actual allocations would be too variable over time to remain applicable.

In addition, it is useful to distinguish between those planning processes which are "substate" because they are statutorily related to a state level agency and program, and those which are "regional" because they are the product of local and/or federal initiative and are not statutorily related to state level agencies and programs.

1. State Comprehensive Planning

This section explores the state level Office of Planning and Research (OPR) and Council on Intergovernmental Relations (CIR) which exist in the statutes as two distinct entities but have now been combined administratively as a single organization within the Governor's Office. CIR exists as an internal division of OPR with only a handful of staff personnel and a comparable budget and political mandate. OPR exists with a somewhat larger staff, budget and potentially significant statutory mandate. Their roles to date have been limited to studies and data assembly, promulgation of guidelines for local general plans and the widely ignored *Environmental Goals and Policy Report*. Even without major new statutory powers, OPR/CIR could exercise significant roles for defining (but not implementing) state and substate land use policies and planning objectives and criteria. To do so, however, would require greater commitment and political support.

Office of Planning and Research

The Office of Planning and Research is the state agency with designated responsibility for comprehensive land use and environmental policy planning. The legislative intent expressed in establishing OPR is that the state's future growth should be guided by an effective planning process and should proceed within the framework of officially approved statewide goals and policies directed to land use, population growth and distribution, urban expansion and other relevant physical, social and economic development factors. OPR is specifically designated to assume primary responsibility for assuring orderly operation of the process of environmental policy development and implementation within state government.[1] Equally clear, however, is that OPR is not vested with any direct implementation or regulatory power over land use, public works or other state, regional or local projects or programs.[2]

a. Legislative History and Intent

The Office of Planning and Research was created in 1970 to replace the State Office of Planning. This legislation, along with the California Environmental Quality Act of 1970, grew out of recommendations made by the Assembly Select Committee on Environmental Quality in its 1970 report, *Environmental Bill of Rights*. OPR was to strengthen the state planning process in order to deal effectively with long range environmental problems in relation to an expanded state environmental quality effort. The Committee determined that the state Office of Planning, then part of the Department of Finance, had been unsuccessful in carrying out the intent of the Legislature, partly because its findings were not taken seriously by either the executive or legislative branches. The Committee recommended replacement of the state Office of Planning by an independent entity reporting directly to the Governor and thereby to better integrate state level planning and decision making functions. The Office was placed under the control of a director appointed by and directly responsible to the Governor.[3] The basic power and responsibility for environmental policy was left to the Governor. OPR was given "primary responsibility for assuring orderly operation of the process of environmental policy development and implementation within state government"[4] and was intended to influence legislative policy through the Governor. However, the Office was specifically denied "any direct operating or regulatory powers over land use, public works, or other state, regional, or local projects or programs."[5] The Legislature intended that OPR should assist in coordinating state agencies and also aid in planning for specific functions such as water development, transportation and natural resources. The "state functional plans" (defined as an intermediate or short range plan for a discrete function of state government) are to be developed according to assumptions and forecasts for state growth and development made by OPR.

b. Functions

Among OPR's specific duties are the following:[6]

(1) To assist in formulating long range goals and policies for land use, population growth and distribution, urban expansion, open space and other factors which affect state development and environmental quality.

(2) To assist state departments and agencies in preparing functional plans in such areas as transportation, water development, open space and recreation in line with overall state planning objectives.

(3) To regularly evaluate plans and programs of state agencies which affect state planning and to make recommendations when needed

(4) To assist the Department of Finance in preparing the state budget as it relates to implementing state functional plans and statewide environmental goals in order to better integrate planning and budgetary functions.

(5) To coordinate development and operation of a statewide environmental monitoring system to pinpoint emerging problem areas or threats to public health, natural resources and environmental quality.

(6) To coordinate state research that relates to growth and environmental quality and to advise the Governor, his cabinet, state agencies and departments, and the Legislature.

(7) To assist the Council on Intergovernmental Relations in coordinating provision of technical aid by state agencies to assure consistency with state environmental policy.

(8) To coordinate with state, regional and local agencies the development of objectives, criteria and procedures for evaluating public and private impacts on environmental quality and to guide the preparation of environmental impact reports by state and local agencies under the California Environmental Quality Act of 1970.

c. Environmental Goals and Policy Report

During the course of statewide planning efforts, by OPR and its predecessor, the two documents which have been produced are significant for what they indicate about existing statewide planning. The California Development Plan was published in 1968 and was intended to be a comprehensive development plan for California's land use. The plan was the product of the previous Administration and was never officially adopted by the later Administration. The second document, the *Environmental Goals and Policy Report.*, published in 1973, was prepared to fulfill the mandate of Government Code section 65041, which required the Governor, through OPR, to prepare, maintain and revise a comprehensive state document. Priority in the Report was to be given to the development of statewide land use policy. It was to contain at minimum (a) a 20 to 30 year overview of state growth and development, (b) a statement of environmental goals and objectives and (c) a description of new policies, programs and other actions to implement statewide environmental goals, including intermediate range plans and actions directed to natural and human resources, and transportation. The Report, after approval by the Governor, was to serve *inter alia* as a basis for judgments about the design, location and priority of major public programs, capital projects and other actions including the allocation of state funds for environmental purposes.

d. Planning Process Assessment

Although OPR was declared by the Legislature in 1970 to be "the comprehensive state planning agency," the statutory scheme is ambiguous and vaguely worded, but specific in denying OPR "any direct operating or regulatory powers" over land use and state/regional/local projects and programs.[7] Thus, and also because OPR was conceived to serve "as staff" to the Governor,[8] its ability to define and realize its equivocal statutory mandate necessarily became a function of its political mandate—its status, authority and budget within the Governor's Office.

Accordingly, it is not surprising that other state level agencies feel that there is no comprehensive state planning process in California. That assessment was reluctantly shared by numerous regional and local planners in field interviews throughout the state. Moreover, OPR itself noted in June, 1974 that, "California does not have what could be described as a state planning process. Rather it has a collection of functional planning processes ranging from the state to the local level, each more or less independent of one another . . ."[9]

These combined assessments ordinarily would be

sufficient to dismiss OPR from any further consideration. Nonetheless, it may be useful in this report, intended to provide a guide to California's land use related planning law and processes, to describe briefly *how* California has no comprehensive planning agency.

In overall summary, OPR can be characterized as a weak—in comparison with the planning agencies of other states—planning agency displaying three familiar symptoms: subsequent statutory irrelevance, proclivity for interagency coordination and propensity for "paper plans."

(1) Subsequent Statutory Irrelevance

Although OPR's statutory creation was greeted initially by California planners, in part because it was to replace the previously impotent State Office of Planning, that enthusiasm has since waned among planners and the Legislature. Specifically, the Legislature in establishing the State Department of Transportation (1972) and the Energy Resources Conservation and Development Commission (1974) ignored any mention or significant role for OPR, even though both agencies will exert very substantial impacts on land use development patterns and allocation of growth.

In addition, as discussed in the next section, the Department of Transportation observed in legislative testimony in July, 1974 that California has no comprehensive land use policy capable of guiding development of the State Transportation Plan. Absent such a policy— and no comment was made upon OPR's Environmental Goals and Policy Report, the Department noted that it was presently acting as the state's de facto land use coordinator and that the state Transportation Plan *will* become California's de facto land use plan.[10] But when queried as to OPR, the Department noted that one of its working relationships with OPR included membership on the OPR sponsored Interdepartmental Program and Policy Coordination Group which met regularly "to review and discuss various planning matters."[11]

(2) Proclivity for Inter Agency Coordination

Perhaps the most salient administrative characteristic of OPR is its penchant for interagency "coordination," "cooperation" and "information exchange." In part, this may simply reflect a statutory scheme in which OPR's actual powers are "to assist," "to regularly evaluate" and "to coordinate" various aspects of the legislatively prescribed planning process. It may also reflect its two principal, federally related duties established by various federal urban planning legislation and programs: (a) state clearinghouse for review of environmental impact reports, A-95 reviews of state/regional/local federal grant-in-aid applications and subdivision maps by state agencies; and (b) state level administration of federal 701 comprehensive planning funds which help subsidize the planning programs of many California cities, counties and councils of governments.

However, while a proclivity for interagency "coordination" currently prevails among most planners in various state agencies, it appears to pervade OPR. Because of the predilection for coordination, crucial policy studies and the assessment of goals is curtailed. The basic question, 'Coordinate for what end?' is never asked. To seriously ask that question, would result in scrutinizing interagency "coordinative" meetings in which information is exchanged, progress is described and little is really accomplished.

It would also in part necessitate the articulation of explicit criteria for resolving interagency conflicts having state/substate land use implications, *i.e.*, the rudimentary development of a state land use policy. The state government, however, "has made no basic commitment with regard to its responsibilities and functions which have a major impact on land use," according to A. Alan Post, the Legislative Analyst.[12] "One of the major reasons why California has in past years made no state commitment to land use planning or controls has been because it has not been public policy to do so."[13]

(3) Propensity for "Paper Plans"

Although OPR was enjoined to prepare the Environmental Goals and Policy Report, it was not directly instructed to develop a state land use plan as such. Rather, in preparing the report, "priority shall be given to the development of *statewide land use policy,* including the recommendations resulting from the *land use planning and implementation program* set forth in Section 4 of the act adding this section."[14] However, Section 4 in part provides: "The Office of Planning and Research shall give immediate and high priority to the development of land use policy. As a first component of such policy, the office shall develop, in conjunction with appropriate state departments and federal, regional and local agencies, a statewide plan and implementation program for protecting land and water resources of the state which are of statewide significance . . ."[15] Although there may be some uncertainty in interpreting the seemingly *prima facie* Section 4 requirements for a statewide land use plan, planning and implementation program, there is little doubt that OPR has not developed the "statewide land use policy" also required by the statute. Thus, state government has not developed a broad policy approach to statewide land use problems.[16]

In lieu of the statewide land use policy, OPR has generated a series of reports in its four year history. Its first efforts were accurately described in a "Cry California" article: "In the critical area of land-use policy . . ., OPR has offered, in place of cogent policy, a patchwork of disconnected reports on almost any state project bearing even a tangential relationship to land-use planning. The office's first progress report . . . presented an impressive-looking, three-phased, 27-month, land-use policy development program which will cost more than $2.5 million in this (1971) fiscal year alone. However, almost all of the funds included in this budget are for projects in other state agencies begun long before OPR was even created and over which OPR has no control. Thus, in the name of a land-use program, $235,000 is assigned to the Division of Forestry for local assistance in watershed and fire protection, and $50,000 is allocated to the Resources Agency for power-plant siting. OPR's share of this $2.5 million budget amounts to only $125,000. In comparison, the Division of Highways, which is not participating in the land-use program, will spend more than $4 million this year on land-use planning activities."[17]

OPR's initial progress report was later followed in 1973 by the mandated Environmental Goals and Policy Report. The statutory scheme envisioned the Report as a dynamic policy document to guide all land use related decision-making at the state level. State actions, especially those of the public works and environmental control agencies, tend to have catalytic effects on substate public and private land use development decisions.

The OPR Report falls far short of the legislative intent, however. It states in broad terms policies concerning development and environmental protection. The state land use goal, for example, is "to develop and maintain a series of land use policies, including standards and criteria, which can serve as a guide to state, regional, county and city planning efforts in order to accommodate growth and natural resource allocation consistent with the protection and wise management of our natural resources."

The following policies are recommended to accomplish the goal:

"(1) that all levels of government making decisions af-fecting land use shall . . . analyze the cause and effect relationships of those proposals and evaluate their social, economic, and natural environmental impacts upon the total environment.

"(2) to provide for a continuing, coordinated and comprehensive planning capability to provide technical assistance where necessary and feasible to planning efforts of local government and private enterprise; and

"(3) that assessment and taxation policies shall not be the dominant factor in guiding land use activities."

Equally broad goals are stated for air quality, noise, pesticides, population, solid waste, transportation, water, and environmental resources and hazards. The document does not contain measureable objectives, recommendations or specific implementation mechanisms for achieving the goals.

The Report itself seems to acknowledge that it was not intended to meet the legislative mandates: it states that the environmental goals and policies merely provide "a framework" within which state and local governments and the private sector *may* set priorities and make decisions. The Report, then, should probably be considered at best a tentative first step towards producing the plan called for in the legislation.

A recent joint study of OPR, by both OPR and the federal Department of Housing and Urban Development (HUD), concluded that there is, in fact, little comprehensive or environmental planning at the state level. Although OPR has conducted many special purpose studies in response to other state agencies needs, some of these studies were unrelated to OPR's specific mandate to produce a comprehensive environmental plan. OPR functioned primarily as the research staff of the former Governor and Cabinet. State funding for OPR was low; indeed, most of its studies were financed by federal grants.

The HUD evaluation in part ascribed OPR's failure to assume a strong land use and environmental planning function to a bias against a state role in planning. State planning was being equated with state control of land use and local zoning. The strong home rule tradition in the cities and counties militates in favor of decentralized, local planning. The former Administration seemed to share this bias, by displaying no strong commitment to state planning as evidenced by OPR's budget and its confining "staff" function in the Governor's Office.

Council on Intergovernmental Relations

a. Introduction

The Council on Intergovernmental Relations (CIR) is an advisory body which, although statutorily distinct from OPR, has been administratively incorporated "within" OPR and thus the Governor's Office. Its best known efforts to date have been to promote regional planning, to promulgate advisory guidelines for the preparation of local general plan elements and to disburse federal planning funds. Its general purpose is to promote "cooperation" and "coordination" by advising federal, state, regional and local agencies. Having no staff or planning, regulatory or implementation powers of its own, CIR also was statutorily conceived as a council to advise the Governor and Legislature. The Council is composed of 22 members appointed to four year terms by the Governor and represents widely diverse interests: cities, counties, special districts, school districts, state and regional officials, and the public.

Its statutory roles are:

(1) To strengthen local government and improve regional cooperation and intergovernmental coordination.

(2) To provide planning advisory services to local government and generally to aid local jurisdictions in achieving local objectives.

(3) To publish a directory of state services for local government.

(4) To maintain communication with local government through field representatives and report new ideas regarding ways to improve intergovernmental relations.

(5) To examine the roles of the various governmental units and recommend changes.

(6) To act as the Governor's ombudsman for local government.

CIR evolved from the Council on Urban Policy which was created in 1963 as an advisory body to the Governor. During 1966–67 it was renamed the Intergovernmental Council on Urban Growth. Finally, with the reorganization of the executive branch of state government in 1968, it assumed the current name of the California Council on Intergovernmental Relations. The statutory scheme also provided that CIR supersedes the Intergovernmental Council on Urban Growth and the Planning Advisory Committee. In addition, it allocated to CIR some functions previously performed by the state Office of Planning (now the Office of Planning and Research).[1]

b. Responsibilities

CIR is responsible for developing long range policies to assist the state and local government units in dealing with growth and development problems and in defining their respective roles. It is to encourage intergovernmental cooperation and coordination as well as to advise the Governor and Legislature. The Council is to develop guidelines for the preparation and content of the mandatory elements required for city and county general plans. The guidelines are to assist local agencies in developing their general plans but are merely to be advisory.[2] Nonetheless, each city and county must annually report the degree to which its adopted general plan complies with CIR's guidelines;[3] the reports are not legally self-incriminating against a non-compliant local government, however.

CIR is expected to provide planning assistance on request to local governments including advice on preparing and implementing general plans. The statute expressly states that CIR possesses no planning, regulatory or implementation powers, however.[4]

CIR is also responsible for dividing the state into regional planning areas, which have no known legal force and effect (and should not be confused with various regional and area planning laws or organizations described in following sections). In developing such areas, CIR is to attempt to include natural physiographic regions containing major watersheds and the land beneficially affected by such watersheds, and subareas having mutual social, environmental and commercial interests. Curiously, recent amendments allow the voters of counties to have some input as to the area in which a county should be placed.[5]

Another CIR role is to encourage regional planning and to render planning assistance regarding regional planning to local governments. CIR has proposed creation of substate planning districts to enable local government to deal effectively with regional issues.[6] It found fault with the proliferation of special purpose agencies and districts which fragment responsibility for land use planning. It argued that the voter visibility of special purpose agencies and districts is low and that they remove functions from the control of local officials politically responsible and responsive to voter needs. Thus, these single purpose agencies and districts diminish the importance of general purpose local governments.

The CIR proposal attempts to retain the traditional home rule approach but on a regional level. The proposal involves creation of areawide (regional) planning organizations to coordinate planning within a region and to allow local governments to resolve planning issues of regional concern. Such areawide planning organizations would be equipped to enforce and implement long range policies and goals. An organization would be composed primarily of local elected officials (mayor, city councilmen and county supervisors) with some state and federal representatives. CIR felt such a system would place planning responsibility in the hands of a body both knowledgeable about regional and local issues and responsive to voters.

Presently there are numerous systems of substate districting. Many state agencies have subdivided the state for administering their programs. Areawide planning organizations would provide a uniform system for administering state programs applied substate. The CIR proposal would result in a single official regional organization in each area, with state agencies working through the planning organization. Each areawide planning organization would have the primary responsibility for the development of areawide plans and goals. Where the state identifies a regional problem, the local governments working together through the areawide planning organization would undertake long range, comprehensive regional planning and the coordinated implementation of regional goals and state policies. Financing for such a scheme would be shared by the local, state and federal governments.

Although the proposal was not vigorously pursued, many policies were opposed to a well-funded, unrelated study for the Governor on intergovernmental relations, which supported special district governance. Moreover, many of its features are now reflected in a recent proposal by the League of California Cities.

c. Planning Process Assessment

CIR has not enjoyed a significant statutory or political mandate. The one visible function that the Council does perform is the promulgation of guidelines for general plan elements. The guidelines are intended to clarify statutory requirements and to instruct local governments in preparing mandatory plan elements, the number of which has mushroomed in recent years.

Sometimes, however, it appears that the CIR guidelines are taken too seriously by local planners in that some planners believe (1) they have legal force and effect—they do not, or (2) they tend to needlessly overload the local planning process—which they do. In field interviews with local planners, considerable criticism was directed both at the proliferating number of mandatory general plan elements and the adequacy of CIR guidelines.

Four principal criticisms emerged. (1) Many of the planning departments lacked staff or budgets to meet statutory deadlines or to prepare plan elements of at least adequate quality. (2) The technical requirements of the statutes and guidelines either were not readily intelligible or, conversely, were technically overarticulated for some elements (e.g., noise) and underarticulated for others (e.g., housing). (3) Some of the elements and guidelines are simply not relevant to many local conditions (e.g., scale, type and planning needs of local government; the open space needs of Watts are significantly different from those of San Bernardino County or Emeryville). (4) The degree of local compliance with the guidelines is not, as a practical matter, uniformly reviewable by a state or regional planning agency. The nearest approximation to a review process potentially occurs at the state or regional (Council of Governments) levels for review of the environmental impact report (EIR) which must accompany each new local general plan or plan element. However, this is a "paper" review process, sometimes honored more by its breach than its observance, and it is indirect, being limited to the EIR which accompanies the plan or element.

The Legislature's proliferation of general plan elements and guidelines, moreover, is being interpreted by some local planners as an implicit state policy of requiring local governments to solve state or regional level problems. Adequate planning for many of the general plan elements transcends the authority and scale of local governments. Effective planning for the housing needs of low and moderate (and perhaps, middle) income families is more of a regional than local problem, while adequate planning for open space preservation frequently necessitates regional and statewide approaches. One observer says, "The state has expected a degree of land use wisdom from local government that the state has not required of itself."[7]

However, it must be noted that the CIR guidelines are symptomatic and reflective of the piecemeal, accretion process by which the California planning law has developed. The state government has not looked seriously at the organization and structure of the California planning process for several decades.

2. State Development Planning

In the absence of an effective state level planning agency and statutory scheme, it was inevitable that substantial land use planning policy and process vacuums would develop. It was also inevitable that de facto state/substate planning would quietly begin to fill some of the state level legislative and administrative omissions. Such has been the case with several single-purpose state agencies which exercise proprietary powers or utilize "their" lands in ways that have profound land use consequences for the state's citizens.

Other state agencies, also of the functional type, pursue their essentially single-purpose mandates by authorizing development of public works projects which tend to have irreversible and massive consequences for land use and growth patterns. For example, in recent legislative testimony, the state Department of Transportation noted that, absent a state land use policy, plan and planning powers, the Department will act as the "de facto statewide planning coordinator" and the State Transportation Plan now in progress will become "the State's de facto land use plan." Caltrans' testimony apparently was made without fear of overstatement or contradiction.

Although the role of state government in directly sponsoring development activity in California traditionally has been restricted to such public works as road and water projects, it need not be so narrowly defined. To illustrate some of the potential for other forms of public development, this sub-section juxtaposes the state Department of Housing and Community Development with Caltrans and the state Public Works Board, another public works body. The legislative, administrative and financial differences between the public works and housing development agencies are stark, however.

Department of Transportation

a. Introduction

The planning process, administration and intergovernmental relationships of the state's transportation program are currently undergoing extensive reorganization pursuant to major legislative changes enacted in 1972. These changes, based upon AB 69, essentially codified the federal planning process and the state/substate role requirements under existing federal highway and mass transit programs,[1] while, in addition, anticipating probable trends in federal transportation program emphasis.

The California legislation may be viewed as having three primary objectives: (1) de-emphasis of road construction in favor of a multi-modal balance between highway and mass transit systems; (2) development of a statewide comprehensive transportation plan by 1976; and (3) development of the State Plan through a "bottom up" planning process which relies principally upon substate transportation plans, in turn based largely upon local general plans throughout the state. However, because these structural changes are not complete, the overall effectiveness of AB 69 cannot yet be determined fully.

b. Organization

At the state level, the AB 69 legislation established the Department of Transportation (Caltrans) to superintend development of the California Transportation Plan and the substate planning process, as well as the financing, design and construction of the state's highway and freeway systems. The law provides for state and substate planning for mass transit systems, but their actual finance and implementation has continued to be reserved to local governments, not to the Department. Thus, while the laws articulated and imposed upon the Department extensive planning requirements for multimodal systems, implementation powers for highways and freeways have remained at the state level, while for mass transit systems they have remained with local or regional agencies.

As a result, Caltrans is best understood as the institutional successor to the former Department of Public Works in terms of continuity of planning, finance and implementation of a single transportation mode—highways and freeways. These functions previously characterized the Department of Public Works, as it attempted to design, develop, maintain, administer and otherwise implement the state freeway master plan (legislatively adopted in 1959) in a relatively cost-effective manner. In addition Caltrans absorbed the personnel and principal constituent of the Department of Public Works, the Division of Highways, as one of six statutorily prescribed internal divisions. The five other internal divisions include transportation planning, mass transportation, aeronautics, legal services and administrative services.[2]

The district offices of the Division of Highways, once under the control and direction of the State Highway Engineer, are now directly supervised by the Director of Transportation and their staffs were enlarged to perform multi-modal transportation planning in cooperation with local and regional transportation planning agencies. These organizational realignments were undertaken to realize better multi-modal planning, liaison and cooperation by the district offices, whose prior duties included continuing, comprehensive and cooperative highway planning at the substate level in association with local and regional transportation planning agencies.

AB 69 also defined an independent and expanded role for the State Transportation Board and implied a considerably diminished function for the California Highway Commission. Until 1973, the Commission was the chief non-legislative body for transportation policy-making and politically a "sacred cow" for state highway interests. For example, at the peak of its administrative influence the Commission, with only nominal legislative review, was able to: (1) designate route alignments for highways and freeways within very broad statutory parameters of the state's freeway master plan; and (2) allocate road construction monies from the State Highway Fund which includes the Highway Users Tax Fund, a substantial and permissive trust fund. The highway trust fund was also established in 1959, the year the Legislature adopted the state freeway master plan, and is financed by a seven cent per gallon gasoline tax. Until recently, trust fund monies were not divertable for non-highway purposes such as development of local or regional mass transit systems.[3]

The emergence of the State Transportation Board under AB 69 can be seen, accordingly, as culminating a process of political, legislative and financial erosion of the powers of the Commission. Underlying factors contributing to the erosion process include shifts in federal transportation policy and availability of federal trust funds for transit purposes, reduction of highway construction funding to the 1952 level, and increasing legislative insistence upon making controversial route decisions, including deletion of proposed freeways under the 1959 master plan. In addition, local governments could in some instances block construction of an unwanted freeway by refusing to close local streets and roads traversing the proposed route.[4] Such local opposition would force the Commission to construct an unwanted freeway completely above or below ground, a very expensive process. For instance, by refusing to close local streets, San Francisco was able to block further extension of the Embarcadero Freeway.

In contrast, the general purpose of the State Transportation Board was declared to be "to advise and assist" the Legislature and Business and Transportation Agency in formulating and evaluating state transportation policy and plans.[5] The Board's powers include the following.

Financial Review. The Board is required: (1) to review the annual budget proposed by Caltrans for "consistency with" the State Transportation Plan before its submission to the Department of Finance; (2) to review financial reports prepared by Caltrans regarding transportation system development, planning, construction and operation by state and substate agencies; and (3) to review and allocate funds from the State Transportation Fund for transportation planning and research.

Plan Review. Plan review responsibilities consist of reviewing: (1) component plans of the State Transportation Plan prepared by the Department and regional transportation planning agencies, including the state freeway master plan and aviation master plan, and (2) transportation implications of major state, regional or areawide comprehensive general plans, including the State Environmental Goals and Policy Report and the State Parks and Recreation Plan.

Plan Adoption and Implementation. The Board is required (1) to assist if requested in drawing boundaries of regional transportation districts, (2) to adopt the California Transportation Plan, prepared by the Caltrans Division of Transportation Planning, for submission to the Legislature by January, 1976, and (3) to monitor implementation of the state Plan.[6]

The role of the Board was further strengthened by two other statutory provisions. Organizationally it became an autonomous body with its removal from the Business and Transportation Agency, the umbrella agency which previously encompassed the Department of Public Works and Highway Commission. Once the Plan is adopted by the Board and Legislature, the Highway Commission, Toll Bridge Authority, Aeronautics Board and Department of Transportation are required to "act in accordance with" the Plan.[7]

c. Legislative Intent

The new institutional framework regarding Caltrans and the State Transportation Board is part of an unusually comprehensive and well articulated law which also clearly defines governmental roles and a more contemporary set of transportation policies. These institutional relationships have important implications for establishing a de facto state/substate planning process. Hence, the state Transportation Plan, described below, could become California's de facto land use plan. And because AB 69 is the most recent legislative expression regarding state/substate roles and planning process, the intent of the Legislature warrants full description.

(1) Role of the State

The Legislature found and declared the role of the state government in part to be to:

"(a) Encourage and stimulate the development of urban mass transportation and interregional high-speed transportation where found appropriate as a means of carrying out the policy of providing balanced transportation in the state.

"(b) Implement and maintain a state highway system which supports the goals and priorities determined through the transportation planning process, which is in conformity with comprehensive statewide and regional transportation plans, and which is compatible with statewide and regional socioeconomic and environmental goals, priorities and available resources."[8]

(2) State Transportation Policy

The Legislature's declaration of California transportation policy is as follows.

"(a) The diversity of conditions in California is such as to require a variety of solutions to transportation problems within various areas of the state. . . . In some cases, future demands, particularly in urban corridors, may prove to be beyond the practical capabilities of a highway solution; while in other cases, environmental conditions may rule out a highway solution. In still other cases, heavy reliance upon highway transportation may prove to be satisfactory for the foreseeable future.

"In all cases, regional and local expressions of transportation goals, objectives, and policies which reflect the unique characteristics and aspirations of various areas of the state shall be recognized in transportation planning, tempered, however, by consideration of statewide interests.

"(b) . . . . The provision of adequate transportation services for persons not now adequately served by any transportation mode, particularly the disadvantaged, the elderly, the handicapped, and the young, should be an integral element of the planning process. . . . It is the desire of the state to provide a transportation system that significantly reduces hazards to human life, pollution of the atmosphere, generation of noise, disruption of community organization, and adverse impacts on the natural

environment. The desirability of utilizing corridors for multi-modal transportation, where possible to improve efficiency and economy in land use, is recognized. The coastal zone should be provided with optimal transportation services consistent with local and regional goals and plans, with the objective of conserving the coastal resource.

"(c) The responsibilities for decision-making for California's transportation systems are highly fragmented. This has hampered effective integration of transportation planning and intermodal coordination. . ."[9]

d. State and Substate Planning Process

The Department of Transportation was directed by AB 69 to prepare the California Transportation Plan for achieving "a coordinated and balanced" statewide transportation system. The Plan is to include mass transit, highway, aviation, maritime and railroad systems and is to be "consistent with the state's social, economic and environmental needs and goals."[10]

The state Plan will be based upon regional transportation plans prepared by regional transportation agencies (or at their request, Caltrans) according to state statutory requirements and advisory department guidelines. In addition, the Plan may include: (1) alternate recommendations for resolving conflicts or omissions in the regional plans which are of "statewide interregional interest"; and (2) recommendations "to promote consistency" among regional plans so as to provide better total system integration, balance and equity "on a statewide basis."[11]

The initial draft of the Plan is to be submitted by the State Transportation Board to the Legislature for adoption by January, 1976, following its own deliberations and a series of public hearings. The hearings "shall solicit" the views of the public as well as various public and private organizations affected by the Plan. "Any objections raised, including, but not limited to, inconsistencies, conflicts, or disagreements between regional transportation plans and the California Transportation Plan, shall be resolved by the board."[12] The Department is required to update the Plan, once adopted, each year for two years and then every second year thereafter and to submit these revised drafts to the Board (not the Legislature) for adoption.[13]

Thus, the state Plan will have considerable force once adopted by the Legislature, because the Highway Commission, Toll Bridge Authority, Aeronautics Board, State Transportation Board and Department of Transportation "shall act in accordance with" the Plan, and the regional plans incorporated by it, "except as otherwise provided by law."[14]

(1) Initial Report to Legislature

Submission of the State Transportation Plan will be the final of three reports required for consideration by the Legislature. It will conclude a legislative review process for preparation of the state Plan, which also has included an initial report and a Progress Report.

As required by a 1972 legislative resolution, the State Transportation Board was to submit to the Legislature a report describing:

(a) Provisions to insure that local communities would have "adequate control" over new transportation development.

(b) Provisions regarding "the need for creation of regional authorities with the responsibility to implement" regional transportation plans, but "taking into consideration the possibility of alternative approaches in view of significant differences among the regions of the state."[15]

(c) Allocation of responsibilities for constructing, operating and control of resources among various governmental units.

(d) Necessary changes in the transportation planning process including planning criteria.

Legislative acceptance of the report (which was subsequently given) was made a precondition to funding preparation of the state and regional transportation plans.[16]

(2) Progress Report

A Progress Report on the state Plan was submitted by the Board to the Legislature by July, 1974 as required by law. The report was to include:

(a) Recommendations as to statewide and regional goals, objectives and policies for all transportation modes.

(b) Proposed application of statutory criteria "which shall guide" the development and evaluation of the state and regional plans. (The statutory criteria for evaluating alternative transportation plans for their land use, economic, taxation, environmental, and social system performance and service levels are described below.)

(c) Information on the organizational status of the Department.

(d) Description of the Department's work program including recommended changes in its planning methods.

(e) Recommendations as to the need and desirability for statutory establishment of regional transportation planning agencies including their boundaries and formation.

(f) Preliminary proposals for "effective state, regional, and local decision-making for transportation" including protection of local communities and designation of implementation roles and responsibilities.[17]

The Progress Report was then updated and augmented for a second submission to the Legislature in January, 1975. The augmented report has incorporated inventories of travel desires, goods movement and transportation facilities; statutory requirements for transportation services; and financial resources for transportation planning, development and operation.[18]

Although the substate planning process in general appeared well underway as of April, 1974, major shortfalls were noted by the Department in its Progress Report to the Board.[19] Among the noted deficiences was the capability of urban versus non-urban regional transportation planning agencies (TPAs). For the urban transportation planning agencies (TPAs), already familiar with the so-called 3C's of highway planning—continuing, comprehensive and cooperative planning under the federal Highway Act of 1972, AB 69 served as "a catalyst" and "their planning efforts shifted into high gear", according to the Progress Report. The non-urban TPAs, however, "have devoted most of their efforts to organizing and developing work programs and goals".[20]

Other "deficiencies" in the substate planning process were noted by the Department, including:

(a) Recognizing and conforming to federal air quality standards.

(b) Inadequate attention given to environmental, citizen participation and financial considerations.

(c) Non-resolution of jurisdictional issues.

(d) Non-resolution of institutional barriers to regional plan and program implementation.

(e) Inadequate attention given to regional transportation needs and deficiencies, measurable goals and evaluation criteria.

(f) Inadequate attention given to recreational travel and commodity movement.

The Department stated, however, that promulgation

of additional state guidelines "will assist" the substate agencies in overcoming some of the deficiencies.

Nonetheless, the Department further stated that because state Plan development must necessarily lag behind the substate plans, "full compliance with all the requirements of AB 69 will not be possible within the given time frame", *i.e.*, by January, 1976. It noted that "little has been done in certain issues" such as recreational travel and commodity movement which present considerable analytical problems.[21]

(3) Substate Planning

The State Transportation Plan rests upon a substate planning process whose principal components are: (a) 41 "regional" transportation plans which incorporate the land use assumptions of local general plans of cities and counties; and (b) so-called "regional" transportation agencies. For purposes of developing the substate plans, a "regional" TPA may be a federally mandated Council of Governments, a statutory transportation agency, or a single county local transportation commission.[22]

Alternatively, at local option, the "regional" transportation plan may be prepared directly by Caltrans. The Department presently has assigned more than 300 personnel to prepare the substate plans for 23 counties, each with its own Local Transportation Commission. Thus, more than half of the 41 substate plans are being prepared directly by Caltrans in association with local officials. Moreover, the term "regional" plan or planning agency is a misnomer in most cases, because nearly all the substate plans and agencies remain at the county level. The only true regional transportation planning is being performed by the statutory transportation agencies, such as those in the San Francisco Bay and Tahoe region or by councils of governments in the Los Angeles and San Diego regions.

Each substate TPA is to prepare a transportation plan "directed at" a coordinated and balanced transportation system that is "consistent with" the region's and state's social, economic and environmental needs and goals. The plans are to include various modes (mass transit, highways, railroads, maritime and aviation) as well as to incorporate appropriate local, state and federal transportation plans. The completed "regional" plan is then submitted to the governing body (or designated policy committee) of the transportation planning agency for adoption following public hearings, and then transmitted to the Department before April, 1975. Thereafter each agency is required to update and resub-

mit its plan annually for two years, and then biennially, to the Department.[23]

(4) Substantive Plan Elements

The legislative scheme imposed comprehensive substantive requirements for both the state and substate transportation plans. However, because the state Plan is to be basically a compilation of the 41 substate plans, AB 69 established common elements for the state/substate plans in order to promote substantive uniformity and thereby to facilitate integration of the substate plans into the state Plan.

At minimum, the state and substate plans are to have a common framework composed of five elements: (a) a statement of goals and objectives, (b) forecasts of needs and deficiencies, (c) a proposed multi-modal transportation system "based on" studies and evaluations of alternative plans, (d) required environmental impact statements and reports, and (e) a "cooperatively" developed implementation program.[24]

In addition, the statute details extensive requirements for generating alternative transportation plans at the state and substate levels. The planning studies are to be directed at proposing alternative plans which reflect various assumptions as to funding, service levels, and "proper utilization of various modes", as well as consideration of "advanced concepts for transportation systems".[25] In evaluating the alternative plans, relationships between transportation and land use, taxation, environment, economic and social factors, policies and goals are to be "considered".

More specifically, the alternative state/substate plans are to be evaluated against six sets of substantive criteria.[26]

(a) Economic—operating costs, capital costs, revenues, impact on local economy and employment, and related public service costs.

(b) Land Use—support of "development pattern" policies, land absorption and multiple use of transportation corridors.

(c) Taxation—tax base and equity.

(d) Environmental—air and water quality; impact on soil, weather, landscape, wildlife and natural resources; and noise, vibration, glare and other effects.

(e) Social—displacement, disruption and relocation; "consistency with social objectives", and "usability by various groups".

(f) System performance and service level—technological feasibility, flexibility, reliability, safety, mobility, accessibility, induced demand, amenity and convenience.

e. Planning Process Assessment

The AB 69 legislation, in specifying state/substate planning process and institutional relationships, closely reflects existing highway and mass transit planning requirements found in federal transportation legislation, programs and administrative guidelines. In summary, the federal planning scheme includes requirements for: organizational arrangements; organization of public involvement; the decision-making process; work programs and staffing; inventory of community and environmental values; goals, objectives and policies; inventories of transportation related data; analysis of data from inventories; forecasts of population, land use, economic and environmental factors in order to determine future year travel demands and system environmental impacts; preliminary needs determination; development and evaluation of alternative plans for all transportation modes; environmental impact evaluation; plan selection and adoption; plan implementation; and a continuing planning process.[27]

The California transportation planning process diverges from the federal planning model—a necessary precondition for funding eligibility of the state's highway and mass transit programs—only in terms of selective emphasis. The state transportation planning process under AB 69, thus conforms to the federal requirements but emphasizes certain aspects. According to Caltrans, emphasis is placed upon citizen participation, environmental assessment of regional transportation systems, coordination among planning agencies, consideration of advanced concepts, planning implementation, and "bottom up" planning from local general plans to regional transportation plans to a State Transportation Plan.[28]

(1) Commitment to Highway and Freeway Development

Sometimes a yawning gap exists between a planning law and the reality of the planning process. Mere enactment of a law may not be sufficient to fully institute a new planning process, especially in the short run. For example, the underlying impetus for AB 69 can be assumed to have been either an enlightened pursuit of a rational state/substate planning process or, alternatively, instinct for survival, following numerous battles with community organizations, conservationists and local officials over the prior overemphasis on highways and freeways as the key to California's transportation needs. Encouraging such a shift were earlier shifts in federal funding priorities; increasing criticism of highway planning by localities, environmentalists and conservationists; the inflationary erosion of gas-tax revenues. With an increasing segment of the highway budget going for maintenance, highway development had peaked in terms of growth potential.

As for Caltrans' continuing but now implicit commitment to highway and freeway development, according to veteran transportation planners, the problem lies in changing Caltrans' organizational environment. Caltrans absorbed more than 15,000 personnel from the former Department of Public Works. Many are highway engineers, who, although undergoing retraining in multi-modal systems, work for an organization which—like its predecessor—still is limited to implementing highways and freeways. Implementing mass transit systems presently requires different forms of governmental liaison, technical assistance, and political skills than are possessed by many Caltrans planners, engineers and administrators.

The new Division of Mass Transportation had an initial staff of 30 persons. Unlike the Division of Highways whose funding is assured by extraordinarily well-financed federal and state highway funds, the bulk of the funding of the Division of Mass Transportation is derived from a state gasoline sales tax whose revenues pass directly through to local governments. The Division's financial purpose then is federal and state grantsmanship for local mass transit systems which it cannot itself implement.[29] Although funding of the state highway and freeway program is now down to the 1950's level, it is still more than adequate.

Finally, it should be reiterated that more than half-23, of the substate transportation plans are being prepared directly by Caltrans personnel in association with county level officials but according to Department guidelines. Hence, a significant portion of the state Transportation Plan may reflect the perspective and assumptions of the district offices whose personnel (in some instances highway engineers reclassified as "transportation planners") may tend to remain committed to highway and freeway development.

(2) Commitment to Air Quality

By way of overview of the intricately complex set of

32

statutory, program and federal-state relationships, it should be noted that AB 69 does not satisfactorily address a critical issue confronting Caltrans-state air quality planning. That issue concerns the relationship of new highway and freeway projects to land use patterns to state and federal air quality standards. The issue is particularly critical in the designated "critical" air basins of California, such as Los Angeles, whose air pollution levels exceed existing national standards. AB 69 basically does two things regarding the transportation/air quality relationship. First, it enunciates legislative policies reflective of current environmental concerns such as the following, "In some cases, future demands, particularly in urban corridors, may prove to be beyond the practical capabilities of a highway solution; while in other cases, environmental conditions may rule out a highway solution."[30] And: "It is the desire of the state to provide a transportation system that significantly reduces hazards to human life, pollution of the atmosphere, generation of noise, disruption of community organization, and adverse impacts on the natural environment."[31]

Secondly, AB 69 provides no well defined or enforceable air quality standards to ensure that new highway projects, the state Transportation Plan or the state/substate planning process are effectively regulated. Rather, it speaks to most of state/substate state plans which are "based on" studies that include alternative transportation plans. These alternative plans are to be "evaluated" in terms of "considering" the relationships between transportation, land use and the environment (including air and water quality) as well as taxation, economic and social factors. AB 69, accordingly, provides for no more than "consideration" of air quality impacts. After two years of environmental impact review of Caltrans transportation projects, the Air Resources Board has found many instances of "inadequate consideration" of their air quality impacts.

It is not clear whether the statutory gap regarding the significance of air quality standards was a legislative oversight. However, it is clear that carefully articulated, enforceable standards potentially could paralyze further highway and freeway development especially in critical air basins. But, what the state law failed to provide in AB 69, the federal environmental and highway statutes and programs have provided. In brief, the federal scheme makes the following pertinent provisions regarding the transportation/air quality relationship.

(a) The federal Clean Air Act of 1970 directs the Environmental Protection Agency (EPA) to approve State Implementation Plans (SIPs) if they can effectively demonstrate air emission strategies, which may include land use and transportation controls.[32]

(b) Section 109 (j) of the federal Highway Act of 1970 required promulgation of federal guidelines to assure that federally aided highways are "consistent with" state plans for implementing regional ambient air quality standards.

(c) The Federal Highway Administration in November, 1973, issued air quality guidelines for federally-aided highway programs which in pertinent part provide: "Comprehensive planning for land use, air quality and transportation are interdependent. These planning activities should be closely coordinated in the conceptual stages and throughout the highway project development process. The (state) highway agency shall follow . . . appropriate procedures . . . to assure that the planning and construction of highways are consistent with the State Implementation Plan for attainment and maintenance of air quality standards."[33]

Accordingly, the combined effect of the federal scheme is to (1) articulate air quality standards which are incorporated in the federally mandated State Implementation Plan (described in the following section), (2) require Caltrans and the substate transportation planning agencies and process to be "consistent with" the federal standards, and (3) note that any "significant deficiencies" will be grounds for withholding federal highway funds.

Thus, the federal "consistency" requirement has the further effect of changing air quality from an environmental "consideration" to an operative transportation planning and project constraint in California. The State Air Resources Board review of the substate transportation planning process as of January, 1974, found "inadequate integration" of air quality constraints. Caltrans responded by instructing the substate agencies to submit alternative plans by Fall, 1974, which met federal standards, as well as transportation control plans in five critical air basins—Los Angeles, San Francisco, San Diego, Sacramento and San Joaquin Valley.

The ultimate test of Caltrans' commitment to air quality will be whether on its own initiative—not due to funding cutbacks, local opposition or legislative pressure—it decides not to proceed with a proposed freeway in a critical air basin.[34] Several such freeways are pending in Los Angeles. "The critical Los Angeles air pollution calls for an immediate solution," according to A. Alan Post, Legislative Analyst, who notes in part concluding his February, 1974, evaluation report on Caltrans that: "The state now cannot make such decisions."[35]

(3) The "De Facto" California Land Use Plan

In its July, 1974 testimony before the Senate Local Government Subcommittee on Land Use Planning, Caltrans representatives described several underlying land use assumptions and implications concerning development of the state Transportation Plan.

First, the state Plan will integrate 41 substate plans which depend on the long range land use assumptions of local general plans throughout the state.[36] Thus, the state/substate plans rest upon local land use assumptions as to population, growth, employment, incomes, housing and so forth. (As later sections of this report make clear, the adequacy of the state's local general plans and planning process is highly variable, ranging from generally excellent to merely adequate to essentially primitive).

Second, Caltrans observed, as have many others, that California lacks a set of "clearly articulated statewide comprehensive planning policies" but carefully noted that this was "not necessarily a statutory deficiency."[37]

Third, it said that, "Lacking clear direction on statewide land use policies, the land use assumptions contained in the aggregated land use plans from the 41 transportation planning regions will become *the State's de facto land use plan*."[38] (Emphasis supplied).

Finally, it indicated that, "If the planning process remains essentially as it is, then Caltrans would continue its catalytic role as coordinator, that is, striving to achieve as much comprehensiveness as possible. It should be realized that Caltrans, and before that, Public Works, has maintained an extensive organization of planners throughout the State and has cooperated effectively with planners at all levels of government for many years. In fact, under existing conditions and because of the necessity for a high degree of comprehensiveness in transportation planning, Caltrans is carrying out the role of *de facto statewide planning coordinator*. This is not the role we think we should have."[39] (Emphasis supplied).

Thus, Caltrans accurately perceives itself, absent a comprehensive statewide land use policy and planning process, as the de facto state planning agency. Yet its transportation planning powers, as derived from the AB 69 legislation, may be somewhat tenuous. Its statutory planning powers entail "coordinating", "assisting", "studying" and developing either "in cooperation with" or "upon request of" substate transportation planning agencies.[40] Caltrans planning guidelines (e.g., air quality) are technically "advisory" for the substate agencies, most of which are county level organizations.

For these and other reasons, a conclusion of the A. Alan Post report on Caltrans is particularly appropriate: "In summary, the state has a comprehensive transportation planning organization, a statutory board of doubtful effectiveness to resolve transportation planning conflicts, a plan to control major construction programs and virtually no capability to resolve transportation problems with local government."[41] In addition, Caltrans is charged ironically with ensuring adequate provision for multi-modal, balanced transportation systems in the State Transportation Plan, while being empowered only to implement automobile-related highway and freeway projects.

Department of Housing and Community Development

a. Introduction

As established in 1965,[1] the Department of Housing and Community Development is responsible for housing and community development activities. The Department, as well as its governing body, the Commission of Housing and Community Development are: (1) to act as an information source for housing and community development programs; (2) to protect and conserve "the large equities that the majority of California residents in most economic strata have now accumulated in single family homes"; and (3) to improve housing conditions of the state's farmworkers.[2]

b. Organization and Functions

A nine-member Commission, appointed by the Governor, establishes departmental policy and may promulgate housing regulations and minimum standards pursuant to various housing related laws, including the State Housing Law, Employee Housing Law and Mobilehome and Mobilehome Park Law. With the Council on Intergovernmental Relations and Office of Planning and Research, the Commission and Department developed guidelines for preparation of housing elements to local general plans and for relocation of households displaced by public work projects. The Department is within the executive department of the state government; its director is appointed by the Governor.

The functions of the Department are: to "assist" local governments and private enterprise on community development and housing matters; to establish, administer and enforce minimum housing standards and regulations pursuant to various housing related laws; to maintain a statistics and research service; to "make recommendations" to the Governor for changes in state and federal housing laws; and to "encourage" planning and other activities intended to increase housing supply and quality. It was required to develop the California Statewide Housing Element and is "responsible for coordinating federal-state relationships in housing" and for "encouraging full utilization" of federal programs which assist "the residents of this state, the private housing industry and local government, in satisfying California's needs."

c. Planning Process Assessment

As a "facilitating" type of agency, the Department has had minor influence upon housing and land use-related planning in the state. This may be attributed to several factors operating within and without the Department. The Department is statutorily weak, with nominal powers and budget. This is exemplified by the Legislature's sweeping but vague mandate that it prepare a statewide housing element which: (1) contains "housing development goals for the forthcoming year and projected five years ahead"; (2) analyzes state and local housing market and code constraints; and (3) presents "recommendations" which will "contribute to" attainment of statewide housing goals.

To date, no part of that mandate has been fulfilled. Part of this non-accomplishment has been the result of inadequate political support both by the Legislature and recent Administration. There have been frequent reorganization and personnel changes within the Department. The statutory language emphasizes "full utilization" of federal programs, rather than establishment of state programs other than those for code regulation and technical assistance. Thus, the prevailing concept was of minimal state involvement for housing planning and construction assistance. The level of program activity reflected a belief that: (1) state government had little role in housing beyond providing information and standards of construction to the private market; and (2) the need of low-income households for decent, standard and sanitary housing could be met satisfactorily by the private market and by utilization of federal housing programs.

Public Works Board

a. Introduction

The state Public Works Board influences the real estate and construction activity of most state agencies. The Board reviews state construction projects funded by the Legislature and approves their construction and timing on the basis of the immediate needs of state agencies, cost considerations and the need for developing public works to relieve unemployment. Under the Property Acquisition Law, the Board must approve land acquisitions by all state agencies except the Department of Transportation, Department of Water Resources, Reclamation Board, University of California and community colleges. It must also approve sales of surplus state property authorized by the Legislature.

b. Organization

The Board is located in the Department of General Services and consists of that department's director as well as the Directors of Finance and Transportation as voting members. In addition, there are four legislative advisory members who are non-voting; two senators are appointed by the Senate Rules Committee and two assemblymen by the Assembly Speaker. Traditionally, the Director of Finance has been chairman of the Board.

The Board has no staff of its own. Real estate staff functions (appraising, engineering, and property evaluation and acquisition) are performed by the Real Estate Services Division of the Department of General Services. Staff assistance in the area of construction is provided by the Budget Division of the Department of Finance.

In addition, the Board is advised by an unofficial screening committee consisting of representatives from the Legislative Analyst's Office, Department of Finance, Office of Architecture and Construction, and Real Estate Services Division.

c. Planning Process Assessment

Although there are several examples of the Board's ability to influence the planning decisions of other state agencies, land acquisition for the state park system is illustrative. Typically, the Legislature allocates funds for parkland acquisition in appropriation measures which do not specify the exact parcels to be purchased but merely articulate general policy. (Various statewide park bond propositions are also of this type.) A recent law appropriated $3 million to acquire coastal land near the mouth of the Russian River. The Department of Parks and Recreation proposed to acquire a subdivided parcel in the area which had previously received a building permit from a regional Coastal Zone Conservation Commission, and the parcel owner was willing to sell without condemnation proceedings. However, the Board would not approve the purchase. It justified its decision on the basis of cost; it felt that the state should not purchase subdivided land if the remaining area was still in undivided acreage. Apparently, the particular parcel was not sufficiently important in the Board's opinion to justify the expenditure. Thus, although the Board cannot make policy, it can veto or effect modification in minor ways of projects proposed by the Legislature and other state agencies.

3. State Environmental Quality Planning

This subsection explores three state agencies directly involved with the planning, regulation and conservation of environmental resources increasingly precious to the quality of human and organic life: air—Air Resources Board, water—State Water Resources Control Board and the coastline—Coastal Zone Conservation Commission. Because their planning functions are linked with regulatory (i.e., permit) powers, the agencies exemplify the emergence of single-purpose environmental constraints and corresponding (but fragmented) sets of de facto land use controls. Moreover, because of their distinctively different legislative antecedents, these environmental agencies provide disparate illustrations of state/substate planning processes, scope of planning programs, institutional accountability and sensitivity to comprehensive land use considerations. Fullest treatment is given to air quality because of its crucial importance to California's future.

California Air Quality Program

The Federal Background

a. Introduction

The public as well as air pollution control agencies are becoming increasingly aware that national ambient air standards should be achieved and maintained by direct regulation of pollution sources and long range, comprehensive land use planning for air quality.[1] Under the federal Clean Air Act amendments of 1970,[2] states must seek to attain ambient standards by new source location review and licensing,[3] emissions standards for new sources,[4] and the detailed review and licensing of new indirect air pollution sources.[5] These enforcement strategies combined with others[6] create a complex set of constraints on the number of pollution sources within an air pollution control area. The amount of permissible dirty air in any one area may vary according to the ambient standards, control equipment presently in use, anti-pollution technology, geophyiscal configuration of the air basin and other factors.

In addition, the Clean Air Act requires states to achieve and maintain ambient standards by whatever other means may be necessary—including land use and transportation controls.[7] The location and intensity of vehicle-related land uses which result in air pollution could be affected by such controls, especially in critical air basins. Other uses could be affected if, for example, an air pollution control strategy requires population or industrial dispersal in order to secure a desired level of air quality.

b. History of the Clean Air Act

Although "the history of federal air pollution control legislation is one of a growing assertion of authority by the federal government,"[8] the federal statutes repeatedly declare that air pollution control is "the primary responsibility" of the states. The Air Pollution Control Act of 1955 provided that the Department of Health, Education and Welfare (HEW) was to research and provide technical assistance to determine the causes and effects of air pollution. Actual federal regulation began in 1963 with the enactment of the Clean Air Act.[9] The Act allowed HEW to investigate local pollution problems, but only if the pollution had interstate consequences. However, HEW's recommendations were advisory and not binding upon the states involved. HEW was to develop air quality guidelines which states were not required to adopt. Direct federal intervention could occur only by a complicated abatement action in cases where pollution endangered health or welfare.[10]

The federal enforcement role expanded with the Air Quality Act of 1967. HEW was to designate eight atmospheric areas for the continental United States. Each area was to be defined on the basis of climate, meterology and topography, all of which influence the ability of air to assimilate or disperse pollution. Using the same criteria, HEW was also required to designate specific air quality control regions, e.g., the Bay Area. Concurrently, air quality criteria for pollutants and information on available control techniques were being developed by HEW. The Act required the states to set air quality standards and develop plans for implementing them. HEW had to approve the standards and plans, but if the state standards were inadequate, HEW could "take action to insure that appropriate standards are set".[11] The states had the primary enforcement role, but if their efforts were ineffective, HEW was directed to abate cases involving interstate pollution upon the unlikely request of the governors of both states.

c. The Clean Air Amendments of 1970[12]

The 1970 Amendments significantly increased federal involvement in intrastate pollution control. While the Amendments reassert that the states have "the primary responsibility" for air quality control, the responsibility now became "one of complying with federal air quality standards."[13] EPA was to promulgate two types of ambient standards: primary—based solely only on health protection considerations, and secondary—based on socioeconomic and public welfare considerations.[14] Within nine months after promulgation of a primary ambient air standard, each state was to adopt a State Implementation Plan (SIP). The SIP was subject to EPA review for attainment of primary standards as expeditiously as practicable. The SIP was also to provide for attainment of secondary standards "within a reasonable time."

In order to avoid "paper plans," EPA regulations require each State Implementation Plan to demonstrate that the state has legal authority to actually implement the Plan, including authority:

(1) to adopt emission standards, limitations and any other measures necessary for attainment and maintenance of national standards;

(2) to enforce applicable laws, regulations and standards;

(3) to abate pollutant emissions in an emergency to prevent substantial health dangers;

(4) to prevent construction, modification or operation of buildings and other facilities which would directly or indirectly result in emissions that would prevent the attainment or maintenance of a national air quality standard;

(5) to obtain information necessary to determine whether air pollution sources comply with applicable laws, regulations and standards including authority to require record-keeping and to inspect and conduct tests of emission sources; and

(6) to require operators of stationary sources to install emission monitoring devices and to make periodic reports to the state on the type and amount of their emissions, and for the state to make such data available to the public.[15]

The EPA regulations speak in terms of state enforcement, but they do not require a state level agency to exclusively enforce the State Implementation Plan. The state agency must retain ultimate enforcement authority, but most enforcement actions can (and do) take place at local or substate levels.[16]

If a state submits an inadequate or no implementation plan, EPA is to then promulgate its own Plan for the state.[17] The 1970 Amendments allow for direct federal enforcement of the SIP. If the implementation plan is being violated, EPA must notify the violator and state involved. After 30 days EPA may then issue a cease-and-desist order or bring a civil action in federal court. Also, if EPA concludes that the State Implementation Plan is not being enforced, it may take over its direct enforcement. No preliminary notice is necessary before state enforcement when violations of new source performance standards or hazardous emissions occur.[18] Moreover, the 1970 Amendments authorize citizen suits against violators of the national emissions standards, limitations or state/federal compliance orders as well as against EPA directly for non-performance of its statutory duties. Actual or threatened citizen suits can potentially assure vigorous enforcement of the federal statute by federal, state and substate agencies.

d. Land Use and Transportation Controls

(1) New Stationary Sources

EPA regulations, based on Clean Air Act provisions,[19] require that the State Implementation Plan include or establish sufficient legal authority in the state/substate air control agencies to prevent construction of new emissions sources if they would interfere with the state control strategy for attaining and maintaining national ambient standards. A state control strategy is a combination of controls designed to reduce emissions levels and can include land use and transportation controls. A new source, then, may be forbidden even if it meets all state and federal emissions standards, if it violates a control strategy for any pollutant.

(2) Indirect Stationary Sources

EPA has further extended control over stationary sources by requiring that State Implementation Plans include authority to prevent construction of indirect sources.[20] Indirect sources are facilities which, while not emitting pollutants directly, can result in the emission of pollutants that prevent attainment or maintenance of a national standard. Facilities such as amusement parks, shopping centers, airports and highways may be indirect sources, because they are magnets for automobiles. EPA has promulgated final rules for the states' indirect source regulations, but it is not clear when they will become effective. Nonetheless, it is apparent that a permit system controlling indirect sources could substantially constrain land use development patterns if major facilities which generate growth, such as highways and airports, are disapproved or are required to shift location.

(3) Other Land Use and Transportation Controls

In addition to reviewing and approving construction of new direct and indirect stationary sources, the federal Act authorizes other land use and transportation controls to achieve national ambient standards. State Implementation Plans must include emissions limitations, schedules and timetables, and "such other measures as may be necessary . . . including, but not limited to, land use and transportation controls."[21]

EPA's implementation of the Act's land use provisions have expanded their potential application for air pollution control. In addition, EPA regulations allow for incorporation of land use and transportation strategies as part of the "control strategy" of the State Implementation Plan.[22]

Despite the fact that the Act and regulations delegate broad authority, there has been little refined articulation of land use planning and transportation controls in State Implementation Plans beyond mandatory new source review procedures. However, EPA may now be forcing states to incorporate land use and transportation planning and controls into their implementation plans. The Agency recently issued a requirement that states submit ten year growth plans for urban or urbanizing areas where attainment and maintenance of national

ambient standards is in doubt.[23] These Air Quality Maintenance Plans are to develop strategies for maintaining ambient standards by regulating the design and location of all new stationary sources. The states are to designate substate air quality maintenance areas which are either (a) currently polluted areas or (b) areas where patterns of land use or development could lead to future air pollution violations. Air quality must be the primary consideration in these substate plans, but it would be unrealistic to assume that other factors, such as energy, transportation, water or sewer controls, would not also be constraints.

The non-deterioration issue will also force land use planning for air pollution control upon the states. *Sierra Club v. Ruckelshaus*[24] held that in so-called pristine areas where air quality already meets or exceeds national standards, State Implementation Plans must ensure that the existing air quality will not deteriorate "significantly." Following the decision, EPA disapproved all state plans because they failed to prevent significant deterioration.[25] EPA has since proposed four controversial, alternate sets of regulations regarding non-deterioration which allow states to consider economic and development factors in setting standards for pristine areas.

(4) Vehicle Controls

While stationary sources are subject to a combined federal/state regulatory approach, with the states having the primary enforcement responsibility, the federal government has preempted the field of motor vehicle controls.[26] Because California's vehicle control program was the most advanced in the nation, the Act created a special exemption for California. EPA must waive federal vehicle emissions standards in California unless it finds (a) that California does not require standards more stringent than applicable federal standards or (b) that such state standards and enforcement procedures are not "consistent with" the federal statutory scheme.[27]

In many urban areas, efforts to control vehicular emissions by testing and inspection programs have failed to meet the carbon monoxide and oxidant standards. EPA has found it necessary that State Implementation Plans for these urban areas contain transportation controls. These plans, as drawn up by EPA in the absence of state action, include strict technological control over pre-1975 automobiles, stationary sources and the times, amounts, places and modes of travel. Some of the EPA proposed regulations may result in severe disruption of the automotive lifestyle.

Air Resources Board

In California the relationship between state and substate air pollution control agencies roughly parallels the federal/state model. The stationary source powers of the substate local agencies predated creation of the state level Air Resources Board, and today the state like the federal government generally plays a supervisory, oversight and, if required, override enforcement role. But, as discussed below, state level enforcement powers have been expanding recently, principally in response to federal air quality initiatives and requirements.

The county level Air Pollution Control District (APCD) for controlling stationary source emissions was established by the County Act of 1947[28], which also provided that the board of supervisors of each county was ex officio to comprise the board of each substate APCD. Regulatory power was conferred upon the county districts authorizing them to establish regulations and a permit system. Under legislation creating the state air pollution control agency, these substate agencies retained "primary responsibility" for controlling air pollution emitted by stationary sources within their respective counties.[29] The only regional APCD in California was initiated by special legislation in 1955. The Bay Area Air Pollution Control District is a special district comprised of the nine Bay Area counties and governed by a board having representatives from both cities and counties.

In response to federal legislative initiative requiring establishment of a single state agency for air pollution control, the Mulford-Carrell Air Resources Act of 1967[30] created the state Air Resources Board.[31] It is responsible for administration, research, development of standards and coordination of air pollution activities. ARB is the designated state agency responsible for implementing the federal Clean Air Act which includes establishing air quality standards as well as air basin and state implementation plans. As the state air pollution control agency, it is to oversee substate stationary source controls and to enforce local standards and regulations when necessary.[32] The Board administers the state's program for the control of motor vehicle emissions[33] while stationary source control remains "the prime responsibility" of the substate APCDs.[34]

a. Statutory Responsibilities

The Air Resources Board is in the Resources Agency and composed of five members appointed by the Governor subject to Senate approval. Its members are to possess certain scientific, administrative and legal qualifications, but they serve exclusively at the pleasure of the Governor and only on a part-time basis. Administrative functions of the ARB are carried out by an executive officer (whom the board appoints) and staff.[35]

Under the federal and state statutory schemes, the Air Resources Board has five principal sets of air pollution control responsibilities:

(1) To divide the state into air basins. This was also the responsibility of EPA under the Clean Air Act Amendments. To date, however, the basin-wide approach has not proven an effective planning or regulatory unit, because most of the substate regulatory functions are carried out by county level APCDs.

(2) To promulgate ambient air quality standards for each air basin "in consideration of" the public welfare including health, illness, sensory irritation, aesthetic values, interference with visibility and "effects on the economy." Although the legislation allows ambient air quality standards to vary among the 13 designated air basins, uniform standards for the entire state were adopted in 1969 and 1970.[36] Federal ambient air standards were promulgated in 1971 in accordance with the Clean Air Amendments, but the state and federal standards differ for some pollutants. In such cases the more stringent standard prevails and is used to determine compliance with the ambient air control program.[37] Although uniform statewide ambient standards are in force, different control strategies for achieving the ambient standards appropriate to each basin have been established by the Air Resources Board.[38]

(3) To promulgate rules and regulations. This consists in large part of the State Implementation Plan as required by the Clean Air Amendments of 1970.

(4) To promulgate emission standards for all stationary and other non-vehicular sources for each basin. This is an example of the ARB's back-up function. The substate APCDs have power to control emissions from non-vehicular sources, but EPA regulations require that the State Implementation Plan includes authority at the state level to adopt emission standards and limitations necessary for the attainment and maintenance of national ambient air standards. Thus, California has a state/substate split of authority for enforcing the SIP as to stationary and other non-vehicular souces. ARB is responsible for adopting stationary standards, but each substate APCD may adopt more stringent standards. If ARB determines that a substate APCD program cannot

achieve and maintain ambient standards, it may assume substate enforcement powers, in which case the state's emission standards become effective.[39]

(5) To develop test procedures to measure compliance with its own stationary emission standards and those of substate APCDs. As the foregoing indicates, "the primary responsibility" for stationary sources is substate but the state must possess authority to oversee the regulations of the substate districts and to intervene should the substate APDSs fail to fulfill their responsibilities.[40] This state level oversight and override role is required by the Clean Air Amendments and EPA regulations for the State Implementation Plans, and assures that state governments retain necessary and effective enforcement powers.

ARB decides whether to override substate control programs on the basis of its own air quality monitoring, review of rules and regulations of the substate APCDs, citizen complaints and state level political and administrative considerations. ARB is empowered to review the rules and regulations of substate APCDs "to assure that reasonable provision is made to control emissions from non-vehicular sources and to achieve the air quality standards established by the board."[41] The Board may also repeal a substate regulation which does not meet its air quality standards and promulgate its own regulation for the substate APCD. Typically, ARB is required to hold a public hearing giving 30 days written notice of its intent to override, repeal and promulgate a substate regulation. However, if the Board discovers that an episodic concentration of air contaminants is presenting "an imminent and substantial endangerment to the health of persons, and that the districts affected are not taking reasonable action to abate the concentration of air contaminants", it need give only 24 hours notice before taking action.[42] In addition, ARB can review, revoke or modify emission variances issued by a substate APCD if "the variance does not require compliance (with emissions limitations) as expeditiously as practicable."[43]

ARB's federally-mandated authority to oversee and override, if necessary, substate APCD regulations or variances for local stationary sources has significant land use implications. Emission controls can influence the location of new and existing stationary sources such as certain types of industrial and manufacturing plants. As was previously mentioned, each county level APCD may set emission limitations that are stricter than ARB's standards. However, there are potential tradeoffs involved between the county's economic and tax base

and its clean air and health of its residents. Significant disparities in substate standards may induce stationary sources to locate in counties with less strict air quality standards if other economic factors (e.g., labor supply, accessibility, land costs, etc.) are roughly comparable. Moreover, the land use implications would be heightened should some substate APCDs, in order to attract or preserve stationary sources, adopt permissive enforcement or variance policies and thereby elevate economic and tax base considerations over attainment and maintenance of relatively clean air.

b. Land Use and Transportation Controls

(1) New Stationary Sources

As required by EPA regulations, the State Implementation Plan must include authority to review and approve new stationary sources. Issuance of permits for new sources is the primary responsibility of substate APCDs which must operate within ARB approved basin implementation plans. Under ARB pressure and threatened intervention, South Coast Air Basin APCDs in 1973 adopted regulations to bring their permit systems into conformity with the State Implementation Plan with regard to excessive ambient air concentrations of pollutants. Four of the substate APCDs adopted the ARB-inspired regulations, but the state agency had to override and promulgate its own regulations for the Orange and Santa Barbara County APCDs.

These new state mandated regulations may also have significant land use implications for the South Coast Air Basin which includes most of the Los Angeles metropolitan region. A new stationary source may be forbidden from a location if its emissions contribute to pollutant concentrations exceeding an ambient standard even though it cannot be proven that the source by itself would violate the ambient air standard. The new regulations in effect subdivide the air basin into pollutant concentration areas. In areas of low pollution concentrations, new sources probably will not be prohibited while in already dense areas, where concentration levels are high, it is more likely that new sources permits would be denied. The new regulations may induce new stationary sources to locate in cleaner areas in order to secure the required permit.

(2) Indirect Stationary Sources

Following EPA's final regulations for indirect stationary sources, urban area APCDs may have to incorporate indirect source controls into their programs. This would require in part estimations of long term effects on land use and development patterns resulting from approval or denial of such indirect sources as new highways, airports, shopping centers, amusement parks, and other major vehicle related land developments. ARB has proposed two levels of indirect source review: (a) a basic program to review sources individually, primarily for localized effects and (b) a supplemental program "which would establish a regional framework for interfacing land use and transportation planning efforts" in the five critical urban air basins.[44] This proposal, and legislation which ARB has proposed to relate land use and transportation planning to air pollution control, envisage a lead role for the substate APCDs while ARB continues as the state agency with oversight and override powers.

(3) Transportation Controls

California was required to submit transportation control plans (TCPs) for the Sacramento Valley, San Diego, San Francisco Bay Area, San Joaquin Valley and South Coast air basins. The control plans are basically measures to reduce automobile emissions, with some discussion of transportation controls designed to reduce vehicle miles travelled. The State Implementation Plan states "that development of traffic control measures and transportation plans for certain air basins is essential if air quality standards in those areas were to be attained."[45] However, transportation planning for developing alternatives to the motor vehicle, including the reduction of vehicle miles travelled, is the primary responsibility of the state Department of Transportation under an interagency agreement between ARB and Caltrans. ARB has also instituted an information exchange with Caltrans, which is preparing the California Transportation Plan.

c. Planning Process Assessment

This section focuses generally upon the federally mandated State Implementation Plan, (S.I.P.) the nature of ARB's response and compliance, and some resulting implications for effective land use and transportation controls in California's critical air basins, the most populated and urbanized areas of the state. The SIP is the primary, state/substate planning instrument to emerge from the federal statutory scheme and the subsequent regulations and control strategies enunciated by EPA.

However, the reader—if he is not to be overwhelmed by technical, bureaucratic and political claims and counterclaims—may appreciate additional background information. Thus, this section is in two parts. The first part prvides a planning process overview of the SIP including its intended purpose as well as observations about the air quality-land use control relationship and the reactive posture of ARB. Since the SIP prepared by ARB was found "not acceptable" by EPA regarding the implementation of land use and transportation controls, some of the *de facto* status quo implications are explored in the second part.

(1) Planning Process Overview of the State Implementation Plan

As indicated earlier, the legal structure of a SIP comprises a mandatory set of state level powers which, however, as part of the state's statutory scheme for air quality, may be delegated to substate control agencies operating at the county level. That legal structure is built upon the following powers:

(a) To adopt emission standards, limitations and other measures to attain and maintain national standards.

(b) To enforce applicable laws, regulations and standards.

(c) To abate pollutant emissions on an emergency basis.

(d) To prevent construction, modification or operation of direct and indirect stationary sources whose emissions will prevent attaining or maintaining national standards.

(e) To obtain information needed to determine air pollution source compliance.

(f) To require stationary sources to install emission monitoring devices, with the state agency in turn making the information available to the public.

(g) To inspect and test motor vehicles and/or to develop transportation control measures and land use control measures.[46]

A SIP should be exactly what it purports to be: a state's plan for implementing the mandatory elements of the federal statutory/regulatory scheme. The state plan of necessity should attempt to orchestrate various state and substate agencies as well as substantive strategies. These substantive strategies, only recently entering the planning lexicon, are known as new stationary source controls, indirect stationary source controls, Air Quality Maintenance Plans (AQMP), and Transportation Control Plans (TCP) which can include reducing vehicle miles traveled (VMT), and parking management plans (PMP).

The end result should be a coherent response for achieving and maintaining national air quality standards and goals.

However, the stationary source and transportation control elements of the SIP submitted by ARB were rejected as "not acceptable" by EPA for failure among other things, to demonstrate adequate state level review and regulation procedures and thus attainment of national standards. Not only was the SIP submitted after the expiration of most plan submittal deadlines,[47] but as a document it is, in the opinion of a former ARB official, "a huge mess. It is a huge bulky bundle of papers, with some strategies, but it is not a plan." A similar conclusion was reached by the Legislative Analyst: "The implementation plan of the ARB is essentially a schedule of control actions rather than a comprehensive plan. It furnishes no guidelines to land use decisions because the plan recognizes air quality control as an end in itself rather than a basis to coordinate reductions of emissions with land use decisions or beneficial changes in land use. . . . When under existing law or . . . indirect source controls, the ARB has to review any local (APCD) air quality decisions, it has no plan, policy or land use basis to review the local decisions."[48]

Two additional background observations should be made. First, there is no direct short term, and hence technically well defined, relationship between land use controls and air quality. A strategy which regulates the type, location and intensity of new development is necessarily a long range air quality strategy and should be viewed as supplementing vehicular and transportation strategies.

A land use strategy, nonetheless, will be as necessary as vehicular and transportation control strategies in a heavily urbanized, critical air basin, according to indirect source control proposals made by EPA and ARB. "In California's major urban areas, 70 to 80 percent of the principal air pollutants can be attributed to the use of the automobile, the same automobile which it has been observed is basic to California's life style and to many of its land use patterns. Much of the remaining nonindustrial, nonautomotive air pollution results from what people do and how they live. It will be necessary to bring all these sources of air pollution under stringent controls if ambient air quality standards are to be met."[49]

How the ambient standards are to be achieved and maintained in the critical air basins has been the subject of divergent federal, state and in some cases, substate approaches. Although there are serious differences in scientific opinion, according to an analysis by the League of Women Voters, a "bureaucratic standoff" currently exists between EPA and ARB "with each agency supporting its stance with its own scientific data, uncommited to joint goals."[50]

Secondly, it should be noted that while ARB (and its predecessor agency) initially pioneered the use of vehicle exhaust controls, its position regarding land use and transportation controls has been reactive to federal initiatives and requirements. The ARB board has stated that it does not want to be the state agency making basic state/substate land use decisions and the attendant political, economic and social tradeoffs.[51] Its position was reflected by development of the SIP which was not only tardy, but basically an attempted response to the federal statutory scheme. Establishment of ARB in 1967 was also in response to federal "forcing" legislation as was its more recent, reluctant entry into the fields of indirect stationary and transportation controls, both of which continue to be pioneered by EPA.

If a "bureaucratic malaise" settled in over ARB as "an agency that has faded from national prominence,"[52] some of the contributing factors are readily apparent. In a state which has traditionally valued a "home rule" ideology and legislatively delegated "the primary responsibility" for air quality and transportation planning to single county agencies, any state level intrusion directly into local land use control is, accordingly going quickly to become "a hot potato." A frequently mentioned statutory deficiency is the composition of the ARB board. Under the state statutory scheme the board consists of five half-time members who serve "at the pleasure" of the Governor, and most of the recent ARB board, previously noted for their "lack of aggressiveness,"[53] were dismissed by the new state Administration.

Finally, a quiet "bureaucratic standoff"[54] continues between ARB and EPA which is being played out in various arenas; including the following interview with Dr. Jan Arlie Haagen-Smit, director of ARB and former university professor:

"Those people in Washington are out of touch with reality. They don't know that I can't tell the Legislature to pass those bills we need. I can't establish and run a transportation system. And the idea of land-use controls—do they think the Govenor is going to give that to the professor from Cal Tech?"[55]

(2) Land Use and Transportation Control Implications

The general effect of the "unacceptable" SIP has been to

leave the state's statutory and regulatory provisions intact for the control of stationary sources and transportation emissions. Although under federal law EPA is to promulgate necessary regulations and assume direct enforcement authority, it may be likely that many in both EPA and ARB believe that the likelihood of such potent federal intervention is highly remote.

In summary, the ARB may not find itself in a position where it must quickly devise and implement land use and transportation plans for achieving air quality. It could then ignore land use considerations and pass responsibility for transportation control strategies to Caltrans, which could substitute traffic control measures for the needed strategies. The stringent requirements of the Clean Air Act may thus not intrude significantly upon the performance of the ARB or EPA.

(a) Land Use Control Implications

The State Implementation Plan was disapproved in part because ARB failed to demonstrate adequate state level review and regulation of new and indirect stationary sources. As indicated earlier, "the primary responsibility" for regulating stationary sources is statutorily delegated to substate APCDs operating at the county level, whose respective boards are comprised ex officio of the local boards of supervisors.

In the opinion of the Legislative Analyst, while the logical basis for administering air quality programs is at the air basin or regional level, "there is no effective structure in existence for that purpose."[56] The state statutory scheme requires APCDs to come together as basinwide "coordinating councils" to coordinate the stationary source planning and federal implementation plans by the member APCDs. Supervisory oversight and override powers, if required, are reserved to the state level ARB. The Legislative Analyst then makes three astute observations: (1) "The councils are not state agencies, but are local agencies with a governing board of local officials." (2) "The ARB has been reluctant to utilize these councils" (3) "For this reason and because of governing board membership problems, the effectiveness of the councils is minimal."[57]

There are varying assessments of APCDs' performance. Because they are single purpose agencies and highly responsive to local governments they may tend to steer away from land use and transportation controls. As an example, in the South Coast Air Basin of the metropolitan Los Angeles airshed, the APCDs are not denying permits to construct new stationary sources,

although the ambient air quality standards are exceeded more than 200 days per year. However, many believe that adequate independent reviews of new source locations are being made by the APCDs.

In contrast, ARB stated in its 1973 *Annual Report* that it has never found it necessary to take direct regulatory action in any local control districts. Rather, its role has apparently been self-restricted to preparing reports on major stationary sources, preparing emissions inventories, suggesting additional regulations and investigating citizens complaints.[58] ARB seems to have been most successful, for example, in persuading the local agencies to accelerate their compliance schedules of some major stationary sources.

As for controlling new indirect stationary sources, such as highways, airports, large parking lots, shopping centers and the like, ARB has proposed legislation that would build upon the substate APCDs to allocate the location of new emissions within an air basin. Once the basinwide emissions allocations were established by the APCDs, local governments would decide upon appropriate land uses which could include new direct and indirect stationary sources. As the Legislative Analyst noted, "this approach temporarily avoids the issue of participating in or guiding the efforts to limit growth and land use" in the five critical air basins already exceeding the national ambient standards. "More important, where the (ARB) board should be disapproving new emissions sources or reducing existing emissions by every means possible, it will still be contemplating dispersing additional emissions."[59]

(b) Transportation Control Implications

The transportation element of the SIP was disapproved by EPA for failure to develop adequate Transportation Control Plans for attaining national ambient standards by 1975 in California's five critical air basins—San Diego, Los Angeles, San Joaquin Valley, San Francisco and Sacramento Valley. Specifically, according to one of the former ARB officials, the transportation element was "unacceptable" because: (1) The technical calculations were internally inconsistent and based on different measurement standards; (2) adequate state level legal authority for assuring effective implementation was not conclusively demonstrated; (3) a strategy or methodology for actually reducing the number of vehicle miles traveled was not proposed; and (4) attainment of national ambient standards by 1975 for all pollutants was not demonstrated, although an extension to 1977 was sought.

The chief effect of the disapproved SIP is that the state Department of Transportation (Caltrans) has "primary responsibility" for developing and executing the transportation control strategies required under the SIP. An interagency agreement in November, 1973 provides in pertinent part that:

Caltrans ". . . shall assist local and regional government in integrating air quality concerns in the evaluation of transportation alternatives . . . The Air Resources Board will assist Caltrans in the development of plans for a reduction of emissions from transportation systems and work with Caltrans on evaluating alternate transportation control measures as a means of reducing air pollution. ARB shall coordinate its activities with Caltrans and call on Caltrans for advice and recommendations regarding traffic control measures for reducing air pollution."[60]

Although the interagency agreement provides for "coordinating" transportation planning with air pollution control, it does not per se ensure development of effective Transportation Control Plans for the five critical air basins. An effective TCP would probably necessitate strategies for reducing automobile usage by reducing vehicle miles traveled. In addition, this should directly influence consideration of alternate transportation systems in the regional transportation plans being prepared under Caltrans "advisory" guidance and indirectly result in long range implications for land use development patterns.

Two diverse viewpoints exist on this issue. The combined effect of the substate TCPs under the State Implementation Plan and the Federal Highway Act requirements for air quality/transportation "consistency" could transform air quality from a "consideration" into a definite planning "constraint." Alternatively, there could be little action due to absent motivation, although ARB could assure that new highway and freeway projects are "consistent with" air quality standards by its environmental impact reviews (EIR). There are difficulties with both viewpoints, however.

First, ARB's environmental review of new Caltrans projects, including proposed freeway development in critical air basins, is activated after the fact—i.e., after Caltrans has already made the basic decision to undertake the project. The most ARB can do is to slow down project development by challenging the environmental analysis contained in the EIR. It does not challenge the basic decision by Caltrans (or other state agencies), for example, that the new freeway is "needed" even though

the ambient air quality of an urban basin already exceeds permissible national limits.

Secondly, it is not commonly appreciated that California has two State Implementation Plans—one prepared by ARB, the other by EPA. The ARB's SIP can be understood, to quote a former official, as "what we have submitted to EPA and EPA has approved." The EPA's SIP includes "what ARB has submitted and EPA has approved, *plus* what EPA has promulgated to make up for ARB deficiencies regarding stationary source and transportation controls, as required by federal law."

The practical effect of two SIPs can have considerable significance for new highway and freeway projects, the official explained. For example: (1) Caltrans decides to build a freeway which must be "consistent with" the Transportation Control Plan (also developed by Caltrans) of the SIP. (2) Because the transportation element of the ARB's SIP contains no well defined strategies, ARB as part of its EIR procedures cannot determine whether the project is "consistent with" its own SIP. (3) Accordingly, ARB will declare that the freeway is "not inconsistent with" the transportation element of its SIP. (4) The responsibility for environmental assessment of the freeway is then shifted de facto from the state ARB to the federal EPA whose SIP contains a transportation element capable of determining project "consistency" with national air quality standards. Thus, this former official observed, "it's very difficult to protect air quality if the "cognizant" air quality agencies cannot agree."

A third difficulty with the ARB-Caltrans agreement was pointed out by the Legislative Analyst. While the two agencies are to "coordinate" air quality/transportation planning, no method is provided for resolving planning and administrative conflicts. Although it has been suggested that ARB could appeal a disagreement with Caltrans to the Governor's Cabinet, the Legislative Analyst commented:

"This is an unlikely event. It is more probable that the problem will remain unsolved, especially if it involves land use or similar local issues. The memorandum provides a convenient resolution of a difficult state problem; it avoids the issue by passing the problems on to local government."[61]

"In air quality and transportation planning the tendency is to avoid significant interrelated policy problems by leaving them to local government to resolve. The state should not look to major expanded state authority with respect to land use or other environmental controls, but should put its existing activities in order."[62]

California Water Quality Program

Water pollution control and its relationship to land use development patterns is emerging to assume an importance equal to the air quality/land use interaction. 1972 amendments to the Federal Water Pollution Control Act (FWPCA) seek the complete elimination of all polluting discharges into navigable waters by 1985. As interpreted by the federal Environmental Protection Agency (EPA) as well as the State Water Resources Control Board, (SWRCB), "navigable" waters are essentially *all* of the state's surface waters. The federal statutory scheme requires private point sources (*i.e.*, those points where waste water is discharged) to install the "best practicable" equipment and other technical controls to limit their discharges by July 1977. By 1983 the "best available" technological controls must be in use for these private point sources. The federal legislation also assumes implicitly that technological advances will be available for waste treatment and industrial processes so that the nation can attain the national goals.

Implementation of the national program has emphasized control of point sources through issuance of permits, grants for constructing waste treatment facilities, planning for water quality and development of water quality standards and allocations. Little emphasis has been placed upon development of non-technological (*i.e.*, non"hardware") control strategies for non-point sources or for point sources other than construction of waste water treatment plants and facilities. Nonetheless, nontechnological control strategies are also necessary. This would seem especially true in California in the development of water quality plans for regional watersheds and in the allocation of grants for new treatment facilities. Both the regional plans and grant allocation system have important land use consequences, especially in developing areas of the state, and could become important leverage points for more comprehensive land use approaches at the state and regional levels.

In addition, shortfalls in developing the new technological controls, which are implicitly assumed in the federal statutory scheme, may necessitate revision of national water quality goals and control strategies. This in turn could influence the state's water quality controls and thus the types of permissible effluent discharges and possible land uses in regard to navigable waters.

Federal Background

a. Legislative History

Amendments to the federal Water Pollution Control Act[1] in 1972 completely replaced the statutory provisions of the previous federal control program. The 1965 federal water legislation and its predecessors were widely criticized for their inability to achieve national water quality objectives. This failure, it has been noted, was due to use of receiving (ambient) water standards, rather than discharge standards, as the basis for enforcement actions.[2] Since ambient standards specify a permissible level of water quality for a body of water, it was difficult to link the discharges of any one of a number of polluters with a violation of the standards and thus difficult to enforce them.

With the 1972 amendments, the federal government assumed a major role in national water pollution control. The Congressional declaration of national goals and policy states that:

(1) The discharge of pollutants into the navigable waters is to be eliminated by 1985.

(2) Wherever attainable, an interim goal of "swimmable" water quality is to be achieved by July 1983, which provides for the protection and propagation of fish, shellfish and wildlife as well as human recreation in and on navigable waters.

(3) The discharge of toxic pollutants in toxic amounts is to be prohibited.

(4) Federal subsidies are to be provided to construct public waste treatment works such as sewage treatment plants.

(5) Basin, areawide and facility planning processes are to be developed and implemented to assure adequate control of pollutant sources in each state.[3]

The legislation is comprehensive and complex, covering all aspects of water quality and pollution control. It requires EPA to conduct extensive research, development and planning programs; to adopt new standards; to regulate industrial facilities and public treatment plants by a federal (or federally supervised) permit system as part of a rigorous enforcement system; and to authorize a massive construction program for municipal sewage treatment facilities.

b. Water Pollution Controls

(1) Receiving Water Standards

Under previous federal legislation, the setting of receiving or ambient water standards was a joint federal/state effort. But the standards "were not designed for use primarily as an enforcement device . . . (t)heir principal objective was the orderly development of our water resources without the necessity of adversary proceedings which inevitably develop in enforcement cases."[4]

Substantively, the water quality standards were made up of three elements: (a) a limited number of potential usages for the water body were developed; (b) the physical characteristics necessary for the desired highest usage of the water body were determined; and (c) a plan for implementation and enforcement of standards was devised. Water usages were to be established after consideration of "economic, health, esthetic, and conservation values which contribute to the social and economic welfare" of the area . . ."[5] Standards for interstate waters were enforceable under both state and federal law. A state itself could set standards for intrastate waters without federal approval.

The designation of specific water usages had potential impacts on land use. If, for example, a stretch of river were designated for residential uses, industrial users would then have to achieve a discharge standard that would maintain the "residential" receiving water standard. Because of the lengthy process for obtaining federal approval of the standards and of associated enforcement problems, in most states the standards were never effective for achieving the legislative goals.

Section 303 of the FWPCA continues in effect the previous state-developed interstate standards but requires that intrastate as well as other interstate standards now receive federal approval.[6] Approval is to be based on the requirements for receiving water standards in effect immediately prior to the 1972 amendments. If the standards were not consistent and if a state does not so adjust them as specified by EPA, EPA could then "promulgate such standards."[7]

Standards approved before the 1972 legislature must be consistent with prior legislation; those promulgated afterwards must be consistent with the 1972 amendments. In general the requirements under either law are the same.[8] Thermal water quality standards under the new legislation are different, however. They must be as stringent as necessary "to protect a balanced, indigenous aquatic population."[9]

(2) Effluent Limitations

The application of effluent standards to point source discharges represented a major shift in enforcement strategy under the FWPCA of 1972. Effluent limitations are "any restriction on quantities, rates, and concentrations of chemical, physical, biological, and other constituents which are discharged from point sources into navigable waters, the waters of the contiguous zone, or the ocean, including schedules of compliance."[10] Point sources are defined as "any discernable . . . conveyance . . . from which pollutants are or may be discharged."[11] Under the effluent control strategy any point source discharge is illegal unless authorized by a permit which established effluent limits. By July 1977 private sources must install the "best practicable" control technology currently available to limit point source discharges.[12] Public treatment plants must meet effluent standards based on secondary waste treatment or better.[13] By July 1983 effluent standards will require the installation of "best available" pollution control technology.

(3) Performance Standards

National performance standards apply to certain point sources constructed after 1972. A "performance standard" is defined as "a standard for the control of discharge of pollutants which reflects the greatest degree of effluent reduction which EPA determines to be achievable through application of the best available . . . control techniques . . . including, where practicable, a standard permitting no discharge of pollutants."[14] It is a standard equivalent to the 1983 effluent requirements. Some of the sources subject to the standards of performance are listed in the legislation, and include major industrial sources such as paper mills, cement manufacturing, iron and steel manufacturing.[15]

(4) Enforcement

Section 402 establishes a permit system for regulating and enforcing effluent limitations for point sources. The permit program may be implemented by either EPA or a state, but a state is expected to eventually assume "primary responsibility" for the granting of permits.

As a prerequisite to EPA approval of a state's permit program, a state must have an approved "continuing planning process."[16] EPA may approve a state permit program if it includes sufficient legal authority:

(a) To issue permits which (1) insure compliance with

applicable effluent limitations, water effluent limitations, performance standards, toxic effluent standards or ocean discharge standards; (2) do not exceed five years; and (3) can be terminated or modified, *e.g.*, for violations or change in conditions.

(b) To issue permits which require inspections, monitoring and on-site entry whenever necessary.

(c) To abate violations of a permit or the permit program, including enforcement sanctions imposing civil and criminal penalties.

(d) To insure that any permit for treatment facilities includes adequate notice to the permit granting agency as to (1) new sources using the public treatment plant, (2) new pollutants, or (3) changes in volume or character of pollutants.[17]

The approved state programs must continue to comply with the FWPCA as amended, and EPA is to withdraw approval if a state fails to remedy any shortcomings.[18] EPA has authority to review every state issued permit and to disapprove it for non-conformance with the FWPCA.[19] Once it determines that a state program is functioning properly, however, EPA may waive its permit review authority.[20]

c. State/Area Planning Programs

(1) State Water Quality Planning

Each state is required by Section 303 (e) of the FWPCA to develop and implement a "continuing water quality planning process" for the purpose of carrying out national objectives.[21] The planning process and subsequent plans are subject to periodic EPA review for consistency with the Act.[22] The process is intended to provide states with the water quality assessment and program management information necessary to make centralized, coordinated water quality management decisions and to encourage water quality objectives which take into account overall state policies and programs, including those for land use and other related natural resources.[23] Through the continuing planning process, a state makes an annual assessment of its progress toward attainment of state water quality standards and develops an annual strategy for directing resources, establishing priorities and scheduling actions.[24]

Central to the planning process is the preparation of basin plans which specify water quality standards, effluent limitations, schedules of compliance, allowable waste loadings and priority lists of needs for construction of wastewater treatment facilities. Analysis is made of "water quality segments" which typically are river sections. Based on the water quality assessments of the various basin plans, a state ranks water quality segments in priority order, and the ranking is then used to direct the development sequence of plans, treatment works construction, permit issuances and other activities.[25] The emphasis is on the control of point sources, such as sewer outfalls, drainage pipes, industrial waste dischargers, etc.; the basin plans (and the analyses of water quality segments) are intended to translate water quality standards for water bodies into specific requirements for identified point sources.[26] The basin plan is to include identification and control of possible non-point pollutant sources (*e.g.*, agricultural runoff, mining effluents and salt water intrusion)[27], but the control powers and grant programs of the FWPCA are not suited to dealing with this type of source.

(2) Areawide Waste Treatment Management Plans

Under section 208, the governor of each state is required to designate areas with "substantial water quality control problems" (generally industrialized, urban areas) and to select for each area "a single representative organization, including elected officials from local governments".[28] Such organizations should have current waste treatment management responsibilities. These organizations are then required to operate "a continuing areawide waste treatment management planning process;" and plans prepared under this "process" must be submitted for EPA approval.[29] Designation attempts to engage agencies with involvement in a wide range of concerns—including land use planning, water sewer planning and coastal zone planning—in order to better relate waste treatment management planning to other planning concerns. If the governor fails to designate a potential planning area having "substantial water quality control problems," local officials, alternatively, may so designate the area under section 208, with EPA's approval. However, the governor may preclude this local designation by making a deliberate "non-designation" of a potential planning area, while reserving the right to designate it at a later date.[30]

A section 208 area planning agency is to prepare a plan identifying the sewage treatment projects necessary to meet anticipated needs. The plan includes construction priorities as well as regulatory programs (a) to regulate the location, modification and construction of treatment facilities and (b) to ensure compliance with industrial pretreatment requirements, state performance standards, and toxic effluent standards and prohibitions. This is all by way of preparation of grant-in-aid applications to EPA. In addition, the planning agency is required to identify the processes and control procedures (including land use requirements) for certain non-point pollution sources and activities. The plan must be consistent with the section 303(e) basin plan and the state regulatory program. The states are encouraged to apply control mechanisms (including land use controls), under the threat of EPA withholding grants and other aid, in order to reduce non-point source pollution. However, the difficulty of applying such controls diminishes EPA's ability to enforce such sanctions.

(3) Grants for Construction of Treatment Works

The 1972 amendments tightened standards for public sewage treatment grants where the previous program had been found to be ineffective. Waste management plans, practices and works must use the best practicable waste treatment technology and should be on an areawide basis and provide for regulating point and non-point sources.[31]

Another criticism of the previous federal grant program was that federal funds were not concentrated in areas of high pollution and often were not effective because antipollution gains from one plant were offset by nearby waste discharges. The FWPCA now tries to eliminate these problems by requiring (1) that proposed plants be consistent with the section 303(e) state plan which must specify funding priorities based on the magnitude of the problem and (b) that the proposed plants be in conformance with the section 208 areawide waste management plan, if one exists and is adopted.

State Water Resources Control Board

a. Legislative Background: The Porter-Cologne Act

While national interest in recent years increasingly focused upon curtailment of water pollution through point and non-point source controls, ambient water standards and comprehensive basin and critical area planning, California, it should be noted, had already "long been in the vanguard of states which have had relatively strong anti-pollution laws."[1] In 1949, the Dickey Water Pollution Act established a state/substate control system administered by nine regional (substate) water boards

under the direction of a state board. The State Water Resources Control Board (SWRCB) emerged in 1967 following the legislative reorganization and combination of the State Water Rights Board and State Water Quality Control Board.[2] "The purpose was to strengthen the state board structure and to combine the two functions of state government so that the quality of affected waters would be considered whenever new water appropriations were considered."[3]

Two years later a vigorous water pollution statute, the Porter-Cologne Water Quality Control Act of 1969,[4] was enacted which has a threefold significance for land use planning. First, the Act retained the nine regional boards but expanded SWRCB's authority to promulgate substate guidelines for the regional boards, to review regional board decision-making and to institute remedial action to prevent pollution and nuisances resulting from improper waste treatment or disposal. Second, more effective administrative and judicial enforcement procedures were provided. For example, new hookups to a public sewer system may be prohibited when the system cannot meet state standards and the new connections would unreasonably impair water quality.[5] Also, important provisions regarding cumulative pollution impacts were established to control individual instances which, if considered separately and alone, may be relatively insignificant. A simple violation of waste discharge requirements is sufficient *per se* for issuance of a cease and desist order by a regional board. Subsequent violations may result in a court order without the need to prove that the particular discharge is causing the pollution problem.[6] This provision for cumulative effects, thus is necessary where several separate discharges contribute to the pollution of a body of water and where it is difficult to demonstrate that any one is the "cause" of the problem.[7] The Act also more closely tied water quality considerations to procedures regarding new applications for water rights.[8] The SWRCB was additionally authorized to institute judicial proceedings to halt pumping of ground water where the quality of such water is threatened with destruction or impairment.[9]

And third, the state's water pollution program not only predated the federal program under the FWPCA but, in addition, provided a model for some amendments to the federal Act in 1972. While many states were proceeding with development of ambient water standards, California had instituted procedures for controlling waste discharges that served as a basis for the federal permit system. The state's requirement of regional (basin) water quality plans was reflected in federal provisions for Section 303(e) state level continuing planning process and Section 208 substate areawide planning for critical areas. Although the California program must meet FWPCA requirements, the state statutory scheme in some aspects remains more comprehensive than the federal. For example, the Porter-Cologne Act makes some provisions for regulating discharges into non-navigable waters such as underground basins and non-point discharges such as agricultural feed lot and irrigation runoff, while the FWPCA does not.

b. Legislative Declarations

The basic tenor of the state water quality program under Porter-Cologne was set by the Legislature's declaration that the people have "a primary interest" in the conservation, control and use of the state's water resources and that the quality of all state waters are to be protected for their use and enjoyment. The quality of state waters are to attain "the highest water quality" which is "reasonable" as indicated by consideration of all present and future demands and the totality of economic, social and other values involved. It was further declared, among other things, that: "the state must be prepared to exercise its full power and jurisdiction to protect" water quality; state waters were "increasingly influenced by interbasin water development projects and other statewide considerations"; and the state program "can be most effectively administered regionally within a framework of statewide coordination and policy."[10]

Further, the legislature declared its intent that the state and regional boards be the "principal state agencies with primary responsibility" for water quality control and coordination. To that end, the state/substate boards are to coordinate "their respective activities so as to achieve a unified and effective" water quality control program.[11]

c. State Water Resources Control Board

The State Water Resources Control Board was established in 1967 and placed within the state Resources Agency, a "super-department" encompassing other boards and departments associated with natural resource administration. The Agency is directed by a secretary appointed by and directly responsible to the Governor.[12] The Board consists of five full-time members, serving four year terms, who "shall represent the state at large and not any particular portion thereof."[13] Eligibility qualifications for each member are specified. Thus, the Board is composed of: an attorney qualified in water

supply and water rights law; a registered civil engineer also qualified in water supply and rights; and a civil engineer experienced in sanitary engineering and qualified in water quality; a member qualified in the "field of water quality"; and a fifth member needing no specialized experience.[14] The Governor also appoints the board's chairman who serves at his pleasure.[15]

The Board is statutorily divided into two divisions, water rights and water quality, although other divisions may be created administratively.[16] The Board may establish a Water Quality Coordinating Committee consisting of at least one representative from each of the nine regional boards.[17] A prior nine-member advisory committee consisting of representatives with backgrounds in agriculture, aquatic biology, economics, environmental science, industrial waste, municipal waste, oceanography, recreational water use and urban planning was abolished by the Legislature in 1972.[18] The SWRCB is the designated state agency under the FWPCA and is empowered, among other things, to certify water quality activities as complying with the federal law, to exercise such federal powers delegated to the state through the FWPCA,[19] to approve applications for federal water quality grants, and to certify priority of projects for federal grants.[20] The Board's other responsibilities include:

(1) Formulating and adopting state policy for water quality control.[21]

(2) Administering a state research program into the technical phases of water quality control.[22]

(3) Coordinating and evaluating the need for water quality related investigations of other state agencies.[23]

(4) Regulating the testing, licensing and use of materials for cleaning up oil in state waters.[24]

(5) Allocating funds to the regional boards as well as oversight review of their actions (or failures to act) and taking appropriate corrective action.[25]

Corresponding to the Board's responsibilities for water quality are even greater powers regarding the intricacies of water appropriations and determination of water rights. The exercise of these powers also has important land use effects.

d. Regional Water Quality Control Boards

California is divided into nine water basins, each under the administrative planning and regulatory authority of a substate Regional Water Quality Control Board. A regional board is composed of nine part-time members appointed by the Governor to four year terms. Composition of the board is statutorily prescribed to assure diversity of membership.[26]

Water quality powers vested in the regional boards, excluding planning powers discussed separately below, include the following:

(1) A regional board may establish requirements for all present or proposed waste discharges not flowing into a community sewer system. Such discharge requirements "shall implement" relevant water quality control plans "if any have been adopted" and consider protection of beneficial uses, regional water quality objectives, other waste discharges and prevention of nuisances. The discharge requirement process is activated by the mandatory filing of a report with a regional board describing any material change or proposed change in the character, location or value of waste discharges.[27] However, a discharge requirement cannot specify the design, location, type of construction or particular method by which compliance is to be achieved.[28]

(2) The discharge requirement system is supported, in event of a violation, by authority in a regional board to issue a cease and desist order requiring either immediate compliance or compliance according to a detailed time schedule.[29] Cease and desist orders may be enforced by a court injunction and/or a civil fine up to $6,000 per each day of violation.[30] The boards may also issue cleanup and abatement orders.[31] Cease and desist orders may also be issued regarding volume, type or concentration of wastes discharged into a community sewer system.[32]

(3) Obtain coordinated action in water quality control, including prevention and abatement of water pollution and nuisances; encourage and assist in self-policing waste disposal programs; require technical investigations by local and state agencies regarding water quality control; request enforcement of water quality laws; and recommend projects for financial assistance to the SWRCB.[33]

e. State/Substate Planning Process

The Porter-Cologne Act additionally instructed SWRCB to formulate and adopt statewide policy for water quality control. Such policy as well as approved regional water quality plans are to become "part of" the California Water Plan once they have been reported to the Legislature. SWRCB, as the statewide policy is being formulated

or revised, is to "consult with and carefully evaluate" recommendations of relevant local, state and federal agencies.[34] The Board is to take into "consideration" the effect of its actions upon the California Water Plan and "any other general or coordinated governmental plan looking toward" water use, development or conservation.[35] State agencies "shall comply with" the state policy for water quality control, "unless otherwise directed or authorized by statute."[36]

Basic guiding principles for the state's water quality policy are statutorily prescribed. The policy is to consist of one or more of the following:

(1) Water quality principles and guidelines for long range resource planning, including ground and surface water management programs as well as control and use of reclaimed water.

(2) Water quality objectives "at key locations" for planning and operation of water resource development projects and water quality control activities.

(3) Other principles and objectives established by SWRCB for water quality control.[37]

The statutory principles constitute the basis for the state policy consisting of 12 general principles adopted by SWRCB in July, 1972 and are weighted heavily toward engineering and economic efficiency considerations.

Each regional board is to formulate and adopt a regional plan incorporating, among other things, water quality control objectives ensuring the "reasonable" protection of beneficial uses and prevention of nuisances. "However, it is recognized that it may be possible for the quality to be changed to some degree without unreasonably affecting beneficial uses." Factors to be "considered" by regional boards in establishing antipollution objectives are at minimum to include:

(1) Past, present and probably future beneficial uses of water.

(2) Environmental characteristics of the hydrographic unit under consideration including the quality of available water.

(3) Water quality that could be "reasonably" achieved through "coordinated" control of all relevant factors affecting water quality.

(4) Economic considerations.[38]

The regional plans are also to contain an implementation program that describes actions and recommendations necessary to achieve regional objectives, a time schedule, and surveillance measures to assure compliance.[39] Most significantly, a regional board either in the water quality plan or in waste discharge requirements may specify conditions or areas where waste discharges are prohibited.[40] Thus, as noted previously, waste discharge requirements "shall implement" the regional plan once adopted.

The planning process is based on the familiar substate/state or "bottom up" approach in which regional plans, to become legally operative, are first to be adopted by the regional boards and then by the state board.[41] In formulating its plan, a regional board is to "consult with and consider the recommendations" of affected local and state agencies.[42] More generally, a regional board "shall" encourage regional planning and action for water quality control as well as "take into consideration" the effect of its actions upon the California Water Plan and "any other" general or coordinating plan involving state water resources.[43] However, the regional plans required by the Porter-Cologne Act are to be superseded in event of conflict by water quality control plans, once adopted, as appropriately required for the state by the FWPCA.

f. Grant Programs

SWRCB administers the 75 percent share federal grants for treatment plants authorized under the FWPCA. The board reviews applications for grants, determines their conformity with state policy for water quality control and adopted regional water control plans, and certifies whether the project is entitled to priority ranking.[44] SWRCB also administers the state water quality control fund which provides 12½ percent grant subsidies for the construction of public treatment and reclamation facilities.[45]

Solid Waste Management Board

a. Legislative Background

There is an obvious environmental relationship between the disposal of gaseous wastes into the air, the disposal of liquid wastes into a community sewer system or the land, and the disposal of solid wastes into the land and/or air and watercourses. Disposal of gaseous, liquid and solid waste residuals typically represents the tail end of economic production and consumption as well as of land use planning. Not only are these residuals the end products or final outputs (unless recovered and recycled)

of an increasingly affluent and populous state, the methods of their disposition may be seen to form interdependent environmental, land use, economic and governmental relationships.

While California's air and water quality programs have a relatively long history, interest in planning for solid waste disposal was comparatively neglected until fairly recently. Solid waste residuals in California traditionally were buried in dumps or landfills and/or burned and allowed to seep into surface and underground waterways. However, since January 1972 a ban was placed upon burning in dumps and agricultural burning was to be regulated according to atmospheric conditions so as to minimize air pollution.[1] The net result has been a shift toward sanitary landfill operations where solid wastes are compacted and covered over with earth daily. Although a well-operated sanitary landfill avoids most air pollution problems because no burning is involved, it also precludes the possibility of potential economic recovery of some solid waste residuals. Significantly, too, it has "the disadvantage of using up another diminishing resource, land."[2]

The cumulative effect quantitatively,. both of increasing consumption patterns and technological innovations (especially, in packaging and containerization) has been variously described and estimated. For example, California's solid waste output in 1973 was likened to "a slab of refuse 100 feet wide and 30 feet high from Mexico to Oregon." Another estimate was that the state would generate 2.5 billion tons of solid waste by the year 2000.[3]

While these empirical conditions were necessary, apparently they were not sufficient for enactment of the state Solid Waste Management and Resource Recovery Act of 1972 and establishment of the State Solid Waste Management Board and attendant provisions for policy, planning and program development.[4] Three additional factors were reported to be integral to the legislative crucible:

(1) Prior federal enactment of the Resource Recovery Act of 1970 and the prospect of substantial federal funding, especially of state research and development activity regarding solid waste disposal and management.[5]

(2) Resolution of governmental jurisdiction conflicts—horizontally between the State Water Resources Control Board and Department of Health; and vertially between the "proper roles" of state and local government for solid waster matters, historically within the latters' purview.[6]

(3) The California Refuse Removal Council, "by far the largest industry representative in Sacramento," which had previously sought creation of an independent state regulatory board which "would include strong industry representation and would exercise its regulatory powers through licensing arrangements. . ."[7]

The sum result may be characterized as an interesting piece of legislation which, for instance, incorporates some state/substate elements of the state transportation planning process, but which yields a state policy of minimum standards—not a statewide solid waste plan and effective implementation machinery. Alternatively, the 1972 Act may be seen as a tentative step by state government into the legislative thicket of state level solid waste planning and management.

b. Legislative Findings and Policy

The Legislature found that traditional methods of solid waste disposal, chiefly land dumps and sanitary landfills, "may not" prove adequate for eliminating environmental pollution and conserving natural resources. The increasing volume and diversity of solid wastes being generated in California, together with traditional, often inadequate disposition methods, were found to contribute to air, water and land pollution; to the production of flies, rodents and litter; to the waste of dwindling natural resources; and to general environmental deterioration. These effects were seen to result from the interaction of various factors including: rapid population increases, decentralized urban growth patterns, industrial expansion, changes in agriculture, transportation improvements, and significantly, a developing technology for the manufacture, packaging and marketing of consumer products. Collectively, these factors operate to place "planning, economic, and resource base limitations upon the availability of land" for solid waste disposal. Accordingly, non-traditional methods which emphasize source reduction, recovery, conversion and recycling of solid wastes were declared essential to the public health and well-being, to the maintenance of economic productivity and environmental quality, and to the conservation of "the state's remaining natural resources."[8]

c. Solid Waste Management Board

The State Solid Waste Management Board (SWMB), essentially a single-purpose planning agency, was charged with initiation of statewide solid waste management policy, a research and development program, and related information and research activities. Its jurisdiction was explicitly circumscribed by a legislative policy enunciating "that the primary responsibility for adequate solid waste management and planning shall rest with local government." The state role in solid waste matters was declared to be basically policy and program development.[9]

The Solid Waste Management Board consists of seven voting members, compensated at the rate of $100 per day for attending meetings, and is located within the Resources Agency. "Balance" provisions apply to the selection and appointment of the voting members who serve four-year terms. Five members are appointed by the Governor, subject to Senate confirmation; one councilman of a city of more than 250,000 persons; one supervisor of a county of more than 500,000 persons; two members representing the solid waste management industries of northern and southern California; and a fifth member representing the public, having specialized education and experience in environmental quality and pollution control. The remaining two members are registered civil engineers with specialized knowledge of natural resources conservation and resources recovery. They are appointed separately by the Assembly Speaker and Senate Rules Committee. In addition, the Director of Health, Director of Agriculture and Chief of the Division of Mines and Geology serve as ex officio but non-voting members.[10]

The Board is assisted by a 25-member, non-compensated advisory body known as the State Solid Waste Management and Recovery Advisory Council. Although the Council's existence expires July 1, 1976, its activities for the interim were prescribed as follows:

(1) Initial preparation and recommendations to the Board of the state solid waste recovery program by July 1974.

(2) Assisting the Board in development of the State Policy for Solid Waste Management.

(3) Review and proposed revision of the resource recovery program and state policy following their adoption.

(4) Recommendations as to each local solid waste management plan submitted to the Board for its approval.

(5) Assisting the Board in its study of "the litter problem statewide."

(6) Assisting various groups in development and implementation of solid waste recycling and recovery programs.[11]

d. State/Substate Planning Process

(1) State Solid Waste Management and Resource Recovery Policy

The Solid Waste Management and Resource Recovery Act makes reference to two kinds of state policy—an overall policy described as the Solid Waste Management and Resource Recovery Policy and another policy known as the State Policy for Solid Waste Management. The difference between the two, in the absence of authoritative clarification, may be subtle as well as significant. The overall or Solid Waste Management and Resource Recovery Policy is to "consist of" the State Policy for Solid Waste Management, substate solid waste management plans, the State Solid Waste Resource Recovery Program and related programs,[12] described below. Thus, the overall policy bears a certain resemblance to, for example, such statutory antecedents as the state level transportation and water quality plans which include, in part, substate plans prepared according to state guidelines.[13] However, since the overall policy appears to serve no necessary purpose, its operative meaning is not clear on the face of the statute. Accordingly, whether the policy is to be a meaningful planning instrument and program or alternatively as it appears, a summing up of constituent parts, is statutorily uncertain. Arguably, such ambiguity would have been avoided from the start if the Legislature had intended a compelling "umbrella" policy.

(2) State Policy for Solid Waste Management

The state Board was required to adopt by January 1975, and thereafter periodically review and revise, the State Policy for Solid Waste Management. The Policy is to include "minimum standards" for solid waste handling and disposal "for the protection of air, water, and land from pollution" based upon two considerations:[14]

(a) Although the state standards "may include" the location, design, operation, maintenance and ultimate reuse of solid waste processing, and disposal facilities, they "shall not include" those aspects which are "solely of local concern . . . such as, but not limited to, frequency of collections, means of collection and transportation, level of service,

charges and fees, designation of territory served through franchises, contracts, or governmental services, and purely aesthetic considerations."[15]

(b) Minimum standards for public health protection as developed by the state Department of Health and which may vary throughout the state according to population density, climate, geology and other factors relevant to solid waste handling and disposal.[16]

In formulating the Policy, SWMB also was instructed to consider recommendations made by the Solid Waste Management and Resource Recovery Advisory Council, Air Resources Board, State Water Resources Control Board, Conference of Local Health Affairs and other relevant agencies.[17]

(3) Substate Solid Waste Management Plans

The state Board was instructed to provide guidelines and necessary technical assistance for the preparation of substate solid waste plans.[18] Each county, "in cooperation with affected local jurisdictions," must prepare a solid waste management plan, that is "comprehensive, coordinated and consistent with" the State Policy as well as any regional or sub-regional solid waste plans.[19] Alternatively, a regional planning agency recognized by the state Council on Intergovernmental Relations (typically a Council of Governments or statutory regional agency[20]) may prepare the plan if authorized by the county and a majority of the cities within the county which have a majority of the incorporated area population.[21]

Regardless of how prepared, the plan is to deal with "all waste disposal within the county" and in addition, with "all waste originating therein which is to be disposed of outside" the county.[22] The Act defines "solid waste" to mean all putrescible and non-putrescible solid and semi-solid wastes, including garbage, trash, refuse, paper, rubbish, ashes, industrial wastes, demolition and construction wastes, abandoned vehicles and parts thereof, discarded home and industrial appliances, manure, and non-liquid vegetable, animal and other discarded wastes.[23] Solid waste "disposal" is defined as "the final deposition" of these wastes "onto land, into the atmosphere, or into the waters of the state."[24] In addition, the plan is to include a mandatory analysis of its economic feasibility and may provide for sub-regional elements covering two or more counties or parts thereof.[25]

A county-prepared plan must be approved by a

majority of the cities within the county which have a majority of the incorporated area population. A subregional plan, however, cannot supersede local solid waste plans unless unanimously approved by all affected local governments. Nonetheless, the plan must be submitted to the recognized regional planning agency for its review and comments prior to ultimate submission to the state Board.[26]

The substate plans are to be submitted to the state Board for approval as to their "compliance with" the State Policy for Solid Waste Management by January 1976.[27] The approval process includes review and recommendation for each plan by the State Solid Waste Management and Resource Recovery Advisory Council, as previously indicated.[28] However, the efficacy of SWMB approval for actual implementation of a substate plan is uncertain as to the following:

(a) State agencies whose activities involve solid waste "disposal" "shall comply with" an approved plan "unless directed or authorized by statute."[29] For example, the State Water Resources Control Board and the Regional Water Quality Control Boards are specifically exempted from activities and programs specifically authorized under the Porter-Cologne Water Quality Control Act of 1969.[30] Similar specific exemptions apply to all other state agencies.[31]

(b) The state Board "shall not approve" any request for state or federal funding of a solid waste management project "not in conformance with" an approved plan. However, no noteworthy state or federal funding program appears to exist at present.[32]

(c) The solid waste management and planning of local government "shall conform to" an approved plan.[33] However, no provision of the Solid Waste Management and Resource Recovery Act is to abridge the power of local government to regulate the handling or disposal of solid wastes, nor the "right of any person to dispose of inert, nontoxic and inorganic solid waste as land fill on his own property," nor the "right of any person to dispose of organic and toxic waste materials on his own property in evaporation ponds from which there is no drainage or seepage."[34]

(4) State Solid Waste Resource Recovery Program

A State Solid Waste Resource Recovery Program was authorized. Essentially a comprehensive research and development program, it was to be drafted initially by the Advisory Council and submitted to the state Board by July 1974, with final adoption by the Board after its review.

One element of the program was to include preparation of guidelines, criteria and financial participation formulas for "a major state-directed research and development program . . . to develop technologically and economically feasible systems for the collection, reduction, separation, recovery, conversion, and recycling of all solid wastes, and the environmentally safe disposal of nonusable residues."[35] The program should be structured to ensure maximum entitlement to federal, state and private matching funds and may include pure and applied research objectives.

A second element is to include special studies and demonstration projects or "the recovery of useful energy and resources from solid wastes."[36] The scope of these investigations: resource and energy recovery methods; public and economic uses of recovered resources; changes in product design, production and packaging to reduce solid waste generation; more effective methods of collection, reduction, separation and containerization; use of the state's purchasing power to develop market demand for recycled paper and other recovered resources; recommended incentives to accelerate public and private resource reclamation and recovery; the effects of existing and alternate policies on solid waste recycling and reuse; and significantly, the relative advantages of "disposal taxes or packaging, containers, vehicles, and other manufactured goods, which charges would reflect the cost of final disposal, the value of recoverable components of the item, and any social costs associated with the nonrecycling or uncontrolled disposal of such items."[37]

A third element provides for pilot projects for solid waste recovery, and possible reuse and recycling, at state institutions.[38]

In addition, the Board is to assume such ancillary program responsibilities as coordination of solid waste management studies by state agencies, a public information program, an information storage and retrieval system, provision of technical assistance, recommend anti-litter legislation, and study of financial assistance methods for local solid waste planning and facilities.[39]

4. State Energy Planning

The public regulation of the supply, distribution and pricing of various forms of energy provides another illustration of how the decision-making and planning processes of state agencies can constitute "back door" controls (or incentives) for land use development and growth patterns. In addition, establishment of the new Energy Resources Conservation and Development Commission, the first state agency of its kind nationally, suggests another insitutional model for comprehensive, integrated planning and regulation of an increasingly critical resource.

Energy Resources Conservation and Development Commission

The Commission is a state level planning and regulatory agency with comprehensive authority to plan for electric energy needs within the state and to preempt, with few exceptions, the certification of all new thermal electric generation facilities. It was created in May, 1974, by the State Energy Resources Conservation and Development Act[1] and became effective on January 1, 1975. The Commission is an example of a state level agency with considerable planning and other governmental authority concerning a particular resource—electricity—that is in short supply. The availability of the resource, however, has a fundamental impact on the intensity and location of new urbanization; hence, Commission plans and decisions could be powerful forces that influence state land use patterns. Further, generating facilities in themselves have a considerable environmental impact on surrounding lands and Commission certifications have the potential for conflicting with local land use policy in the interest of statewide and areawide energy needs.

a. Legislative History

The 1974 Act evolved from a number of prior actions at the state level in response to the difficulties experienced by electric utilities in running the gamut of multiple permit agencies and in obtaining final authorization for new and expanded generating facilities. In 1966, a Power Plant Siting Committee that included seven representatives from state environmental agencies was formed in the Resources Agency. Electric utilities submitted plans for new facilities to the Committee prior to seeking needed state and/or federal licenses. If this resulted in an approved preconstruction agreement, the environmental agencies agreed not to contest necessary state and federal approvals. This still left the initiative in the utilities to select energy form and site and constituted a reactive rather than planning role for the state. A state planning role was created in 1970 by enactment of the Power Plant Siting Coordination Act[2] which directed the Re-

sources Agency to develop a twenty year plan for optimum location of new and expanded generating facilities. These were to be suitable from an environmental standpoint. In addition, the plan was to contain recmendations of the types of fuel to be used.

The 1974 Act is a culmination of these two prior initiatives, but goes much further in involving a single state agency in both facility planning and preemptive regulation as well in energy conservation and research and development.[3]

b. Legislative Intent

The basic intention of the Act is to centralize into one state agency most of the responsibility for assessing future electricity demands, evolving a plan to meet those demands and to reduce them where they are the product of waste and inefficiencies; to make appropriate tradeoffs between environmental and energy values; and to administer a single certification process in order to lessen the time between application and certification. In these quests, the new state Commission is granted exclusive authority to set forth and administer standards applicable to new generation facilities (except air and water quality standards). The Commission thus has the authority to preempt all other standards applied heretofore by other state agencies and by local governments (including local general plans and zoning ordinances) except, presumably, standards contained in air implementation plans and water quality effluent limitations. Moreover, to a large extent, multiple proceedings before such agencies as local planning commissions, local legislatures and the Public Utilities Commission (which dealt with site location, design and performance standards) have been consolidated into a single proceeding before the new Commission. Further, the new agency is primarily responsible for the preparation of the environmental impact report which must accompany any proposed facility.

c. Organization

The new Commission is part of the Resources Agency. It is a five member Commission,, with staggered five year terms, appointed by the Governor with the advice and consent of the Senate. There are two additional nonvoting members, the Secretary of the Resources Agency and the President of the Public Utilities Commission. It is a fulltime, compensated commission whose members are supposed to represent the state-at-large (rather than geographic regions or special interests) and reflect at least four types of expertise: engineering and energy supply, administrative law, environmental protection and ecosystems and economics of natural resources. One member is to be from the public-at-large. There are very strict conflict of interest provisions.

The statute provides for Commission appointment of an executive director and of an administrative advisor. The latter, who is to be an attorney, is directed to "insure that full and adequate participation by all interested groups and the public-at-large is secured" in the activities of the Commission.[4] The statute provides for a surcharge on electricity rates to pay for the operations of the Commission.

d. Powers and Duties

The Commission's responsibilites are four-fold. It is involved in forecasting and planning, certification of facility sites, research and development, and contingency planning for periods of energy shortage. In addition, it has limited authority to prescribe building standards designed to save energy consumption. The two land use-related responsibilities are described below.

(1) Forecasting and Planning

The Commission is charged with continually assessing trends in consumption of electrical energy and other energy forms and with analyzing social, economic and environmental consequences of these trends. In addition, it is to collect and evaluate utility forecasts of future supplies and demands of energy and fuels, independently analyze these in relation to growth forecasts and "formally specify statewide and service area electrical energy demands to be utilized as a basis for planning the siting and design of electric power generating and related facilities."[5] Further, the Commission is directed to compile local, regional, state and federal land use, safety, environmental and other standards to be met in designing, siting and operating generating facilities; and then to adopt its own standards which, except in the cases of air and water quality standards and areas of federal preemption, can, at the Commission's discretion, supersede the standards of the other agencies.[6]

The statute provides in considerable detail for biennial submissions by all electrical utilities, consistent with a Commission-provided methodology, of five, ten and twenty year forecasts of loads and resources of their service areas, facilities required to service such loads including general locations and types of fuels, other potential system capacities and projected fuel costs. Copies of these submissions are to be sent to relevant state agencies (e.g., the PUC, OPR) and affected local governments. Local governments are asked to respond in terms of population growth figures, land use implications and impacts on general plan elements. Following these responses, the Commission is to prepare its own report which contains its own conclusions regarding impacts of proposed facilities and measures necessary to ameliorate harmful impacts, anticipated five and ten year demand levels to be used as a basis for certification of facilities and twenty year forecasts as a basis for its recommended conservation program. The report also is to identify on a statewide and service area basis facilities that will be required. This report, as well as biennial reports described below, are not to be adopted finally until after public hearings.

Beginning in 1977, and thereafter biennially, the Commission is to prepare a comprehensive report identifying emerging trends and the levels of statewide and service area energy demands for each year of the forthcoming five, ten and twenty year forecasts in order to provide a basis for state policy, including the approval of new sites. In this regard the Commission is directed to prepare continually updated overviews of statewide growth and development as these relate to future requirements for energy, "including patterns of urban metropolitan expansion, statewide and service area economic growth, shifts in transportation modes . . ."[7]

This is to be followed in each of the biennial reports with a statement of "the level of statewide and service area electrical energy demand for the forthcoming 5-and 10-year . . . period which, in the judgment of the Commission,, will reasonably balance . . . growth and development, protection of public health and safety, preservation of environmental quality, maintenance of a sound economy . . ."[8] These "levels" are to serve as the basis for the planning and certification of new facilities. In addition to the foregoing, these reports are to contain a list of existing facilities where expansion is feasible during the following ten years, a list (with location) of appropriate sites for new facilities and types of fuels to be used, and a forecast of potential adverse impacts associated with meeting twenty year demand forecasts.

The foregoing describes a planning process and updated biennial plans whereby the new Commission, in arriving at authoritative appropriate target levels (upon which facility planning and certification are to be based), balances economic, social and environmental considerations and can determine, in large measure, where expansion will or will not occur.

(2) Certification of New Facilities

Much of the statute is devoted to the Commission's role as the repository of nearly exclusive power (to the extent permitted by federal law) to certify all new electric generating sites and related facilities. The procedural model is interesting: other state agencies and local governments are to make recommendations to the Commission; hearings are to be held; comment is to be made on otherwise applicable local general plans and zoning; certifications must be consistent with Commission's own plans and standards; the Commission must cause an EIR to be prepared.

The Commission's authority is not entirely exclusive: a permit from the Coastal Zone Conservation Commission is still required; air and water standards adopted by other agencies are applicable; a PUC certificate of convenience and necessity is still apparently necessary in selected cases; and the Legislature has listed a number of areas of critical environmental concern (e.g., parks) where new facilities presumptively would be barred. Nevertheless, the Commission's certification powers are considerable.

Public Utilities Commission

a. Organization and Functions

The Public Utilities Commission (PUC) consists of five members appointed by the Governor, with the consent of the Senate, to six-year staggered terms. The Commission regulates the services and rates of certain privately owned utilities and transportation companies; public utilities are not under its jurisdiction. The PUC exercises its authority through three channels: licensing the operation of plants, equipment, apparatus or facilities of a public utility; the certification of public convenience and necessity for construction of a new plant or expansion of an existing facility; and review and approval of power plant siting. Decisions are based on standards and criteria, as articulated by the PUC itself, relating to such factors as community values, recreational and park use, historical and aesthetic values, environmental quality considerations, performance and design, and site location.

With enactment of the state Energy Resources Conservation and Development Act of 1974, much of the licensing and power plant siting authority for electricity generating facilities was transferred to the new Energy Resources Conservation and Development Commission. It is contended, however, that the "certification of public convenience and necessity" still would be a requisite for expansion or construction of an electricity generating facility. As for preparation of environmental impact reports, the new Energy Commission is likely to assume the lead role, replacing the PUC in matters relating to electricity generation and transmission facilities.

b. Planning Process Assessment

Since the availability of utilities and transportation services are two important factors affecting the intensity and location of growth, PUC decisions have major impacts on land use development patterns in the state. Further, utility and transportation facilities have considerable effects on local environments and surrounding areas. Thus, the PUC in making its decisions is performing a de facto planning role which could cause serious disruption of local and regional planning decisions. Unfortunately, the Commission has almost no research and planning staff to properly evaluate the comprehensive, long-term planning implications of its decisions. As indicated in several investigative studies of the Public Utilities Commission, failure of the Commission to achieve its mandated goals can in part be attributed to the quality of the commissioners themselves and their actions in undermining the independence of the PUC staff. This further aggravates the serious shortcomings associated with the lack of planning.

5. State Natural Resources Planning

The need to manage California's natural resources has resulted in several single-purpose agencies which combine resource conservation, development and planning functions, although with varying degrees of emphasis and efficacy. The State Lands Commission, Department of Parks and Recreation, and Department of Fish and Game are all natural resource-type agencies which could be alternatively categorized under "environmental" and "development" headings. To do so, nevertheless, would diminish their integrated managerial responsibilities which comprise environmental constraint and resource development functions.

Coastal Zone Conservation Commission

The California Coastal Zone Conservation Commission and six regional commissions possess important planning and regulatory responsibility for land use in the coastal zone. Any attempt to restructure land use controls in California will, therefore, deal with the CZCC role most carefully, particularly in light of the strong voter support given to it in its enactment.

a. Legislative History

The Coastal Zone Conservation Act of 1972 was initially adopted as an initative, Proposition 20, approved by the state's voters in November, 1972. Previously, several coastal zone conservation bills had been introduced without success in the Legislature.[1]

The resulting legislation states that "the California coastal zone is a distinct and valuable natural resource belonging to *all the people*." (Emphasis supplied.) The coastal zone is a "delicately balanced ecosystem" and its permanent protection a paramount concern to present and future residents of the state and nation. Thus, "it is necessary to preserve the ecological balance of the coastal zone and prevent its further deterioration and destruction."[2]

The Act's definition of the coastal zone is important for determining the planning jurisdiction of regional commissions. "Coastal zone" is defined as: "that land and water area of the State of California from the border of the State of Oregon to the border of the Republic of Mexico, extending seaward to the outer limit of the state jurisdiction, including all islands within the jurisdiction of the state, and extending inland to the highest elevation of the nearest coastal mountain range, except that in Los Angeles, Orange, and San Diego counties, the inland boundary of the coastal zone shall be the highest elevation of the nearest coastal mountain range, or five miles from the mean high tide line, whichever is the shorter distance."[3]

The Act intends to protect the coastal zone by "a comprehensive, coordinated, enforceable plan for orderly, long-range conservation and management" to be known as the Coastal Zone Conservation Plan.[4] Recognizing that harmful development could occur during interim plan preparation, the Act requires that development occurring in a "permit area" be consistent with statutory objectives. A permit system is established to regulate such interim development and is discussed below.[5] To prepare the Plan and to administer the permit system, the Act established a statewide body, the Coastal Zone Conservation Commission and six regional (substate) commissions.[6]

b. Organization

The Commission consists of six representatives from the regional commissions and six public members.[7] The membership of the regional commissions is split evenly between local governments and the public.[8]

The size of the regional commissions varies generally according to the number of cities and counties within their region. Thus, four regional commissions have 12 members each, while the North Central Coast Regional Commission (Sonoma, Marin, San Francisco Counties) has 14 and the Central Coast Regional Commission (San Mateo, Santa Cruz, Monterey Counties) 16.[9] All supervisors are to be appointed by their boards of supervisors, all city councilmen by the local city selection committee (except for Los Angeles and San Diego), and all delegates from regional agencies by their respective agencies.[10] Public representatives are appointed by the Governor, Senate Rules Committee and Speaker of the Assembly.[11]

The composition of the state and regional commissions allows local government interests and expertise to be represented, but precludes local officials from assuming a predominant role. The Act, however, has been criticized for adding yet another type of agency to California's already complex substate governance scene.[12]

c. Powers and Duties

The state and regional commissions are empowered to accept grants, contributions and appropriations; to contract for outside professional assistance; to pursue judicial remedies through the state Attorney General; and to adopt regulations to carry out the Act.[13] In addition, the commissions may request the advice and services of federal, state and local agencies. A regional commission may request staff assistance from any federally recognized regional planning agency within its jurisdiction.[14]

The primary powers of the state and regional commissions relate to preparing the Coastal Zone Conservation Plan and administering the interim permit system.

(1) The Plan

The Coastal Zone Conservation Plan is intended primarily to conserve and protect the coast of California. The Act requires the Plan to be consistent with four objectives. First, the overall quality of the coastal zone (including amenities and aesthetic values) is to be maintained, restored and enhanced. Second, the existence of optimum populations of all species of living organisms must be continued. Third, the utilization and preservation of all living and non-living coastal resources must be provided for in an orderly, balanced way which is consistent with sound conservation principles. Fourth, irreversible and irreparable commitments of coastal zone resources must be avoided.[15]

The Act specifies the basic elements and features to be included in the resulting Coastal Plan. The public interest in the coastal zone is to be precisely and comprehensively defined. The ecological and planning principles used in determining the suitability and extent of permissible development in the coastal zone must be enunciated. Other Plan elements are mandated, including land use, transportation, conservation, public access, recreation, public services and facilities, ocean minerals and organic resources, population, and educational or scientific uses. The Plan must also include elements for reserving coastal zone land or water for certain uses or for prohibiting certain uses in specific areas. The powers, funding and governmental organization necessary to carry out the Plan must be spelled out.[16]

The regional commissions are active participants in preparation of the Plan. Each regional commission must prepare its own set of definitive conclusions and recommendations, including areas which should be reserved for specific uses or within which specific uses should be prohibited, and submit them to the state Commission by April, 1975.[17] The Commission must adopt a coastal Plan and submit it to the Legislature for its adoption and implementation by December, 1975.

Thus, a final decision on the coastal zone is yet to come. The present institutional and planning structure is only temporary, because the Plan will propose permanent mechanisms for coastal zone management. After submittal of the Plan, legislation must be enacted to implement it. According to its annual report, the Commission's goal for its planning program is ''to arrive at a set of policies to guide future conservation and use of coastal resources—a constitution for the coastline.''[18] The Plan will have two parts: policies of statewide importance, and substate policies that are compatible with the statewide policies but sensitive to the special needs of each region.

(2) The Permit System

The permit system is an interim measure. Since the Plan would not be submitted until December, 1975, and could not be implemented until the following year at the earliest, the danger existed that interim development could irreparably damage the very resources which the Plan was to preserve and protect.

To forestall this, the Act vests interim regulatory powers in the state and regional commissions. Any development begun after February, 1973, within a ''permit area'' (and on which substantial construction had not previously been performed) must be approved by a regional commission.[19] A permit area is smaller than the coastal zone. While the permit area extends seaward to the state's jurisdiction (three miles) as does the coastal zone, the landward boundary of the permit area extends inland only 1,000 yards from the mean high tide mark.[20] The area under the jurisdiction of the San Francisco Bay Conservation and Development Commission is specifically exempted.[21] Urban land developed and stabilized to a residential density of four or more dwelling units per acre by January 1972, and commercial or industrial land stabilized before that date, may be excluded from the permit area.

The fact that the permit area does not cover the entire coastal zone planning area has been criticized. Development of inland sections of the coastal zone could significantly affect coastal resources while the plan is being formulated. If the Act had included the entire coastal zone as its permit area, the regional and state commissions could better guide development of all lands while the plan was being prepared. On the other hand, the administrative burden of reviewing every new development within the entire coastal zone might have been overwhelming.

The permits granted by regional commissions do not replace other state, local or regional controls on development.[22] The interim permit system constitutes another layer of approval. It is a necessary, but not sufficient, authorization because another authority may deny a permit and block development.

The permit system is two-tiered. An applicant, after receiving local approval, seeks a permit from a regional commission. Simple majority approval by the regional commission, and by the state Commission on appeal, is required.[23] In certain cases, however, a two-thirds extraordinary majority is required, both by a regional commission and the state Commission on appeal. The following types of development require a two-thirds majority:

(a) Dredging, filling or otherwise altering a bay, estuary, salt marsh, river mouth, slough or lagoon.

(b) Any development which would reduce the size of beach or other area usable for public recreation.

(c) Any development which would reduce or impose

restrictions upon public access to tidal and submerged lands, beaches and the mean high tide line where there is no beach.

(d) Any development which would substantially interfere with or detract from the line of sight toward the sea from the state highway nearest the coast.

(e) Any development which would adversely affect water quality, existing areas of open water free of visible structures, existing and potential commercial and sport fisheries or existing agricultural uses of land.[24]

Before issuing any permit, a regional commission must find that the development will not have a substantially adverse environmental effect and is consistent with the Act and coastal Plan objectives. The burden of proof is on the applicant.[25] All permits are subject to conditions designed to allow access to beaches and recreation areas, to reserve recreation areas and wildlife preserves, to provide for solid and liquid waste treatment, and to avoid the danger of floods, landslides, erosion, siltation or structural failure during an earthquake.[26] Exempt from the Act are persons who acquired vested rights in a project under a local building permit issued prior to November 8, 1972.[27]

No permit is required for repairs and improvements to existing single family residences totalling less than $7,500, for maintenance, dredging of existing navigation channels or for repair or maintenance activities which do not enlarge an existing structure.

The state Commission acts only in an appellate capacity, except that it may prescribe the procedures for permit applications and their appeal. The state Commission may not, on its own motion, review a permit decision by a regional commission; thus, the permit applicant or any person aggrieved by permit approval must appeal when a permit is granted. This is in keeping with the Act's declaration that the coastal zone is a resource belonging to "all the people." The term "aggrieved," however, may limit standing to persons with a direct interest that would be affected by the proposed development. Appeals are de novo and must be heard and decided in the same manner and by the same vote as applications to the regional commissions. The state Commission may affirm, reverse or modify a regional commission's decision, and the state Commission may decline appeals if it determines that no substantial issues are raised.

In addition to allowing any aggrieved citizen to file an administrative appeal, the Act specifically provides for citizen suits in state courts. Standing is given to "any person" to bring suit against violators and to recover civil penalties under the Act. To encourage such suits, the successful plaintiff is awarded costs of the litigation including reasonable attorney's fees.[31] The general public also has the right to bring citizen suits to ensure proper performance of the commission.

State Lands Commission

a. Organization and Functions

The State Lands Commission is an independent agency under the direction of a board composed ex officio of the Lieutenant Governor, State Controller and Director of Finance. Created in 1867, the Commission has exclusive responsibility for administering ungranted and unpatented public lands owned by the state or under its control, including vacant school lands, tidelands, submerged lands, swamp and overflowed lands, and beds of navigable rivers and lakes. It has statutory power to sell, lease or dispose of land under its jurisdiction, provided that the transaction is in "the public interest" and is authorized to approve or disapprove permits for the private use of state lands, such as offshore oil drilling in submerged lands within state jurisdiction. It has broad powers to exchange state tidelands and submerged lands for publicly or privately owned lands. The exchange must be in the best interests of the state for one of the following purposes: improvement of navigation; aid to reclamation; flood control; or "to enhance the configuration of the shoreline for the improvement of the water and upland." The Commission has no power to acquire land for the state beyond acquisition of an easement to inaccessible public land for the purpose of facilitating its sale.

Legislation enacted in 1970, and amended in 1973, prohibits the Commission from selling or granting land under its jurisdiction unless certain stipulated requirements are met.

The Commission was to submit to the Legislature by January 15, 1975, a final report which identifies those lands determined to possess significant environmental values and which recommends additional actions necessary to assure their permanent protection. Additionally, the Commission was to adopt regulations as part of the recommended actions. Future sale of land by the Commission must be substantiated by a finding made at a public meeting that the sale is necessary for "the health, welfare or safety" of the people or that such land is determined to be of little environmental value.

On land leases, the Commission is required to comply with specified environmental impact report requirements.

Department of Water Resources

The Department of Water Resources (DWR) probably is best known for the State Water Project and Aqueduct and California Water Plan, undertakings related to its primary functions of conservation, development and transportation of the state's water resources. Located within the Resources Agency, the Department is the product of a wide ranging reorganization and consolidation in 1956 of the state's water resource activities including the Department of Finance as well as the former Office of State Engineer, Division of Water Resources and Water Project Authority.[1] The state Reclamation Board is a part of the Department and is now in the process of being consolidated with it.

a. Departmental Organization

The Department is under the control of a director appointed by the Governor, subject to Senate confirmation. The director "holds office at the pleasure of the Governor"[2] and "shall organize the department with the approval of Governor, including establishment of regional branch offices."[3]

Exercise of the Department's rule-making (regulatory) power is divided between the director and California Water Commission, a nine-member body having general policy-making powers except as described below. Seven commission members are appointed to four-year terms by the Governor, with Senate approval, following selection on the basis of: general educational and business qualifications; familiarity with problems of water control, storage and beneficial use; balanced geographic representation; and engineering experience. Two public members, also appointed to four-year terms, are to have "an interest in and knowledge of the environment."[4] Commission members and the director may be removed from office for corruption, incompetency or dereliction of duty.[5]

As to making rules and regulations, the Commission "shall confer with, advise, and make recommendations to the director" regarding matters within his jurisdiction, which relates exclusively to internal administration and management. All other rules and regulations "shall be first presented by the director to the commission" for its approval.[6] In making major departmental decisions, procedures and policies, such as departmental recommendations to the Legislature, the Commission and director "shall be in agreement whenever possible." In event of disagreement, "the views of the director shall prevail," but a report is to be filed immediately with the Governor, Senate President and Assembly Speaker.[7]

Other powers of the Commission include reporting to the Legislature annually on construction progress and operation of the State Water Project,[8] conducting necessary investigations and hearings,[9] hiring an executive officer[10] and the naming of State Water Project facilities.[11]

The state Reclamation Board cooperates with the U.S. Army Corps of Engineers in planning and constructing flood control projects on the Sacramento and San Joaquin rivers and their tributaries. It is the governing body for the Sacramento and San Joaquin Drainage District and is responsible for the maintenance and operation of flood control projects under federal and state regulations. The Board is empowered to acquire project lands and rights of way within its 2700 square mile jurisdiction which covers about 50 percent of the water in the state.

b. Principal Planning Powers

(1) California Water Plan

After the conclusion of World War II, the state in the late 1940's undertook studies leading toward a long-range plan for comprehensive development of water resources.[12] The eventual result was the California Water Plan (not to be confused with the former State Water Plan adopted by Statute in 1941)[13] which was adopted in 1959.[14] The Plan is to serve as "the guide for the orderly and co-ordinated control, protection, conservation, development, and utilization of the water resources of the State,"[15] and may be amended as needed by the Legislature and Department.[16] Adoption of the Plan, however, did not constitute approval of specific projects or water transportation routes.[17]

The State Water Project known formally as the State Water Resources Development System also was approved in 1959, with the Legislature authorizing a $1.75 billion state bond issue to finance system construction.[18] The bond issue was approved by the voters in 1960; revised estimates place total Project costs at approximately $3 billion.

(2) Water Exportation

In order for the Legislature to determine the availability of water supplies for export from the watersheds of their origination, the Department is instructed to conduct investigations and hearings and to report its findings to the Legislature. The investigations are to determine watershed boundaries and the quantity of water originating therein; the quantity of water "reasonably required for ultimate beneficial use" in the watersheds; the amount of water, if any, available for export from the watersheds; and areas of the state "which can be served by the water available for export from each watershed."[19]

(3) Multiple Use Planning

The Department is to undertake planning for public recreation uses and fish and wildlife preservation as part of its general project development activities for water facilities. The legislative purpose is to provide for multiple use of state water storage, conservation and regulation facilities, and for the planning and acquisition of real property concurrently with land acquisition for water facilities.[20] Further, the Legislature intended that there be "full and close coordination of all planning for the preservation and enhancement of fish and wildlife and for recreation in connection with state water projects.[21]

Thus, DWR's facility planning and construction activities are to give "full consideration" to recommendations, "to the extent . . . consistent with other uses of the project," made by local and federal agencies, and the Departments of Fish and Game, Parks and Recreation, and Navigation and Ocean Development.[22] Recommendations for recreational purposes, for example, may include camping, fishing, picnicking, hunting, boating, water contact sports and associated facilities such as campgrounds, parking lots and the like.[23] These recommendations are to be part of its general project formulation activities "through the advance planning stage, including cost/benefit analysis, recreation land use planning and local acquisition.[24]

(4) Ground Water Basin Protection

A significant portion of the state's water, as found by the Legislature, is stored, distributed and furnished by ground water basins that are subject to overdraft, depletion, saline intrusion and pollution.[25] To prevent degradation or irreparable damage to such basins, the Legislature intended "whenever money is appropriated for the purpose," that the Department undertake investigations, studies, plans and design criteria for construction of

projects deemed "to be practical, economically feasible and urgently needed."[26] In addition, it was intended that state and local agencies submit project construction plans and design criteria to DWR for its review, evaluation and necessary revision. The Department may provide technical assistance to these agencies, and is to transmit the results of its studies, investigations, plans and design criteria to the State Water Resources Control Board and regional water quality boards for possible inclusion in state/substate water quality policy, plans and waste discharge controls.[27]

A "designated floodway" which may endanger life or significantly restrict the floodway's carrying capacity is prohibited.[28] A "designated floodway" is the stream channel and that portion of the adjoining flood plain required for the construction of a flood control project such as levees.[29] The state shall not appropriate funds for land acquisition as part of a flood control project if the local agency fails to establish appropriate land use regulations following completion of a federal project report and subsequent DWR classification of the area as a "designated floodway."[30]

Department of Parks and Recreation

The Department of Parks and Recreation is an executive department within the Resources Agency and operates under policies set by a nine member Parks and Recreation Commission that is appointed by the Governor and subject to Senate confirmation.

The Department has broad powers for administering, developing, planning and operating park and recreation facilities in the state. It may acquire or lease property so as to enhance and maintain the state's outdoor recreation resources and facilities. It maintains a comprehensive plan for development of outdoor recreation resources and coordinates state and local agencies having an interest in planning, developing and maintaining these resources. It designs, constructs, operates and maintains recreational facilities at state water projects, and manages the lands and water surfaces of such projects for recreational purposes.

The Department is one of the state agencies which can have major impact on the state's land use planning decisions. As the lead agency in developing and maintaining statewide recreation plans, it is directly involved in a statewide planning process. Three plans of major importance have been prepared by the Department, adopted by the Commission, and approved by the Secretary of Resources and Governor: the State Park System

Plan, the California Coastline Preservation and Recreation Plan, and the California Outdoor Recreation Resources Plan. These plans, particularly the latter, represent the official policy positions of the Department.

Department of Fish and Game

The Department of Fish and Game, within the Resources Agency, is established under the Fish and Game Code and governed by a five member Fish and Game Commission. The Commission was created in 1940, with its members appointed by the Governor subject to Senate confirmation. It is authorized to regulate the taking or possession of birds, mammals, fish, amphibians and reptiles except for commercial purposes, and is to promulgate rules and regulations relating to the state's fish and wildlife. It is empowered, among other things, to review and approve proposed projects involving the acquisition of land and water for ecological reserves.

In addition to the Commission, the Legislature established a Wildlife Conservation Board under the Wildlife Conservation Act of 1947. The Board's primary responsibility is to select and authorize acquisition of land and property for recreation purposes as well as the preservation, protection and restoration of wildlife in the state. It may construct facilities on property it has acquired, to be financed chiefly by the Wildlife Conservation Fund.

The Department of Fish and Game is charged with a wide range of duties as administrator of the Fish and Game Code. It is to develop criteria for determining whether a species or subspecies is endangered and to make a biennial inventory of threatened species. It is to manage, control and protect spawning areas on state lands. The Department also conducts research programs and coordinates water quality activities as they affect fish and wildlife. The Department may establish ecological reserves and acquire property for conservation purposes. Under various programs, the Department now owns, manages and maintains approximately 120,000 acres and is responsible for carrying out construction projects on property acquired under the Wildlife Conservation Act.

As part of its administrative function, the Department prepares and is primarily responsible for the implementation of a state fish and wildlife plan. However, because of a limited planning function, the Department minimally influences state land use planning decisions. Its planning is most direct and significant for those areas sheltering endangered or rare species including habitats.

Department of Navigation and Ocean Development

The Department of Navigation and Ocean Development is primarily responsible for those ocean-oriented activities of state government not otherwise subject to the jurisdiction of the Coastal Zone Conservation Commission, including the coordination of marina and small harbor development and beach erosion control. In the field of planning and environmental protection, it was responsible for preparing the Comprehensive Ocean Area Plan (COAP) in 1972, which could have had a direct impact on land uses in the coastal areas but was not adopted or implemented. The Plan largely constituted the work of background consultant studies and included only limited, vague policy statements by the Department. The Department's ocean-related planning functions have been largely superseded by the California Coastal Zone Conservation Commission and the various state and regional coastal plans currently in progress.

B. REGIONAL PLANNING LAWS AND AGENCIES

There is no dearth of land use planning activity at the regional level in California. Three types are identifiable. The first and most pervasive is comprehensive regional planning, which has, typically, long range land use, environmental and growth management ramifications. While most of this is undertaken by Councils of Governments, these plans have uncertain implementation bite at present. The second is functional planning which has land use implications, e.g., regional transportation planning. The third is environmentally oriented or critical area regional planning, where the planning process is supported by meaningful regulatory powers for plan implementation. Thus, although different kinds of regional level planning exist in California, regional planning in general remains less developed and more fragmented than the state level planning processes, thereby constituting a substantial omission in a coherent statewide planning process.

1. Regional Planning Enabling Laws

Several California statutes enable local governments to create regional and subregional planning organizations. Interestingly, however, the statutes specifically designed for the purpose have been little used (two of the three have never been used and the more successful regional planning organizations, such as the Association of Bay Area Governments (ABAG), are the result of negotiated agreements under the Joint Exercise of Powers Act.) This and the following subsection explore both the regional planning enabling acts and the Joint Exercise of Powers Act. In all these instances the state has merely enabled local governments to act together; it has not mandated such action nor established a supervening regional authority.

District Planning Law

The District Planning Law was enacted in 1957 and exemplifies an early attempt at regional planning as performed between two or more counties. A district plan is generally defined similarly to a local general plan, i.e., "a comprehensive, long-term general plan," although by statutory conception it emphasizes only physical development. At minimum, it is to consist of:

(a) Principal findings of fact, problems and opportunities for the district;

(b) A statement of major objectives, principles and standards;

(c) Land use recommendations reflecting economic and population trends; and

(d) Recommendations concerning need and location of public facilities as well as for areas well-suited for open space, industrial, agricultural and special uses.

A planning district is composed of two or more counties, and the district board consists of representatives designated by the respective board of supervisors and city selection committee for each county. All district board members, who serve four-year terms, thus must be elected public officials; no provision is made for citizen representatives.

The major function of a planning district is to prepare and revise a district general plan that is "based on" comprehensive physical, economic, social and governmental studies and which shall "aim at" coordinated physical development within the district. In preparing the plan, the district board shall "seek to harmonize" it with the general plan of the cities and counties. Also, in preparing the plan, the board shall "actively seek" the cooperation and advice of member cities and counties and other relevant organizations.[1] This law has never been used.

Regional Planning District Law

The Regional Planning District Law was enacted in 1963. Unlike its predecessor, the District Planning Law whose plan element requirements run approximately two pages, the statutory requirements for a regional plan under the Regional Planning District Law are stated in one paragraph, of two sentences: "Regional plan, as used in this chapter, means a comprehensive, long-term general plan for the physical development of the region, and land outside its boundaries which in the board's judgment bears relation to its planning. The regional plan shall consist of a text and a map or maps, and such recommendations of the regional planning board concerning current or future problems as may in its option affect the region as a whole and are proper for inclusion in the regional plan."[2]

Significantly, however, "A regional plan shall be advisory only and shall not have any binding effect on the counties and cities located within the boundaries of the regional planning district . . ."[3]

The Legislature's intent is based upon a finding of "a fundamental interest in the orderly development of the urban regions of the State . . ."[4] This interest is to be realized through preparation and maintenance of a "long-term, general plan for the physical development" of urban areas that acts as "a guide" for local governments and those state agencies responsible for public works construction. The state's continuing urban growth was found to create problems of interjurisdictional spillover. Planning by cities and counties can be strengthened "when conducted in relation to studies and planning of an urban regional character." The orderly and harmonious development of urban areas, as well as the needs of future generations, is best assured by studying, forecasting and planning for such physical growth and development.[5]

A regional planning district is statutorily authorized for each regional area designated by the Planning Advisory Committee. However, a district does not become operational unless approved by the legislative bodies of two-thirds of the counties and two-thirds of the cities comprising the designated region. Nor may such a district come into being if two-thirds of the cities and counties are engaged in regional planning under a joint powers agreement. Like the District Planning Law, members of the regional planning board are to be selected by cities and counties separately, and all members except one must be an elected public official serving as a supervisor, mayor or city councilman. That one exception is a "citizen-at-large" member of the board who is selected by the other board members.

In order "to facilitate effective and harmonious planning and development," all local legislative bodies and planning agencies within the district are to file with the board their general plans, general plan elements, other published plans, zoning ordinances, official maps and subdivison regulations. These requirements also pertain to state agencies whose plans and other materials relate to regional planning or physical development. These documents, among others, are to be considered by the district board in preparing the regional plan. In addition, the district may publish its own reports concerning regional resources and problems, "related to the physical growth and development, living conditions, beauty, or prosperity of the region, or any part thereof."[6]

This law also has never been activated.

Area Planning Law

The Area Planning Law originating in 1947, does little more than enable counties and cities to undertake joint planning functions. Because the same purpose may be realized through a joint powers agreement, the Area Planning Law appears unnecessary. The law authorizes cities and counties to establish an area planning commission whose domain may include populated areas, unpopulated areas and unimproved areas lying within or without cities. A commission's functions are to be "in accord with a plan for organization, functions and financing mutually agreed upon by the cooperating counties and cities." To this end, a commission may employ personnel and consultants and hold a joint meeting with city or county planning commissions.[7]

Several area planning commissions were created during the early 1960's. Their accomplishments were largely confined to plan documents which resulted in little joint or separate implementing action.

2. Joint Powers Agreements

a. Introduction

California law provides a mechanism by which units of government can agree to jointly exercise any power common to all of the participants. The Joint Exercise of Powers Act, first adopted in 1949, sets forth very general provisions which regulate agreements among cities, among cities and counties, and even among local governments and state and federal agencies.[1] The statutory device has been used by units of local governments to serve more efficiently the needs, and to solve the problems, of larger geographical areas, while at the same time retaining local control over these areawide activities. The types of functions which may be so performed are extremely diverse. Thousands of intergovernmental contracts in California, enable cooperation among governments for providing public services such as hospitals, sewage facilities and mutual police protection.

Many of these activities can have a significant impact on land use. For example, construction of local flood control projects, maintenance of open space as parks[2] and provision of utility services have been undertaken by local bodies exercising their powers jointly. But, more importantly for present purposes, joint powers agreements have formed the basis for numerous government associations currently exercising planning functions in California. Operating under a variety of names, these voluntary, cooperative arrangements are known as Councils of Governments (COGs). The history, statutory framework, current operation and shortcomings of these associations are discussed below.

b. Developement of COGs

An increasing awareness of the need to view planning problems from an areawide (regional) perspective, rather than suffer the limitations of existing jurisdictional boundaries, led to formation of voluntary governmental associations in the late 1950's. Primarily as a result of federal incentives beginning with the federal Highway Act of 1962, these informal associations began to take on formal structure as Councils of Governments. A relatively stable source of funding was a 1965 amendment to the federal Housing Act of 1954, which provided to them federal grants under the "701 program" of the Department of Housing and Urban Development.[3]

A common denominator of large metropolitan regions of California was a desire to form governmental associations and thereby to address problems of overlapping service areas and fragmented local authority. In other areas of the state, COGs were formed typically in reaction to federal legislative requirements and incentives. For example, in order to receive federal grants for open space preservation or water and sewer projects, an areawide planning process is required which includes a plan with housing, water, sewer and open space elements.[4]

The federal Intergovernmental Cooperation Act of 1970 established the basis for regional review of federal grant applications—the A-95 procedure—by interjurisdictional bodies.[5] Similar federal requirements are increasing in number and becoming more stringent. However, local officials sometimes support areawide (regional) planning organizations both to satisfy requirements of federal grant-in-aid programs and occasionally to preclude establishment of larger and stronger regional agencies by the state or federal government.

c. Joint Exercise of Powers Act

The statutory authority for most such intergovernmental planning merely enables cities, counties, special districts and other entities to reach voluntary agreements among themselves. The types of governmental units which may become parties to joint powers agreements is broadly defined,[6] although in practice cities and counties are generally the parties for planning purposes. The parties must have in common that power which they propose to exercise jointly and be authorized to enter such an agreement by their legislative bodies.

Because many diverse activities may be carried out, the statute is of general applicability and requires only that the accord "state the purpose of the agreement or the power to be exercised" and "provide for the method by which the purpose will be accomplished."[7] No additional formal procedures are required to initiate a joint powers agreement, except when the agreement is to create a separate agency or entity which administers the agreement, such as a COG. In this case, the separate entity need only file a short notice of its existence with the Secretary of State.

The powers of the separate entity or agency are those specified in the agreement. They are to be exercised subject to the same legal restrictions as if exercised by one of the contracting parties. However, the agreement is to designate one of the parties for this purpose, and this determines the nature of the legal restrictions relevant to the exercise of the joint power. No uniform organizational structure is required by the enabling legislation and, consequently, many different joint powers agencies exist. The statute provides only that the governing body of the separate agency may be composed exclusively of locally elected officials from the member governments, such as city councilmen and county supervisors. The close correspondence between representation on the COG governing body and locally elected officials is almost univeral practice in California. There is no statutory provision for citizen representatives. And because separate agencies are formed voluntarily, existing jurisdictional boundaries are necessarily adopted by the joint powers agency, whether they be logical or illogical for planning purposes.

The statutory scheme is specific only as to financing the joint powers agency. However, even in this field, the state law provides few absolute requirements. For example, financial resources to carry out the agreement may be derived from many sources, including personnel, equipment or property contributed by the parties, or by advances of public funds to be repaid as provided by the agreement. Revenue bonds may be issued to finance the construction of exhibition halls, sports arenas and "other public buildings." It is noteworthy that the statute provides COGs with no authority to tax area residents or to issue bonds for other purposes. Similarly, the debts of a separate joint powers agency are to be the debts of the parties "unless the agreement shall specify otherwise."[8] Thus, of the numerous aspects of government cooperation which legitimately may be subject to state authorization, few are addressed, and even these amount to no more than the whiff of mere suggestion.

Most COGs are formed under the Joint Exercise of Powers Act. As noted, a few voluntary associations utilize the Area Planning Commission Law, but no planning body was ever activated under the Regional Planning Law or the District Planning Law—probably because the formation requirements are more onerous and the resulting agency would have nearly the same powers as a joint powers association.[9] Thus, few areawide planning organizations in California have relied upon statutes designed specifically for that purpose.

d. Operation of COGs in California

Because the parties to a joint powers agreement self-determine the nature and purpose of their association, no two COGs need be alike. Associations of governments in large metropolitan areas have preceded other COGs and, as a general rule, have more funding, larger staffs and more numerous programs. In many areas, any movement toward bona fide "regionalism" has been met with firm opposition. Accordingly, there is substantial variation in the operation of COGs throughout California.

(1) Single-county COGs

The earliest associations of governments in California were formed in the metropolitan areas of San Francisco, Los Angeles and Sacramento. Each of these COGs included five or more counties as members while COGs in other areas were created later and are usually based in only one county. The latter are known as "single-county" COGs, even though several associations which were created more recently cover two or more counties. Because these non-metropolitan COGs were characteristically formed in reaction to federal incentives and requirements their initial responsibilities were in the fields of air and water pollution and highway planning. At present, the major functions of single-county COGs are: A-95 clearinghouse review; areawide planning; and provision of technical assistance to member governments.

(a) Clearinghouse Review

Although associations created under the Joint Exercise of Powers Act (or Area Planning Law) may formulate regional plans and policies, plan implementation powers to date are principally derived from the federal government. COGs are certified by the federal Office of Management and Budget to act as regional clearinghouses for the review of local grant applications in order to determine conformance of a proposed project (or program) with the regional plan. The A-95 regional review process encompasses 140 separate federal grant-in-aid programs. Section 401 of the Intergovernmental Cooperation Act of 1970 provides that federal grants-in-aid should be disbursed consistent with state, regional and local planning. The federal government may deny grant funds for a project (or program) which the regional agency finds to be in conflict with the regional plan. The regional plan, thus, may be supported by denial of federal subsidies to conflicting projects.

A recent survey of seven single-county COGs in California indicated that the A-95 review process is needed but not effectively used at present.[10] The comments made by these COGs on local grant applications were rarely critical, rarely constructive and typically rendered the A-95 review a mere "rubber-stamp." Several reasons were given for the disappointing performance of these county-level organizations. Most applications processed through the A-95 review process were not viewed by the COGs as having sufficient areawide significance to warrant comment by other local governments. Moreover, it is very difficult to assess areawide significance of a project (or program) without reference to a comprehensive areawide plan or other pre-established criteria. For many single-county COGs, there is no plan of sufficient detail or scope to provide a basis for meaningful review of grant applications. In addition, local officials hesitate to criticize applications of other jurisdictions, and often expect the same unquestioning support for their own projects; this "log rolling" can of course evolve in any organization.

The failure of federal and state government to insist upon consistent compliance with A-95 requirements has been cited as another reason why many COGs do not emphasize the review process. In November 1973, the federal government attempted to make A-95 reviews more effective by requiring a local government within a COG jurisdiction to include a memorandum of agreement with the COG as part of its grant-in-aid application. Despite shortcomings, the A-95 review process can be an important method of intergovernmental information sharing.

A related review and comment process has been undertaken recently by some COGs. As discussed later, the California Environmental Quality Act of 1970 (CEQA) requires preparation of an environmental impact report (EIR) for certain activities of state, regional and local governments.[11] CEQA implementation guidelines provide that the responsible agency is to consult with any organization it believes will be concerned with the environmental effects of the proposed project. Moreover, "the EIR process should be combined with the existing planning, review, and project approval processes", and it is suggested that government agencies utilize existing regional clearinghouse to distribute EIRs.[12] Similar consultation and comment procedures involving COGs have been implemented through the National Environmental Policy Act of 1969 (NEPA).[13] Also, COGs have new opportunities to influence land use policy decisions through regional plan review procedures articulated by the federal Housing and Community Development Act of 1974.

(b) Areawide Planning

The primary rationale for COGs is their potential role as areawide planning bodies. While the rhetoric of areawide planning is often voiced, many single-county COGs have done little tangible planning of any kind, whether functiona, environmental or comprehensive.[14] Their areawide planning has been largely reactive to federal and state requirements, e.g., transportation planning. When broader, comprehensive planning is undertaken by the county-level COGs, it is rarely "direct" but rather efforts at "coordination" of the existing activities of local city and county planners. One handicap is the confusion, and in some cases hostility, which exists between the COG and local planning staffs.

(c) Technical Assistance Services

Many single-county COGs provide technical planning assistance to member governments, although, of course, of varying scope and importance. The most common assistance has been to aid smaller cities in preparing the general plan elements required by state law. Because these services are funded by general membership dues, larger governments often feel they are supporting their own planning as well as the planning of other cities. At times, county planning departments have viewed COG technical assistance as in conflict with their own capacity to provide the same services.

(2) Metropolitan Area COGs

The larger, metropolitan area COGs perform the same three basic functions as the single-county COGs, but with increased funds, larger professional staff and enhanced cooperation from member jurisdictions. In addition, these COGs undertake activities which the smaller COGs cannot perform. The Southern California Association of Governments (SCAG), the Association of Bay Area Governments (ABAG) and the (San Diego) Comprehensive Planning Organization (CPO) are examples of intergovernmental cooperation under joint powers agreements.

(a) Southern California Association of Governments

Established in 1965, SCAG is the largest COG in California and is engaged in programs which affect more than ten million people in its 38,000 square mile region, which includes Los Angeles, Orange, Riverside, Imperial, San Bernardino and Ventura counties. Nearly 80 percent of the municipalities in the area are members.

The organization's General Assembly is composed of one elected official and one alternate from the six member counties and 120 member cities, with the City of Los Angeles having three delegates. The General Assembly meets only twice a year; thus, the Executive Committee is SCAG's real decision-making body. This 18-member committee is composed of three delegates from the City of Los Angeles, one delegate from each county, one delegate from a city in each county (chosen by member cities in the county), and three at-large delegates (chosen by the Executive Committee). Local officials also serve on seven policy committees which deal with specific areawide problems, including land use, grants, environmental quality, housing and community development and transportation planning. In addition, ten advisory committees provide technical information to the policy committees.

SCAG is an established and increasingly active association of governments. In 1973, SCAG began a technical assistance program to provide planning aid to communities of less than 50,000 residents. The Association is the designated metropolitan clearinghouse for A-95 grant reviews and environmental impact reviews, and commented on nearly 1000 projects seeking $300 million in federal grant requests in 1973. For the first six months of 1974, this figure had risen to over $335 million. Processing of this volume of applications and reports is the job of policy committees and the Executive Committee, which also serves as a review board for each proposed project. After several years effort, a Regional Airport System Plan was adopted by SCAG as the first completed element of a regional transportation plan. Also in 1973, regional planning goals and policies developed by the policy committees were approved by the Executive Committee and General Assembly. Together with previous general guidelines and new regional growth forecasts, the goals and policies comprise the Southern California Development Guide which serves as a reference point for SCAG decision-making.

Recent activities of selected SCAG policy and advisory committees indicate the range and type of programs undertaken by the COG. The Housing and Community Development Committees guide SCAG's responsibilities to coordinate regional plans and to create action programs under section 701 of the federal Housing Act of 1954, as amended, as well as to monitor housing-related legislation, inform local officials and publish technical documents.

More concrete steps have been taken in transportation planning. The Association is charged under federal and state legislation with developing a coordinated multimodal transportation plan to solve the momentous traffic, air pollution and energy problems of the region.[15] Statutory provisions require transportation projects to be part of a comprehensive regional plan so as to qualify for state and federal funding. The areawide plan must be ready for adoption by April 1975, and if approved, will become part of the State Transportation Plan to be submitted to the Legislature.

Another part of SCAG's responsibility is development of a "unified work program" for the transportation planning agencies in the region. For fiscal year 1973-74, more than $2.5 million in planning grants were awarded under this program. Significantly, this planning process includes such agencies as local rapid transit districts and informal associations of governments for Ventura, San Bernardino and Imperial Counties. Currently, local agencies are preparing detailed subregional plans for incorporation into the regional plan. The first major effort at the COG level has been to develop the Critical Decisions Plan which will facilitate early decisions on the most pressing transportation issues. An important facet is to measurably improve regional air quality according to federal and state requirements. In addition to evaluating five transportation alternatives, the Critical Decisions program is based upon the land use and population projections of SCAG's growth forecasting.

The Land Use and Growth Policy Committee recently launched the broadest, and potentially most far reaching, activities of SCAG to date. The committees and review processes rely upon policies of the Regional Development Guide. Prior to 1972, two preliminary forecasts and allocations of population and land use had been made, but changes in demographic trends and public attitudes suggested corresponding revisions. Drawing on diverse governmental and private data sources, a Progress Report: Growth Forecast Revision was published in September, 1973 and estimated a 1990 regional population of 12.3 to 12.9 million people, revising downward an earlier population forecast of 13.9 million. SCAG then developed three alternate "spatial allocation patterns", ranging from concentrating growth in existing urban centers to dispensing low-density growth in peripheral centers. The adopted growth forecasts, briefly summarized here, provide reference points which guide SCAG's A-95 and environmental reviews and functional planning. (Growth forecasting is not, however, to be equated with growth management programs which actually implement regional policies, none of which exist at the regional level in California.)

(b) Association of Bay Area Governments

The first COG in California was formed in 1961 for the San Francisco Bay Area. The Association of Bay Area Governments was organized "for the permanent establishment of a forum for discussion and study of metropolitan area problems of mutual interest and concern . . . and for the development of policy and action recommendations."[16] At present 85 of 92 cities, and seven counties in the region are members. Special districts and other interested units of local government may participate in ABAG as non-voting, cooperating members.

ABAG is funded by state and federal grants which are matched by annual local contributions and amount to ten cents per resident of each member city and county. The Association's 1974-75 budget is approximately $1.6 million, of which about 30 percent comes from local government.

ABAG policy is determined by the General Assembly, meeting at least twice a year and composed of elected officials of its member governments. The General Assembly adopts the budget and reviews major policy actions of the Executive Committee. This latter is composed of 35 members appointed by boards of supervisors, mayors and city councils, and reflects the relative population size of each county. The Committee meets monthly to make operative decisions, consider grant applications, control expenditures and make policy recommendations. These bodies are assisted by a professional staff of 70 persons with specialized training.

As noted in this report, the San Francisco Bay region is home to many single-purpose statutory agencies, including the Bay Conservation and Development Commission, (BCDC), Metropolitan Transportation Commission (MTC), Bay Area Sewage Services Agency (BASSA), Bay Area Air Pollution Control District (BAAPCD) and two regional coastal zone conservation commissions. As part of its role as the regional comprehensive planning agency, ABAG considers close cooperation with these single-purpose agencies indispensable. Thus, ABAG has a joint policy committee with MTC to review those land use issues of the regional transportation plan which have implications for ABAG's own Regional Plan. Also, it has joined with other governmental units to form the Bay Delta Resource Recovery Board. As provided by the Coastal Zone Conservation Act, ABAG is represented on both regional commissions within its jurisdiction.[17] Also, as part of its growth policy formulation, ABAG is working closely with BASSA in designing enforceable sewage service strategies to achieve orderly growth in the region. BASSA is a regional single-purpose agency created by the Legislature to develop, adopt and implement a comprehensive waste water treatment plan for the Bay Area. Thus, ABAG has been able to mute, but not overcome, the fragmentation of planning in the Bay Area.

Major regional planning has been underway in the Bay Area for more than two decades. The first substantial effort at studying the entire area was made by the San Francisco Bay Area Rapid Transit Commission between 1951 and 1957. This was followed by 12 major planning studies of regional significance. Though the total planning has been relatively large, its initiative and direction has been scattered very broadly, much of it performed in response to state and federal requirements. Thus, a 1970 study of a unified planning program prepared for ABAG concluded:

". . . Despite large expenditures, there has been relatively little funding or organizational support to build a pool of local talent and information, to carefully correlate and coordinate plans and programs, or to establish priorities on the basis of a comprehensive view of area-wide needs. In fact, the diffusion of initiative and responsibility has actually produced significant amounts of duplication, inefficiency, and even fruitless and confusing conflict."[18]

Partially in response to early recognition of this fragmentation and overlapping governmental authority, ABAG since 1966 has generally supported creation of a limited regional government for the Bay Area. Recognizing the inability of a voluntary agency to perform difficult acts with sufficient authority, ABAG, in a statesmanlike manner, has proposed that a new regional agency be established by the Legislature. The proposals and implementation would include regional planning functions and also give the new agency new responsibility for other functions which over time, would be expanded to include additional areawide functions, as well as gradual absorption of the single-purpose statutory agencies. This movement toward an areawide authority has been reconsidered, debated and firmly opposed by some legislators. An attempt to consolidate ABAG with four other regional agencies was defeated in August 1974,[19] but a similar bill has been resubmitted.

ABAG has also undertaken numerous studies of regional needs and problems. Beginning with consideration of uniform building codes and an inventory of regional open space in 1962, the Association has published 18 studies ranging from population and labor force pro-

jections, to regional geology, to development regulations and housing costs. Recent major planning efforts include the comprehensive Regional Plan: 1970–1990, the Regional Housing Plan and the Regional Ocean Coastline Plane, utilized by the coastal agencies.

ABAG is currently pursuing a major study of growth policy in the Bay Area. The two principal reasons for adopting a regional guide for local growth decisions are: ". . . (1) individual communities responding to their own electorate and sense of priorities, and limited by their own resources have not been able to solve pressing regional problems such as adequate housing, environmental protection, and management of the pace of growth itself; and (2) local autonomy is already being rapidly eroded by the establishment of independent functional regionwide agencies with strong regulatory and program responsibilities in transportation, sewer and water facilities, and environmental protection. Under these conditions, the real issues are not will local prerogatives change, but how and under what conditions, and with what voice for local government."[20]

Specific ABAG activities proposed for the next three years include development of: agreements between ABAG, the nine Bay Area counties and regional cities which would establish growth rates and distributions for areas of the region; and agreements between ABAG and the single-purpose agencies to ensure that all regional agencies are planning according to the same growth projections.

(c) Comprehensive Planning Organization

The Comprehensive Planning Organization (CPO) is a single-county COG covering nearly 1.5 million persons in its jurisdiction, which comprises San Diego County and 13 local cities. The organization was originally formed in 1966 under a joint powers agreement which was re-executed in 1972 in somewhat different form. It is governed by a 14-member board of directors and an executive committee appointed by and from the board. With a staff or more than 40 persons and a burgeoning metropolitan region, CPO is one of the most active COGs in the state. Its major responsibilities are intergovernmental coordination, preparation of a regional comprehensive plan, disbursement of monies from the local transportation fund, review of federally assisted local projects (A-95) including environmental impact review, airport land use planning and review, and regional review of certain state initiated and assisted projects. It has recently completed an open space plan and is currently working on a regional transportation plan.

Like all other single-county COGs, CPO has suffered problems of planning coordination with the county and its major city (San Diego). There has been some hesitancy to invest the organization with additional authority both because of a long tradition in the area of home rule and of occasional wariness of what is perceived as a research-oriented program. The quality of CPO's reports is widely acknowledged, but their technical focus and regional orientation mean they sometimes go unheeded. Because it has limited power beyond A-95 review, CPO cannot get involved fully in major county and city decisions.

e. Planning Process Assessment

From this brief look at California's single-county and metropolitan COGs, it may be concluded that a major problem is the absence of an adequately defined role. Although most COGs state their function to be comprehensive regional planning, there are many divergent viewpoints as to what that means in practice. Programs vary greatly from one COG to another, and uncertainty exists within many COGs as to their proper relationship to existing governmental units.

Of course, such a result is not unexpected. The lack of a well-defined purpose and position is virtually ensured by the statutory basis of COGs. Ignoring the three regional planning enabling laws, nearly all COGs have relied upon the very broad provisions of the Joint Exercise of Powers Act—a law intended to serve equally well as the basis for cooperative library arrangements, joint convention centers and intercity street maintenance. The Act is essentially a non-statute which leaves the most important considerations to the voluntary agreement of the parties.

It can be argued, then, that the state has abdicated its responsibility for fostering areawide planning to the federal and local governments. Many planning requirements delegated to COGs are related to review of federal grants-in-aid. Since local governments are the draftsmen of the joint powers agreements, and their elected officials the members of the COG governing body, the real constituency of associations of governments is local government—and not the residents of the region. Without guidance at the state level, areawide planning in California—at least to the extent it is generally considered necessary for rational development and conservation policies—may become a battleground between local parochial protectionism and increasing federal requirements (and impatience).

Yet, whether out of a need to satisfy federal requirements or a desire to solve problems requiring a regional perspective, associations of governments will remain a fact of life for the foreseeable future. Moreover, recent court decisions in California and elsewhere require that local land use regulations be adopted within the framework of a comprehensive regional scheme.[21] With such forces underlining the importance of COGs, it seems appropriate that the state legislatively recognize their existence.

The several deficiencies of the current COGs and associations of government are logical points of departure and merit reiteration:

(1) They are voluntary associations, and member governments may withdraw whenever they choose (although the government would remain subject to the COG's authority as the A-95 clearinghouse for the area).

(2) Because they have no well-defined role by the state statutes, COGs are subject to claims that they are violating the "home rule" tradition.

(3) Also because their role is not statutorily defined especially as to local and single-purpose regional agencies, there is excessive overlap, fragmentation and conflict among governmental units.

(4) COGs have no taxing power and so must depend on federal grants and voluntary contributions from their members.

(5) They have no legal power to regulate or acquire land and, except for the A-95 grant review process, must depend on the acquiescence of their members to enforce their plans. Moreover, effective administration of the review process is undermined by the sometimes apparent indifference of state and federal agencies.[22]

(6) With local governments as their real constituency in practice, COGs generally have not attracted the attention of area residents. Neither the issues as presented nor the nature of their decision-making process have had much effect on citizen interest.[23]

(7) Areawide agencies have not altered the distribution of political power in the region. Representatives of the member governments generally retain significant loyalty to the local unit.[24]

(8) State law has established no standards or guidelines for the comprehensive areawide plans. Moreover, at present, the state has no procedures for designating

Areawide Planning Organizations; that function is left to the federal Department of Housing and Urban Development.

Despite these inadequacies, it should be noted that COGs have developed to serve specific needs and these needs will continue well into the future. With proper statutory guidance, their potential is clear. Yet, in California, there have been no major structural changes but only the mildest of reforms. "Relationships within many reorganized systems are remarkably like those in the preorganization world. Metropolitan institutional reform has changed little, not because it cannot, but because little has, in fact, been attempted."[25]

3. Regional Statutory Agencies

The state has statutory regional and sub-regional entities, usually single-purpose special districts, which are stewards of particular functions which have land use implications. Examples include the San Francisco Bay Area Air Pollution Control District Board, Bay Area Rapid Transit District (BART), and Alameda-Contra Costa Transit District. One such district—a regional transportation commission—exemplifies problems and opportunities posed by such an institutional arrangement.

Metropolitan Transportation Commission

The Metropolitan Transportation Commission (MTC), which covers the nine San Francisco Bay Area counties, is one of two statutory agencies in California engaged in regional transportation planning. The other, the California Tahoe Regional Planning Agency, is described below.

All regional transportation planning agencies (RTPAs) may be classified as statutory or non-statutory. As a statutory agency, MTC was created as a single-purpose planning agency under special state enabling legislation (AB 363) in 1970, which specified planning, organization, finance and other powers unique to the agency. The Commission is linked to the comprehensive planning process through legal agreement with the Association of Bay Area Governments. However, the statutory existence of MTC precludes ABAG from assuming a primary transportation planning role for its region. However, in the Los Angeles region, the Southern California Association of Governments is the primary RTPA.[1]

The other 39 RTPAs in California were created either in response to federal transportation program requirements or to state legislation (SB 325). Multi- and single-county RTPAs in urbanized areas were organized in response to federal requirements imposed by the Department of Housing and Urban Development and the Federal Highway Administration. The non-urbanized RTPAs were organized in response to California state requirements under SB 325, and with their creation came special state legislative mandates.[2]

a. Legislative Intent

The Legislature intended that MTC be supported by local, state and federal governments, and particularly, be eligible for transportation and general planning funds from federal, state and local sources "which would normally be available for . . . the region." MTC and Caltrans were instructed to negotiate contracts so that federal-aid highway funds, as well as matching funds from the state highway trust fund, may be used by the Commission for regional highway and street planning. The Commission was to seek federal planning and research funds from the Department of Housing and Urban Development. In addition, the Commission was to negotiate "equitable agreements" with regional cities, counties and transportation districts to provide for its general support.[3]

b. Organization

MTC exists as a "local area planning agency," independent of state government, to provide comprehensive transportation planning for the region, composed of the City and County of San Francisco and the Counties of Alameda, Contra Costa, Marin, Napa, San Mateo, Santa Clara, Solano and Sonoma. The Commission is governed by a 19-member board, as follows: two representatives each from San Francisco, Alameda, Contra Costa, San Mateo and Santa Clara counties; one member each from Marin, Napa, Solano and Sonoma counties; and one non-voting member each from the state Secretary of Business and Transportation and the federal Departments of Transportation and Housing and Urban Development. Each appointee serves a four-year term; no provision is made for citizen representatives. Selection of board members is to be based upon their "special familiarity" with transportation problems and issues.[4]

MTC superseded the Bay Area Transportation Study Commission and its interim successor, the Regional Transportation Planning Committee, by assuming their planning and related responsibilities.[5] It was required to develop a regional transportation plan by July, 1973, based upon the following considerations:

(a) The previous plan recommended by the Bay Area Transportation Study Commission, as modified by the Regional Transportation Planning Committee;

(b) Ecological, economic and social impacts of existing and future regional transportation systems upon housing, employment, recreation, environment, land use policies and the economically disadvantaged; and,

(c) Short and long-term regional plans adopted by ABAG, San Francisco Bay Conservation and Development Commission, and the State Office of Planning and Research, as well as other organizations concerned with regional planning.[6]

At minimum, the scope of the regional transportation plan was to include state and federal highways, transbay bridges, mass transit systems and interfaces of multi-modal systems. In addition, the plan was to estimate regional transportation needs for a ten-year period, to schedule transportation priorities according to these needs and to develop a financial program. The financial program was to include (a) a proposal for financing construction and operating costs for each segment of the regional transportation system, and (b) consideration of revenue sources "without regard to any constraints imposed by law on expenditures from such sources." The latter provision apparently is an oblique reference to the state's highway trust fund and other vehicle-related funds whose revenues were exclusively earmarked for highway-related purposes. Thus, MTC was also instructed to recommend appropriate legislation to the Legislature to secure such financing.[7] The regional transportation plan is to be reviewed continuously and revised as needed, with such revisions officially adopted annually. In addition, the Commission was to study the relationship of regional harbors and airports to surface transportation and their role within a regional transportation system.

c. Powers

In addition to planning and finance, the Commission was provided three sets of powers for generally assuring compliance with the regional transportation plan and policies. The Commission is to review and approve all applications for federal and state financial assistance by local governments and transportation districts for their "compatibility with" the regional transportation plan be-

fore submission to the funding agency.[8] Its approval is required for: (a) construction of a new transbay bridge; (b) modification of existing bridges for additional lanes of traffic or rapid transit facilities; and (c) any new multi-county transit system using exclusive rights of way.[9] The Commission is to provide "all available assistance" to public transit systems so as to ensure adequate feeder service to multi-county systems. However, its statutory relationship to the state Highway Commission, now attached to Caltrans, is ambiguous. On the one hand, the Highway Commission "shall conform to" the regional transportation plan and priorities schedule, but on the other hand, it "may deviate from" the plan and schedule where construction of the federal interstate and state highway systems manifest "an overriding state-wide interest."[10]

San Francisco Bay Conservation and Development Commission

The state Legislature has created several powerful planning and regulatory agencies which have as their primary focus balancing development and conservation in geographical areas containing special environmental characteristics. Each, in practical effect, can negate all local planning permits issued within their regions although it cannot institute regionally desirable development over local objections. These agencies stand as models for a "critical area approach" similar to that in yet to be adopted national land use legislation. The first of these created was the San Francisco Bay Conservation and Development Commission (BCDC).

BCDC, a regional regulatory and planning agency for the San Francisco bayshore, served as a model for the Coastal Zone Initiative (Proposition 20) of 1972. Under that initiative, it still retains permit authority through an exemption of San Francisco Bay and adjacent lands. Thus, BCDC may become a prototype for regional agencies with land use regulatory powers, which may gradually provide more specific plans and regulations within a broader policy framework.

a. Legislative History

The legislative impetus for preventing further filling of San Francisco Bay grew out of public pressure, chiefly the Save San Francisco Bay Association and public reaction to *The Future of San Francisco Bay* by Mel Scott. After several unsuccessful attempts, the 1964 Legislature succeeded in creating the San Francisco Bay Study Commission which existed for one year and had nine members. Within six months, the Commission proposed creation of a Bay Conservation and Development Commission.

BCDC operated under the McAteer-Petris Act from September, 1965 to November, 1969. During that period it was instructed: (1) to prepare, and report back to the Legislature in January, 1969, a "comprehensive and enforceable plan for the conservation of the waters of San Francisco Bay to the maximum extent possible" by a permit system regulating filling and dredging in the bay. The Bay Plan was published in January, 1969. The McAteer-Petris Act was subsequently amended so that BCDC essentially embodies the program set forth in the Bay Plan.

b. Legislative Intent

The rapid rate of bay filling probably was the first successful environmental rallying point for citizen groups. Accordingly, the Act recognizes that haphazard, uncoordinated filling threatens the Bay itself, jeopardizes the welfare and enjoyment of present and future residents, and potentially harms wildlife and the natural environment. A single governmental body is needed to evaluate individual projects in relation to the entire bay.[1] The shoreline is to be improved, developed and preserved[2] to make the bay more accessible to essential ports, water related industries, airports, wildlife refuges, recreation, desalinization plants and power plants.[3] Thus, the Bay Plan should provide suitable locations for these uses and thereby minimize the necessity for fill. Maximum feasible public access should be part of the planning of these uses.[4] Salt ponds and managed wetlands deserve special protection by either dedication or public purchase. If development is authorized in such areas, maximum public access consistent with the project should be provided, and the maximum amount of water surface area should be retained.[5]

Additional filling of San Francisco Bay is subject to other limitations in the Act. Fill is authorized only when the public benefit clearly outweighs the public detriment from the loss of water areas but should be carefully limited.[6] An Opinion of the Attorney General held that BCDC cannot allow fill for non-water-oriented uses.[7] Fill for any purpose, whether water-oriented or not, is to be authorized only if no alternative upland location is available and should be minimal, avoiding harmful environmental effects and establishing a permanent shoreline.[8]

c. Organization

BCDC is composed of 27 members. One member each is appointed by the U.S. Army Corps of Engineers and the Environmental Protection Agency. State government representation includes one member each appointed by the Business and Transportation, Finance, and Resources Agencies, and the State Lands Commission. Also, a member of the San Francisco Bay Regional Water Quality Control Board is a member of the BCDC board. Nine county representatives are selected from the boards of supervisors of the nine Bay Area counties. The Association of Bay Area Governments appoints four city representatives, one each from the north, east, south and west bay areas. Each city representative must be an elected official. Seven representatives of the public, five appointed by the Governor and one each by the Senate Rules Committee and Speaker of the Assembly, comprise the remaining membership of the Commission.

d. Powers and Duties

Preparation and continuing review of the Bay Plan, as well as administration of the permit system are BCDC's primary responsibilities.

(1) The Plan

The Plan was to treat the entire bay as a single planning unit to avoid local bias. All characteristics of the bay were to be examined in detail, including water quality, ecological balance, economic interests and industrial deep water uses. In addition, a study was to examine current and proposed uses of the bay and shoreline and the general plans of adjoining cities and counties. The Bay Plan was to be based on the study. In the 1969 amendments to the McAteer-Petris Act, the Legislature found that the Commission had prepared "a comprehensive and enforceable plan for the conservation of the water of the bay and the development of its shoreline."[9] Emphasizing the importance of continuing review, the Legislature stated that the 1969 plan was an interim plan.[10] Any change in the Bay Plan must be consistent with the Act's policies. If a proposed change would revise a policy or standard adopted under the Plan or define a water-oriented land use, a two-thirds vote of approval is required of Commission members.[11]

The Plan is no mere policy document but an implementable guide which is tied to the administration of shoreline permits. In addition to the Bay Plan, BCDC was to establish boundaries for water-oriented priority land uses within its 100 foot shoreline jurisdiction. A change in land use boundaries also requires a two-thirds vote of the Commission. This provision enables BCDC to develop locational controls for the siting of "water-oriented priority land uses."

(2) The Permit System

To better protect the shoreline and bay, the Commission may issue or deny permits for projects that would fill, extract materials or substantially change a water, land or structural use within the area of its jurisdiction.[12] The Commission's jurisdiction is the San Francisco Bay, a strip of land 100 feet wide along the bayshore, saltponds, managed wetlands and certain waterways.

BCDC's power to regulate fill does not preempt city and county controls. An applicant still files for a permit with the local government.[13] If the project requires local approval, the city or county investigates and files a report with the Commission. The San Francisco Bay Regional Water Quality Control Board also reports on the water quality ramifications of the proposed project. Nonetheless, a permit is automatically granted if the Commission fails to act within a specified period of time.

Permits may be granted subject to conditions. Thirteen votes of Commission members are needed for permit approval. (This number constitutes a majority, because the federal members cannot vote on permits.) For a proposed project within the shoreline band but outside the boundaries of "water-oriented priority land uses," a permit must be issued, unless the project fails to provide maximum feasible public access to the bay and shoreline.[14]

(a) Enforcement and Appeal

Criminal and civil enforcement provisions are stipulated by the Act. Any person who performs activities requiring a permit without obtaining one is subject to citation as a criminal misdemeanor or to a cease and desist order. A cease and desist order may contain terms and conditions, including the immediate removal of fill or other material or a compliance schedule which leads to permit approval.[15] Violators of a cease and desist order may be liable for fines up to $6000 for each day of the violation.

Two aspects of the enforcement system should be noted. First, appeal and final resolution lies with the state court system. Second, there is no provision for citizen suits as under the Coastal Zone Conservation Act, which confers standing to the public to sue the Coastal Commission itself and violators of the coastal permit system.

(b) Exemptions

A "grandfather" clause exempted some projects from permit requirements. No permit was required for projects which were fully approved and begun before September 17, 1965.[16] Also, projects within the 100 foot shoreline strip, saltponds and managed wetlands were exempted if the developer had a "vested right." A right to develop is deemed to have vested if, prior to September, 1969, a person in good faith and reliance upon a local ordinance permit authorizing the particular use undertook "substantial" construction and financial liability for the project.[17]

An automatic exemption is extended to public service facilities such as water, gas, electric or communications facilities, and sewer, storm water, petroleum, gas or other pipelines.[18] Planned community developments on filled land which were approved and begun before July, 1969, were excluded from the Commission's jurisdiction except for additional fill or extraction of materials.[19]

Tahoe Regional Planning Agency[1]

a. Introduction

Regional planning for the Lake Tahoe basin began in the late 1950's. The Lake Tahoe Area Council sponsored consultation among planning commissions for all counties in the basin. The Tahoe Regional Planning Commission was subsequently formed and developed the 1980 Regional Plan. The Plan estimated that although the basin could accommodate a maximum summertime population of 400,000 in 1980, local governments should strive for a 1980 summertime limit of no more than 300,000 persons. The Plan had no authoritative force except as a general guide to local officials for their own planning, zoning and subdivision controls. It did, however, serve to focus attention on the Tahoe problem and to provide some perspective.

The two state Legislatures, California and Nevada, then created the Lake Tahoe Joint Study Committee to consider proposals for preserving the Tahoe basin as a natural resource. The Committee's report recommended formation of "a governmental entity of general purpose but of limited functions, designed to supplement and coordinate, not to supplant or displace, the local governments of the Region." Specifically, the Committee recommended establishment of a bi-state agency to enforce land control standards and to act as an intermediary between local governments and also with the federal government.

The California Legislature adopted the Committee's proposal with modifications in 1967. Agency membership was decreased from 15 to ten by dropping the five at-large members. The Nevada Legislature made other changes. Concurrent majorities of the representatives from each state were required to approve Agency decisions. The powers of the new Agency were limited to matters "general and regional in application." The bill removed the Agency's power to veto public works projects of the states. The primary responsibility for planning was shifted from the Agency itself to a subordinate, advisory planning commission. The Nevada version was accepted by the California Legislature, which amended its bill of 1967. Congress ratified the interstate Compact in December, 1969, and the Agency came into being in 1970.

b. Organization

The bi-state Compact recognized what had become apparent even before the initial attempts at regional planning in the 1950's—that, "the waters of Lake Tahoe and other resources of the Lake Tahoe region are threatened with deterioration or degeneration. By virtue of the special conditions and circumstances of the natural ecology, developmental pattern, population distribution and human needs in the Lake Tahoe region, the region is experiencing problems of resource use and deficiencies of environmental control."[2]

The Compact also recognized the necessity for an areawide planning agency with power (a) to adopt and enforce a regional plan for resource conservation and orderly development, (b) to exercise effective environmental controls, and (c) to perform other essential functions.[3] Such an agency would be instrumental in planning and regulating comprehensively so as to maintain an equilibrium between the region's natural endowments and its man-made environment.[4]

To achieve areawide planning and regulation in the region, the Tahoe Regional Planning Agency was created by the Compact. A majority of the Agency's board membership is from local governments. One member is appointed by the boards of supervisors of El Dorado and Placer Counties and one by the City Council of South Lake Tahoe. The California appointee must be an elected official. For the Nevada local government members, one member is appointed by each of the boards of county commissioners of Douglas, Ormsby and Washoe Counties. Any Nevada appointee must be a resident of the county from which he is appointed and

may be a member of the board which appoints him. The Nevada members from county government must disclose all economic interests acquired after appointment. The remaining four representatives on the ten-member governing board are appointed by the two state governments. One is appointed by the Governor of each state. The California member is subject to Senate confirmation; he cannot be a resident of the region and must represent the public at large, presumably to ensure a voice for non-resident users. The remaining two representatives are the Administrator of the California Resources Agency and the Director of the Nevada Department of Conservation and Natural Resources.[5]

A quorum for the transaction of agency business occurs when a majority of the representatives from each state is present. A majority vote of each state's representatives is required to approve any matter.[6] Thus, the requirement for dual majorities of both state delegations may not promote the concept of a governing body acting cohesively to solve regional problems.

The Agency board also appoints the advisory planning commission with equal representatives from California and Nevada. The mandatory commission members total 17 and represent primarily local planning, health, environmental and developer interests.

c. Planning

In preparing the plans or plan amendments required by the Compact, the advisory planning commission, which has primary planning responsibility, must hold at least one public hearing, then recommend a plan or amendment to the Agency board for adoption. The board may adopt, modify or reject the proposal or, alternatively, it may initiate and adopt a plan without first referring it to the planning commission. Thus, while the Compact delegates the responsibility of plan preparation primarily to the planning commission, the Agency itself may also assume that function.[7] Additionally, a governmental unit or the owner or lessee of real property may propose amendments to the plan which affect the jurisdiction of the governmental unit or the individual's property.

The plan and its amendments were officially adopted by the Agency as an ordinance. Thus, the plan assumes legal authority as a guide to preservation and development of the Tahoe Basin, because the Agency's ordinances are enforceable against violators. The regional plan is to include the following elements.

(1) A land use plan setting criteria and standards for the

uses of land, air, water, space and other natural resources within the region, including the indication and allocation of maximum population densities.

(2) A multi-modal transportation plan for integrated development of a regional transportation system.

(3) A conservation plan for preservation, development, utilization and management of the scenic and other natural resources of the basin.

(4) A recreation plan for development, utilization and management of the recreational resources of the region.

(5) A public services and facilities plan for general location, scale and provision of public services and facilities.[8]

The plan is to harmonize the needs of the region as a whole. The plans of the cities and counties within the region and of state, federal and non-governmental organizations which affect the region must also be considered. While there is no requirement for citizen participation beyond public hearings, the Agency and planning commission are to seek the cooperation, and consider the recommendations of state, local and federal agencies; public and private educational and research organizations; civic groups; and private individuals.[9] The regional general plan as finally adopted is enforceable by TRPA as well as by the states, counties and cities of the region.[10]

The Compact recognized that TRPA would assume its regulatory functions prior to adoption of the completed general plan. It instructed the advisory commission to recommend a regional interim plan to be adopted within 90 days by the TRPA board. This plan was to include statements of (a) policies, criteria and standards for planning and development, and (b) plans, projects and planning decisions necessary for the Agency to exercise its substantive powers.[11]

d. Powers

As with the Bay Conservation and Development Commission and Coastal Zone Conservation Commission, TRPA's planning is tied to its regulatory authority. The bi-state agreement authorizes the Agency to adopt ordinances, rules, regulations and policies necessary to implement the interim and regional plans. The form of the regulations is prescribed. Each regulation is to establish a minimum standard applicable throughout the basin, but any city or county may adopt a higher standard. Standards must apply, but are not limited, to the following:

water purity and clarity; subdivision; zoning; tree removal solid waste disposal; sewage disposal; land fills, excavations, cuts and grading; piers, harbors, breakwater or channels and other shoreline areas; waste disposal from boats; mobile home parks; house relocation; outdoor advertising; flood plain protection; soil and sedimentation control; air pollution; and watershed protection.[12]

Nevada's legislation, as accepted by California, added to the Compact a proviso that ordinances, whenever possible without diminishing the interim or general plan, should be restricted to general, regionwide matters. Specific local ordinances, rules, regulations and policies which conform to the interim or regional plan are, accordingly, left to the states, counties and cities.[13] Another Nevada legislative provision which became part of the Compact further limited the authority of the Agency. TRPA ordinances are to recognize any business or recreational establishment individually licensed by state law if (1) it was licensed by February 5, 1968, or (2) it was to be built on land appropriately zoned under an adopted master plan by February 5, 1968.[14] This provision essentially removes gambling casinos, which must be individually licensed in Nevada, from the jurisdiction of the Agency if they fall under one or both categories.

A final weakness in the Agency's regulatory power relates to its inability to deny approval to public construction projects, ". . . which may substantially affect, or may specifically apply, to the uses of land, water, air, space and other natural resources in the region, including . . . public works plans, programs and proposals concerning highway routing, design and construction." These are referred to the agency for its review, as to conformity with the regional plan or interim plan. A public works project which is initiated and is to be constructed by a department of either state shall be submitted to the agency for review and recommendation, but may be constructed as proposed.[15]

Nevada insisted upon adding these provisions to the Compact, probably on the theory that a bi-state agency should not be able to prevent construction projects by state agencies. In California, however, such projects are subject to the approval of the California Tahoe Regional Planning Agency (CTRPA).[16]

CTRPA is a governmental instrument of the State of California and essentially supplements TRPA. Its powers parallel those of TRPA, except that all public works projects must be reviewed prior to construction and approved by the Agency for compliance with the CTRPA's adopted regional general plan.[17] Those projects submitted to the CTRPA must receive its approval before they can be submitted to the Tahoe Regional Planning Agency.[18]

As mentioned above, the states, counties and cities in the region as well as TRPA have the authority to enforce the regional general plan. The Agency is also empowered to police the region to ensure compliance with the plan, ordinances, rules, regulations and policies. The Agency may institute court action to compel a local jurisdiction to enforce the TRPA ordinances.[19] Violation of an Agency ordinance is a misdemeanor.[20] There is no provision in the Compact or in the California legislation enabling citizens to sue the Agency to perform its duties or to sue private violators of the ordinances.

C. LOCAL PLANNING LAWS AND AGENCIES

Despite the emergence of state/substate and regional agencies and programs in recent years, predominant control over land use still rests with local government. Cities and counties are authorized by state enabling legislation to prepare a general plan and to implement the plan legally in exercise of their state-delegated "police power" so as to promote the general welfare. Although recent federal, state and regional initiatives in planning have been necessitated by inadequate land use control by local government, proposals for reform generally reserve significant responsibility for the local level.

1. Local Planning Institutions and Performance

a. Changing Concepts of Local Planning

At the local level, planning may be conceived as a comprehensive and coordinated guide for community development and conservation.[1] Thus, a general plan should approximate a consensus as to future objectives for development and conservation, analyze land use issues in relation to social and economic goals, and serve as official policy for the city or county on these matters. The state Planning and Zoning Law envisions the general plan as "a pattern and guide" for orderly "physical growth and development" as well as conservation of open space land, and as "a basis" for the efficient expenditure of funds "relating to the subjects of the general plan."[2] This traditional approach to land use planning, culminating in the general plan, begins with projections of economic growth for the local area that are based on regional and local trends. It anticipates the local potential for capturing part of the larger regional growth and thereby estimates future local populations. The economic and population projections are then translated into estimates of demand for industrial, commercial, residential and public land uses. The land supply is evaluated for suitability of each type of land use, including analysis of location, accessibility, size, availability of utilities, and physical characteristics such as slope and soil stability. The traditional approach often has contributed to costly pollution, urban sprawl, loss of prime agricultural land and destruction of natural amenities and resources or at best, has proven inadequate to mitigate these potent problems.

These failings and others have led to the current reevaluation of local planning. In response to much thoughtful criticism, the land use planning process is now evolving on three fronts. First, the basic objectives and assumptions of planning have been continually redefined. The quality of the natural environment within and around urban areas has assumed importance alongside the traditional concern for the quality of the man-made environment. The positive benefits of economic growth balanced against negative costs are assessed. Population growth projections are no longer accepted without question and may be challenged by parallel projections of deteriorating environmental quality. Land use planning in a comprehensive framework is increasingly viewed as a means of deciding how much and when, as well as where, growth ought to occur.[3]

Second, there is an increasing search for usable environmental information and objective criteria for deciding the appropriate allocation of new urban activities. Increasingly, studies are made of environmental constraints on development and the visual and psychological perception of surroundings. Some land inventories are being based upon an area's ecosystem and usually stress the independent significance of plant and animal communities. The practice of cost/benefit analysis is being further refined by application to land economics and fundamental reexamination of its assumptions.

Third, the emphasis in land planning has shifted away from data interpretation and formulating long range plans toward being able to implement local planning policies. Too often the plans have been quickly ignored, with zoning and other land use regulations being determined by factors outside of adopted planning policy. Many observers conclude that plans must consider the timing and sequence of urban development as well as providing a static picture of the community at some future endstate. Efforts to correlate land use regulations, planning and decision-making of legislative bodies have produced embryonic steps toward comprehensive "land use guidance systems."[4]

Some local governments in California have been among the leaders in each area. To a large extent, innovative land use programs are being developed by individual cities and counties in response to particular problems of uncontrolled growth and environmental degradation. These innovations, in turn, have led to a serious questioning of the conventional planning practices and of the laws which dictated, or at least suggested, these practices. To some minor extent also, state legislative change prodded local governments to improve traditional planning approaches.

b. Planning Organizations and Institutions

Each city and county is to establish a planning agency.[5] Its prescribed planning functions are development and maintenance of the general plan, development of specific plans "as may be necessary or desirable," periodic review of the local capital improvement program and "such other functions as the legislative body may provide."[6] At the city level, the agency may be a planning department, planning commission or the function may be assumed by the legislative body itself. Counties must have a planning commission. Thus, given the latitude of the statute, institutional arrangements for planning take different forms in different local jurisdictions. Although the names and functions vary, the following description is generally applicable.

The planning department is the professional body which undertakes studies requested by the city council or board of supervisors, researches proposals for changes in land use and makes recommendations to the planning commission and the local legislative body. Although the planning department usually acts only in an advisory role, it can be influential.

A planning commission usually exists along with the planning department and is composed of citizens appointed by the local legislature. The method of appointment and terms of office are governed by local ordinance, but state law provides that the planning commissions of counties and general law cities have five to nine members.[7] The commission's functions include the preparation of the general plan, its periodic review, and recommendations to the legislature in drawing up implementing ordinances. In some cities, the commission handles most of the day-to-day administration of land use ordinances, thus relieving the city council of the burden. Planning commissions were originally intended to "humanize" land regulation and transmit the desires of the community's citizens. However, many observers contend the commission sometimes, merely echoes those who appoint its members, or at least insulate them from controversial issues.

Partially in reaction to uneven concern for and consideration of citizen opinion by planning commissions, other forms of citizen participation have been attempted. Some cities have established citizen advisory councils by area or function to debate policy issues and matters pending local decision. At the county level, there has been use of counterpart municipal advisory councils or municipal area councils, which provide advisory decision-making for unincorporated areas (the name "municipal" notwithstanding). Other local governments have merely adhered to the general suggestion of state law that they "consult with their public officials and agencies, public utilities and various groups and citizens generally in formulating the general plan."[8] A 1971 survey indicated that 84 percent of cities and 79 percent of counties at times have utilized existing citizen groups for advisory purposes.[9] Generally, citizen participation is increasingly viewed as an essential ingredient of successful and effective planning, and formal advisory councils or informal but organized groups are becoming important, although extra-statutory, institutions of local planning.

Coordination among local, regional and state agencies has been an important experiment at attempting to transcend limitations inherent with many local institutions but no prescribed system exists for rationally resolving local planning conflicts. The law, as indicated above, requires a planning agency to "consult with" public officials and agencies to maximize coordination of plans and site locations for public facilities.[10] When a city planning agency is "considering" a general plan or plan element, it is to refer the plan to the county planning agency, contiguous county and city, and every county and city within the city's planning area. Similar provisions apply for county general plans. Because the general plan should also attempt to harmonize the plans and programs of special districts, the statute also recommends its prior reference to the Local Agency Formation Commission. The purpose is to inform neighboring local governments and solicit comments, although their comments have no binding effect and no procedure is prescribed for resolving planning conflicts. Ironically, the statute goes on to describe its own referral provisions as "directory, not mandatory" and that non-compliance in no way affects the validity of the plan or element.[11]

·Local planning statutes do not provide for regional coordination nor identify specific requirements for state-local coordination except that: (1) the open space element is sent to the Secretary of the Resources Agency;[12] (2) the housing element is prepared according to regulations promulgated by the Department of Housing and Community Development;[13] (3) any state agency responsible for a transportation facility is to provide information as to noise levels.[14] Additionally, as discussed more fully below, the Council on Intergovernmental Relations (CIR) has developed guidelines for the preparation of general plans, and local governments are to submit annual reports describing their compliance with the guidelines.[15]

c. The General Plan

Each planning agency is to prepare, and each local legislature to adopt "a comprehensive, long-term general plan" for the "physical development of the jurisdiction" and land outside its boundaries related to its planning.[16] The plan may be prepared so as to be adopted piecemeal or in its entirety, and for all or part of the jurisdiction.[17]

State law requirements which prescribe the substantive content of the general plan apply to charter as well as general law cities and all counties.[18] In general, the California Constitution declares that a county or city may adopt and enforce "all such local, police, sanitary and other regulations as are not in a conflict with general laws."[19] Activities of general law cities may be regulated by the laws enacted by the Legislature which apply to such cities.[20] Charter cities, on the other hand

have charters providing for some degree of rule and may self-determine how to regulate matters of strictly local importance or "municipal affairs"[21] However, matters of "statewide concern" are reserved to the Legislature, regardless of a city's status as a charter city. In the planning field, state statutes declare that no law restrict a charter city's planning process, except that a general plan be adopted by the local legislative body and that it contain the prescribed mandatory elements.[22] Thus, charter cities may establish different procedures for the adopting, administering and implementing of their general plans but must abide by state laws prescribing their substantive content. Of course, a charter city may by ordinance or in its charter, assume any obligation imposed by the state's general laws.

The first California act enabling (but not requiring) cities and counties to adopt general plans was passed in 1927. In 1929, the adoption of plans was made mandatory for those local governments establishing planning commissions in order to aid in administering zoning ordinances. In 1947, 20 years after the first enabling act, state statutes made it mandatory for each city and county to adopt a general plan. In 1955, the first legislative attempt to determine the content of the general plan was made by requiring the inclusion of mandatory elements in each plan. Probably few legislators at the time foresaw the future implications of that evolution.

In its present form, state law declares that the general plan shall include "a statement of development policies" and "a diagram or diagrams and text setting forth objectives, principles, standards, and plan proposals."[23] Within this general statement, there are a variety of views as to desirable forms which comprehensive land use plans should take. Because land use decisions are complex and sometimes require a considerable degree of flexibility, "policy plans" have become popular. These plans set forth the local legislature's policies for land development and are enforced as individual cases arise. However, the dangers of favoritism and a desire to make firm decisions before developers begin to exert pressure have encouraged more specific planning for undeveloped areas. Policy plans may be the only feasible alternative where necessary data has not been gathered. However, in such cases, detailed studies must be made on a project-by-project basis. In the long run, more detailed plans, amended regularly, and backed by adequate economic and environmental data are needed.[24]

A more precise, substantive description of general plans is given in the statutory requirement that each general plan "shall include" the following mandatory elements:[25]

Land Use—This element designates the proposed general distribution, location and uses of land for housing, business, industry, open space (including agriculture, natural resources, recreation and scenic beauty), education, public buildings and grounds, solid and liquid waste disposal facilities and other categories of public and private uses. It includes a statement of the standards of population density and building intensity. The land use element also identifies areas subject to flooding, and these provisions are to be reviewed annually. This element especially should be closely tied to local social, environmental and economic goals. The land use element is to be developed concurrently with the circulation element, because transportation systems are frequently major determinants of housing and land use.

Circulation—The circulation element generally describes the location of existing and proposed major roads, transportation routes, terminals, and other local public utilities and facilities. It is correlated with the land use element and should reflect the scenic highways element, acceptable noise levels, natural resources such as air quality, the housing element, population growth and other environmental concerns.

Housing—This element should attempt to make adequate provision for the housing needs of all economic segments of the local community. To be realistic, the housing element should deal with very difficult financial and institutional problems as well as social and political obstacles, such as neighborhood opposition to racial, economic or social integration and resistance to multiple unit housing for low and moderate income households. Active citizen participation and support is especially important for preparing and implementing this element.

Conservation—This element is devoted to conservation, development and utilization of natural resources, including water, forests, soils, rivers, harbors, fisheries, wildlife, minerals and other natural resources. Because of the close relationship of the conservation, open space, seismic safety and scenic highways elements, some planning agencies are combining them into a comprehensive element for environmental resources.

Seismic Safety—The seismic safety element identifies and appraises seismic hazards, such as susceptibility to surface ruptures, ground shaking, ground failures and effects of seismically induced tidal waves. It includes an appraisal of mudslides and slope stability. In addition, the element should establish: acceptable risk levels for life and property; disaster contingency planning; and implementation through revised building codes, zoning, building inspections and public awareness of seismic hazards.

Noise—This element is to specify noise level contours for existing (and projected) major transportation facilities and to recommend appropriate site and route designations. Any public or private entity responsible for constructing or maintaining a transportation facility is to supply appropriate data describing present and projected noise levels. Maximum levels are to be established for each category of land use; this element is particularly important in preparing the housing, land use and circulation elements.

Scenic Highways—This element provides for establishment, development and protection of scenic highways under applicable provisions of the Streets and Highways Code. Actions necessary to protect scenic corridors, such as control of land uses, outdoor advertising, earth-moving, landscaping and building design and appearance, are to be included.

Safety—The safety element should articulate protection from fires and geologic hazards through, for example, evacuation routes, peak water supply requirements, minimum road widths, clearances around structures and geologic hazard mapping. The purpose is to incorporate safety considerations into the planning process and possibly to combine this element with the seismic safety element.

Open Space—The open space element is intended to protect the natural environment. The Legislature enacted a separate article dealing with open space lands to "assure that cities and counties recognize that open-space land is a limited and valuable resource which must be conserved wherever possible."[26] Open space lands are broadly defined to include lands for natural resources, agriculture, recreation, scenic beauty, watershed or ground water recharge and wildlife habitat. Premature or unnecessary conversion of open space is discouraged. Cities and counties were required to adopt and submit to the Secretary of the Resources Agency a plan for comprehensive, long-range preservation of open space lands. The plan must contain an "action" program consisting of specific steps (e.g., zoning, subdivision control, dedication, acquisition and controlled growth policies) which the local legislative body intends to pursue.[27] Government Code section 65910 specifically required adoption of an "open space zoning ordinance" by December 31, 1973, which was consistent with the element.

In addition to the nine mandatory elements, the law suggests optional elements for recreation, community design, redevelopment, public services and facilities, public buildings, housing, transit, transportation, and expanded elements dealing with circulation and housing.[28]

Listed below are the current deadlines for adoption of mandatory elements by the local planning agency:[29]

Land Use	1955
Circulation	1955
Housing	1969
Conservation	December 31, 1973
Open Space	December 31, 1973
Seismic Safety	September 20, 1975
Noise	September 20, 1975
Scenic Highways	September 20, 1975
Safety	September 20, 1975

Although these elements are declared to be "mandatory," no sanctions are provided in the statutory scheme for non-compliance by local governments. Some observers believe that the only legal consequence of failing to adopt a mandatory element by the specified date would be to expose the local government to a lawsuit seeking to compel preparation and adoption.[30] Land use regulation based on the incomplete general plan would be allowed to remain in effect. The Legislative Counsel has offered a contrasting view. Under this interpretation, a local plan is not the required general plan unless it includes every mandatory element.[31] Thus, a zoning ordinance or subdivision map could not be considered "consistent with" an incomplete plan as now required by state law. One possible consequence is that failure to adopt a mandatory element would, in effect, create a moratorium on approval of subdivision proposals. In sum, the legal requirements are not yet clear, but in the absence of a definitive judicial decision, local governments face no immediate sanctions for failure to comply with state law.

The open space element is the only general plan element which is backed by prohibitions. The statute requires that all local government actions acquiring, disposing, restricting or regulating open space be "consistent with" the open space element. Furthermore, no building permit, subdivision map or open space zoning ordinance may be approved unless it is "consistent with" the open space element.[32] Additionally, an open space element is necessary for reimbursement to offset reduced property tax revenues for land designated as open space conservation areas under the Williamson Act.

Such mandatory elements were not always required by state law, and even when required, an unfortunately large number of local governments prepared various elements inadequately or not at all. A 1973 survey of general plan activity in California indicated widespread non-compliance with state law.[33] Information received from 225 of 407 cities and 40 of 58 counties resulted in the following findings as of early 1973:

(a) One county and 25 cities did not have a general plan.

(b) Sixty seven percent of the counties and 38 percent of the cities had adopted a housing element which was "required" since 1969.

(c) While only 27 percent of the counties had a conservation element, 57 percent were in the process of preparing one. Although due by December, 1973, 16 percent of the cities had then not yet undertaken any activity with respect to this element.

(d) The most serious deficiency was indicated for the seismic safety, scenic highways noise and safety elements, with a majority of the cities having taken no steps toward their preparation as of early 1973. Counties responded with similar figures.

In an attempt to improve the quality of local general plans, recent state legislation directed the Council on Intergovernmental Relations to develop guidelines to aid local governments in meeting their statutory planning responsibilities.[34] Some knowledgeable observers state that the demands of these new guidelines have overburdened the planning staffs of smaller communities. Beginning October, 1974, each city and county planning department must submit its annual report to the Council or otherwise indicate how well its general plan complies with CIR's guidelines. The local general plan must include the recently mandated seismic safety, noise, safety and scenic highways elements within a year of CIR's adoption of the respective guidelines. CIR is empowered to extend the deadline in individual cases of extreme hardship.

A 1974 survey by CIR revealed a mixed pattern of compliance by local government to the Legislature's command for timely completion of the mandatory plan elements. On the favorable side, 66 percent of the cities and 76 percent of the counties had completed the housing and conservation elements, respectively, representing substantial improvement since the 1973 survey. On the negative side, the following data may be indicative of the current state of the local planning process and its responsiveness to state level direction:

(a) Although all local governments were required to respond to the 1974 Survey, 42 of 407 cities did not.

(b) More than 60 percent of both the cities and counties had failed to complete the noise, seismic safety, scenic highways and safety elements. Although all 58 counties responded to the survey, the counties as a group lagged significantly behind the cities in completing the noise, seismic safety and safety elements, perhaps due to larger planning areas.

(c) Although building permits, subdivision maps and a mandatory open space zoning ordinance must all be "consistent with" the local open space element, only 86 percent of the counties and 92 percent of the cities had adopted the element by October, 1974.

(d) If the open space element is excluded, then less than 90 percent of the cities and counties as groups had failed to achieve satisfactory completion of the eight other mandatory elements. For the cities, 84 percent had completed the circulation element, 81 percent the conservation element and 89 percent the land use element. For the counties, 83 percent had a completed land use element. Additionally, it is noteworthy that the survey merely measures local compliance in terms of quantifiable data, thus providing no qualitative indicators of, for example, adequacy, utility and internal consistency of the plan elements.

California law also allows local governments to prepare "specific plans", which should not be confused with general plan elements.[35] While specific plans are based on policies and objectives similar to general plans, they are land use regulations and apply to particular tracts of land. If specific plans are adopted, they must include all regulations, conditions, programs and proposed legislation necessary for implementing the mandatory elements of the general plan. Specific plans can include zoning provisions, require land to be set aside for parks, and implement many of the controls discussed in a later section.[36] The specific plan can apply to only part of the area covered by the general plan.[37] Once a specific street or highway plan is adopted, no street can be improved nor sewer connections or other street improvements authorized unless in conformance with the specific plan.[38] Similarly, after adoption of a specific plan for open space, no street, sewer, public building or public work can be undertaken until the planning agency reports conformity with the specific plan and the local legislative body makes a finding of consistency.

d. Planning Process

The process by which local planning institutions produce a general plan with the prescribed content is also specified by state law. However, this statutory guidance does not extend to every step of the process. A substantial portion of modern planning activity has reflected the initiative of individual local governments. The following description of the current process is widely followed, although it necessarily varies by character of community.

The typical first step in the development of a general plan is the undertaking of planning surveys. These investigations are a collection, compilation, review and analysis of basic data relating to the physical, environmental, economic and social conditions in the community.

California law does not require or even suggest investigation or preliminary studies. As a result, the early steps in preparing general plans vary greatly from city to city. But because voluminous and comprehensive information is a prerequisite to rational planning, such studies are generally undertaken despite the fact that they are time-consuming and expensive. Of course, financial or other limitations on a local government may well mean that the necessary preliminary work is not adequately performed.

A second stage is the determination of community goals. Through various mechanisms, input from many segments of the citizenry is funneled into the planning agency. To encourage widespread consultation, state law suggests that the planning agency "generally" "shall consult and advise with" public officials and agencies, public utilities, various organizations, and citizens to secure the "maximum coordination of plans" during the formulation of a general plan.[39] However, no specific procedures nor any specification of adequate public input is defined. The resulting consensus is generally embodied in a statement of policies and objectives. These should form the rationale for the subsequent policies and proposals contained in the plan.

Formulation of the general plan itself involves the identification of alternative patterns of development and their relationship to community goals. Alternative plans are tested for physical, financial and political feasibility. More frequent use is being made of cost-benefit studies which compare the community costs of alternative land uses (loss of tax revenue, extension of public services, increased demand for public facilities, for example) with the respective benefits of the use. Finally, the plan which seems to optimize the chosen goals and development is selected for fuller amplification and consideration by the local planning agency.

Because this planning activity may take considerable time, it is important that a local government be able to preserve the present characteristics of the community area, especially in areas where imminent development is likely, and thereby to ensure that the plan is not outdated by the time it is adopted. Accordingly, California law provides that local government may adopt an "interim ordinance prohibiting any uses which may be in conflict with a contemplated zoning proposal."[40] Although the section speaks of zoning proposals, it also allows interim measures where the general plan, upon which all zoning ordinances are based, is under consideration. Interim ordinances are enacted for four months duration, but may be extended for up to a total of two years.

The procedures for the formal adoption of a general plan are set forth with some particularity. A city or county planning commission must hold at least one public hearing before approving the plan or plan element.[41] Notice of the hearings is to be published in a newspaper of general circulation in the jurisdiction. A majority vote of the commission is required for approval.[42]

The general plan is then transmitted to the city council or county board of supervisors and another public hearing is held.[43] No changes in the plan as approved by the planning commission may be made by the local legislature until the proposed change has been referred to the commission for a report.[44] Adoption of the plan or any part or element is accomplished by resolution of the local legislature. Copies of the adopted county general plan are sent to the planning agencies of all cities in the county; adopted city plans are sent to the county which may include them in the county general plan.[45]

After adoption of the plan, the planning agency is directed to submit an annual report to the local legislature on the "status of the plan and progress in its application."[46] The agency should "endeavor to promote public interest in an understanding of the general plan."[47] These legislative directives suggest, but do not require, what many planners consider an essential practice—continuing review of the plan. While the general plan is not always formulated as a flexible instrument in part to avoid being bent to suit the later wishes of particular interests, it is also not intended to be a rigid inexorable prescription for the future. Over time, technological changes, new forces within the community and a better understanding of past errors necessitate amendments to the plan. This is particularly true when the plan is adopted element-by-element over a period of years, a procedure practiced with increasing frequency. Continuous review is needed to harmonize the elements and to determine which element is the next logical aspect of the plan deserving attention. However, in the absence of review requirements in state legislation, a 1971 survey showed only 46 percent of the cities and 21 percent of the counties had specific policies for periodic review.[48]

Conversely, continuous amendments of the general plan would deprive it of all effectiveness. Moreover, it is desirable to consider several changes at the same time, so that their cumulative impact on the plan can be better understood. Thus, a recent statute prohibits more than three amendments of any mandatory element in any one calendar year.[49]

e. Planning Process Assessment

A recent nationwide survey of local planning agencies focused on their awareness and practice of environmental quality planning.[50] Among the study's conclusions were the following: (1) planning agencies tend to add environmental goals to a broad range of concerns and are traditionally biased toward urban values, comprehensiveness and balance among multiple objectives, rather than addressing specific environmental problems; (2) governmental fragmentation, inefficient distribution of responsibility among agencies and dispersal of financial resources has hindered introduction of environmental issues into planning; (3) agencies are not satisfied with the present intergovernmental framework, and suggested stronger state legislation and improved intergovernmental coordination, primarily at state and federal levels; and (4) local planning currently is a weak point in environmental improvement efforts because it often lacks technical capacity and is not fully utilized by higher governmental units. Despite innovative programs in some communities, most local planning agencies in California also suffer the same deficiencies.

Many of these shortcomings can be traced to inadequacies and omissions in the state legislation. The planning law is intended to serve general functions. First, it attempts to describe clearly the limits of authority and responsibility but includes both unnecessary detail and uninstructive generalities. Second, it attempts to spell out steps in the process but omits other essential steps and procedures. Third, the law and guidelines attempt to set a qualitative standard for resulting plans but fails to require adequate funding, staff, organization, incentives or penalities.

The mandatory institutions for local planning were conceived in a simpler time, and with modern demands and needs, a rethinking of the entire structure is in order. Some observers contend that representatives of special interests too frequently have been appointed to planning commissions with the result that its role as a citizen forum has been weakened. This deficiency is not remedied by the vague legislative injunction to "consult with" citizens and organized groups. Because no regularized procedures for consultation are established, none need take place. This statutory mandate literally can be satisfied by inaction.

The law does require two hearings during the process of adoption, but such safeguards may be inadequate if affected and interested citizens lack sufficient information or lack political muscle to assert their views before the legislature.[51] Moreover, as one observer has noted, ". . . government agencies rarely respond to interests that are not present in their proceedings. And they are exposed . . . only to the views of those who have a sufficient economic stake in the proceedings to warrant the substantial expense . . ."[52] In addition, the public can often make a greater contribution to informal non-adversary proceedings than formal hearings, since they are more often equipped to deal with general concepts and propositions than specific technical proposals.

The law provides for a single "planning agency" to be created by the individual local government, an admirable goal when planning was in its infancy. But today, with proliferating planning functions and bodies, the statute's requirement has not kept pace by defining precisely the composition of each body or their respective functions. For instance, if the planning commission is intended to contribute significantly to preparation of a comprehensive plan, the law's aspirations are often denied in practice. In fiscal year 1974–75, the seven-member Contra Costa County Planning Commission held 60 meetings and disposed of 1002 matters. These dealt primarily with zoning and subdivision review; only 19% were in other categories.[53] Thus, specifying the precise number of members of a planning commission can be interpreted as a Legislature's attempt to conceal a notable lack of guidance on more important matters.

Foremost among organizational deficiencies is the absence of a statutory provision for effective intergovernmental coordination. Referrals to other jurisdictions for comment may mean little if the reviewing agency has inadequate supporting information, staff or guidance from the Legislature as to which matters deserve closest attention. The fact that referral is a mere formality, easily honored in the breach, is underscored by the statute's own provision that failure to refer proposed plans will not invalidate them when adopted.[54]

The fragmentation of government which hinders effective local planning most severely is the absence of a mandatory consideration of planning from the regional perspective. One knowledgeable observer has stated the problem quite simply as follows:

"In the United States, satellite cities and towns and largely rural counties have often had the planning and zoning power; typically only small parts of their respective metropolitan complexes, they have acted in their own narrow interests, without regard for the effect of their actions upon the entire metropolitan situation. Their plans and actions have not been subject to review or control by any metropolitan, state, or federal agency, except to the very limited extent that was involved in state or federal grants. There is only one way to end such a situation: to bring about a fundamental reform of local government on the basis of the metropolitan or city region principle, or alternatively to transfer planning . . . to higher level regional units of government."[55]

Even if such major reforms are considered inappropriate, it is clear that the current institutional scheme, growing up under hesitant, piecemeal and ad hoc guidance from the state, only exacerbates local parochialism. The present narrow view of local land use decisions has been partly caused by decentralized decision-making. The task is divided among professional planners, inexpert planning commissions and local politicians. No state standards are prescribed for commission qualifications. Even though the position is part-time, commission duties require more time than lower income level persons would be able to sacrifice from their regular jobs. Because of the limited time available, even current commissioners must rely heavily on professional planning staffs. Consequently, some commissions may be reduced to a mere "rubber stamp" role.[56] Furthermore, functioning at times as a buffer between the technical bias of the staff and the political bias of the local legislature, produces a peculiar techno-political character in their view of planning issues. Because commissioners are appointed, at least ostensibly, because of their demonstrated concern for the community, it is quite difficult for them to recommend a proposal which would benefit the region but burden the local jurisdiction.

Although the law purports to regulate the preparation, adoption and revision of general plans, it is a spotty effort. No direction is given for the early stages of plan formulation. Local governments have been left to their own initiative in devising effective methods of study and preliminary investigation, with varying degrees of success. In contrast, the major British planning statute places heavy emphasis on the inventory of existing conditions.[57] Recent advances in gathering relevant ecological data and cost-benefit analysis still are ignored by the California statute. Prescribed procedures for periodic review of the general plan are non-existent.

The low quality of many plans has long concerned the planning profession and most recently, the Legislature. Requiring additional plan elements was not as successful as it might have been because inadequate funding of planning staffs, and sometimes local resistance, made it impossible to meet statutory deadlines. The Legislature responded by extending the time periods, not once but several times. As the mandatory elements were gradually adopted, it became clear that the uneven quality of some plan elements necessitated a more complete description of state expectations and the CIR guidelines were recently promulgated. However, it is not yet clear to what extent these piecemeal measures have improved local planning. Smaller communities contend they are overburdened by guidelines. The guidelines attempted, commendably, to respond to a variety of conditions and needs but this led to considerable complexity and problems of communication and comprehension. Annual progress reports to CIR may offer some monitoring, but there is no provision for state review or comment on the general plans themselves. Progress at the local level has at times outdistanced the legislative concept of general planning. For example, some local jurisdictions now prepare subjurisdiction plans (e.g., downtown plans) which are not considered in state law.

Another serious statutory omission is the absence of methods to enforce state planning requirements. Deadlines for general plan elements have been adopted, but those local governments which do not comply suffer no penalties. No general provisions for citizen enforcement exist in the planning law. Until recently, only the open space element was backed by realistic enforcement pro-

visions, which declare that "no building permit may be issued, no subdivision map approved, and no open-space zoning ordinance adopted unless the proposed construction, subdivision or ordinance is consistent with the local open-space plan."[58] Presumably, if no open space element were adopted, development within the jurisdiction could be halted by legal action.

Because general plans themselves have no direct legal effect,[59] the gap between an existing plan and its implementation has long been the greatest single deficiency in the local planning process. Cities have been able to pass zoning ordinances without any reference to the long-range objectives embodied in the general plan. A 1973 survey of local planning departments in California found that 48 percent of the counties and 56 percent of the cities described their zoning ordinances as "not consistent with" their general plan.[60] A 1973 study by the Association of Bay Area Governments reported that zoning in the region did not support the policies and intentions of most local general plans.[61] Consequently, one California law professor notes that "the plan is seldom taken seriously."[62] Another observer has called local planning "a design for irrelevancy."[63] Writing of the California planning experience, still another commentator suggests:

"The apparent element deficiencies in substance, political motivations of local legislative action, the confusion between planning and zoning and possible inadequate capital improvement expenditure programs leaves one pessimistic as to the day-to-day effectiveness of general plans."[64]

Recognizing the discrepancy between plans and implementation, the Legislature recently has required that zoning be made "consistent with" the general plan.[65] However, the new requirement has led to considerable uncertainty among local officials as to its precise meaning, and it is not clear that planning and its implementation will be more closely related than before.

Contacted a few months before the "consistency" deadline of July 1, 1973 (which was subsequently extended for six months), 57 percent of California cities stated they would not meet the statutory deadline.[66] But the difficulty of imposing any "consistency" requirement can be traced not only to the failure of the legislation to define the term more precisely but also to the lack of precision in other portions of the planning law.

2. Local Planning Implementation

Standing alone, the adoption of the general plan by cities

and counties has no impact on the land use patterns within the jurisdiction. Because the plan itself has no direct legal effect, it needs implementation through a wide variety of land use controls. In times and places where local planning was in its infancy, the existing combination of zoning ordinances and other regulations constituted a de facto "plan", because such controls were the only expressions of development policy. As planning has become more widespread and sophisticated, new types of implementing controls have been devised. With an emphasis on the emerging forms of land use regulations, this section discusses major methods used to implement planning policy in California.

Zoning

Zoning is the tool most frequently employed to regulate the use of privately owned land. As an expression of the police power, zoning must be used to promote "the public health, safety and general welfare"[1] within very broad limits. The power to zone is delegated by the state to cities and counties through enabling legislation and the California Constitution.[2]

The state zoning legislation governs the activities of general law cities in California. Although charter cities are not subject to the restrictions of the enabling laws in most respects,[3] many local jurisdictions have incorporated the state statutes into their charters. The language of the state zoning law is quite broad and expressly states the Legislature's intention "to provide only a minimum of limitation in order that counties and cities may exercise the maximum degree of control over local zoning matters."[4]

a. Forms of Zoning

State statutes specify in very general terms the types of zoning ordinances which may be enacted. Government Code section 65850 lists the major forms of zoning which have been used to implement the general plan.

The most traditional type of zoning is "use zoning." Cities and counties may regulate the use of land and buildings by restricting areas within their jurisdiction for industrial, business, residential, agricultural and other purposes.[5] Zoning ordinances classify such uses in great detail. In major urban areas, several types of commercial zones are created by ordinance, typically with hundreds of separate, specific kinds of commercial uses listed within the zones.[6] Because it is often not feasible to list every conceivable type of use, some ordinances allow "other similar uses" which may be permitted within a

given zoning classification. In this situation, an official or administrative body of local government has discretion to determine on a case-by-case basis which particular uses are "similar." Where more modern approaches are used, a set of "use classifications" attempts to describe generic categories, thereby limiting administrative discretion.

Early zoning ordinances were based upon a scale of intensity, with agricultural or single-family residential considered the least intense use and heavy industrial use the most intense. Under a "cumulative" zoning scheme, each district increasingly allowed more intense uses, but did not prohibit less intense uses. Thus, for example, other uses besides residential were not allowed in single-family residential districts, but nearly all uses, including residential, were permitted in industrial districts. Increasingly, however, local governments have turned to "exclusive" zoning, under which only carefully tailored uses are permitted in each district. Some communities provide for industrial zones as exclusive as the residential zones. A detailed scheme of "exclusive" zoning can provide for more direct and precise control of land uses than "cumulative" zoning.

Height and bulk zoning ordinances also are very common. Local governments may regulate the number of stories and the total bulk of buildings as well.[7] Other types of zoning used to control the density or intensity of development include minimum lot requirements per dwelling unit, specification of the percentage of a lot which may be occupied by a building (coverage) and floor-area ratios. As zoning has become more sophisticated in controlling the urban environment, regulations have been adopted which regulate appearance and form—signs and billboards, position of buildings on a lot, even the actual physical form and relationship of structures.

Early efforts at planning and zoning envisioned a preplanned, rigid and static pattern of development and, at some future time, a stable local economy and community. These projections of distinct bands or blocks of residential, commercial and industrial uses for every community soon proved unfounded in the face of intensive growth pressures and changing development practices. Modern zoning had to be transformed into a flexible and, occasionally, ad hoc device. Some more recent types of flexible zoning are as followed.[8]

The "special use permit" or "conditional use" allows a use different from that specified in the ordinance when conditions prescribed in the ordinance can be satisfied. The suitability of the area for the proposed use, rather than hardships due to the uniqueness of the property, must be demonstrated. For example, even though a district is zoned for residential use, such projects as a rest home or a boarding house may be compatible with the neighborhood.

Cluster zoning provides for a fixed ratio of housing units to acreage and requires the units to be "clustered" or built close together. A landowner who plans to subdivide his parcel would be permitted to build his quota of houses on only a small portion of the land, leaving the rest for open space. Incentives are sometimes used to encourage, but not to require, clustering.

Floating zoning is a more flexible approach. A "floating district" is described in the zoning ordinance, but the district is not located on the zoning map until the need arises. The ordinance simply describes what can be done in the floating district, such as building apartment houses, and lists the circumstances under which the city council will consider zoning property for that use. A floating zone ordinance might permit construction of 50-unit apartment houses in lots over five acres which also meet other specified conditions. Whenever a landowner acquires a lot which fits the description in the ordinance, he can request the city council to rezone his property for the "floating zone" use.

Planned unit development zoning (PUD) is a type of floating zone which applies to parcels of land to be developed as a single entity and according to a comprehensive plan. The PUD zoning unit generally contains a residential housing cluster of prescribed density and appropriate commercial and public facilities to serve the residents.

Conditional, or contract, zoning is the most flexible zoning device and enables a city or county to bargain with developers for certain concessions. A city, for example, may agree to rezone land in a residential district for a hospital, but require the developer to surround the hospital with landscaping and take steps to blend it into the neighborhood.

However, the trends in zoning are centrifugal. Along with the movement toward greater flexibility and administrative discretion, there has been a concomitant development of highly specific, almost scientific techniques. In some cases, a zoning ordinance may establish performance standards rather than listing permitted uses. In an industrial zone, for example, the ordinance may set standards for noise, smoke, heat, odor, vibration, radiation and other adverse effects stemming from use of the lot.[9]

Specific plans are receiving increased attention be-

cause as plans they can avoid the archaic legislative mandate for minimum, uniform and general regulations, characteristic of zoning. Among the provisions which must be included in these plans are height, access, location, preservation of landscape features, views, form and placement of structures and landscaping. They may be set forth in a variety of ways, all of which have development regulatory effects. Also, the specific plan has new importance because it has become a prerequisite for rural subdivisions, and is being considered as a local prerequisite for other large-scale developments.

Impact zoning has come to mean the application of a "performance" or "operational assessment" approach to anticipated effects. Because of the ubiquitous EIR in California and the resulting widespread availability of information regarding development effects, this approach has received considerable attention. Along with cost-benefit analyses, it could be merged into a more refined method for comprehensively estimating environmental, economic and other impacts in quantifiable ways.

Seismic or "hazard" zoning has begun to involve highly technical specifications of distances from major and minor faults, building intensities, etc. This must reflect the Alquist-Priolo Geologic Hazard Zones Act where the State Mines and Geology Board develops policies and criteria concerning development proposed within special hazard zones, as defined by the State Geologist. Cities and counties must regulate within these zones according to Board policies and criteria. (Additionally, the Board reviews geologic/seismic reports relating to proposed hospital sites and subdivisions for exposure to undue hazards.)

b. Zoning Procedures

The main thrust of state zoning legislation is to specify procedures for the enactment and administration of zoning ordinances. A zoning ordinance, amendment to a zoning ordinance, and similar land use regulations must be adopted by general law cities and counties as provided by state law.[10]

While the regulation of one type of zone may differ from other types of zones, "all such regulations shall be uniform for each class or kind of building or use of land throughout each zone."[11] As noted below, this requirement does not demand strict uniformity in all cases, since differences between parcels of land may justify different treatment.

The basic procedure followed by local governments

subject to the general laws of the state is the same for a zoning text change and a zoning map change. The city council or board of supervisors, planning commission or landowner may initiate a proposal. In most places, the commission receives the zoning request first and then sends it to the planning department for study and a determination as to whether the rezoning is consistent with the general plan. The department's recommendation is forwarded to the planning commission. In cases where the request is to rezone more than ten acres, the report of the planning department must be in writing and made available to the public.[12]

The planning commission is required to hold a public hearing on the proposal and file with the local legislature a written recommendation including a statement of reasons for the recommendation and the relationship of the proposed zoning to applicable general and specific plans.[13] The city council or board of supervisors then may approve, modify or disapprove the recommendation and must hold a hearing on the matter in certain circumstances.[14]

State legislation also governs, to some extent, the administration of previously adopted zoning ordinances. Because the strict application of ordinances to particular property may be unfair to the landowner or unnecessary to effectuate the local plan, exceptions to the ordinance may be granted in some circumstances. A "variance" may be granted when "because of special circumstances applicable to the property . . . the strict application of the zoning ordinance deprives such property of privileges enjoyed by other property in the vicinity and under identical zoning classification."[15] The conditions set forth in the state law apply to general law cities and counties, while charter cities, of course, can set their own standards. In practice, however, the power to issue variances has been much abused in the past.[16]

Variances (and special use permits) are not administered in the same way that zoning and rezoning proposals are processed. Local procedures vary, and the city or county may create a board of zoning adjustment, zoning administrator or board of zoning appeals.[17] In other jurisdictions, the planning department or planning commission itself evaluates applications for variances and special use permits. In this case, the decision may be appealed to the city council or board of supervisors.[18]

c. Consistency of Zoning and Planning

As mentioned above, a major shortcoming of local planning has been the wide discrepancy between the general plan and the ordinances implementing the plan. Frequently, for instance, zoning regulations have been adopted which are divorced from the future land use indicated by the local plan. Thus, in too many cases, the foresight and considered judgments embodied in a general plan have been relegated to the library.

In response to this serious deficiency, the Legislature in 1971 enacted legislation which required county or city zoning ordinances to be "consistent with the general plan of the county or city" by January 1973.[19] Because of the difficulties faced by local governments in complying within this time period, the deadline was extended to January 1974. Uncertainty over the meaning of "consistency" led to a further attempt at defining the term. A zoning ordinance is "consistent with" the local general plan only if the local jurisdiction has an officially adopted plan and if the "various land uses authorized by the ordinance are *compatible with* the objectives, policies, general land uses and programs specified in the plan."[20] (Emphasis supplied.)

Despite this clarification, there is still no real consensus as to the meaning of "consistency". The Council on Intergovernmental Relations has adopted the following guideline: "The Zoning Ordinance should be considered consistent with the general plan when the allowable uses and standards contained in the text of the Zoning Ordinance tend to further the policies and designated uses in the general plan and do not inhibit or obstruct the attainment of those articulated policies."[21]

The effect of such declarations is simply to make clear that a complete correspondence between zoning and planning is not required. However, although planning and zoning have not been made synonymous, the extent to which the zoning ordinance may diverge from the current land use designations of the general plan has not been determined. No appellate court in California has yet been asked to rule on this question.

The consistency requirement is directly enforceable through legal action by residents and property owners within the city or county.[22] However, in contrast to recent legislative provisions for implementing the open space element of the general plan,[23] no specific sanctions were articulated to encourage local compliance with the "consistency" requirement—the Legislature chose to remain silent on the matter.

Apparently, zoning ordinances can be adopted even though they are not "consistent with" the general plan. A citizen suit filed within 90 days of adoption of a new or amended zoning ordinance, as required by statute, would likely result in no more than an order to the local jurisdiction to make the zoning compatible with the plan within a reasonable time.[24] In fact, state law now provides that following an amendment of the general plan or a plan element, the zoning ordinance shall be amended to reestablish consistency "within a reasonable time."[25]

Subdivision Regulation

Although zoning is the most prevalent tool used by local government to implement the general plan, the police power also enables cities and counties to control development through subdivision regulations. Subdivision is the process by which a developer acquires a piece of land and divides it into improved or unimproved lots which he then sells.

The conversion of large amounts of open space land to suburban development through subdivision can be regulated by local government so as to carry out the objectives of the general plan. Because developers must file maps of their proposed subdivision with the local government, the jurisdiction's authority is exercised by approving, disapproving or conditioning approval of the maps.

Recognizing a relationship between the subdivision process and implementation of the general plan, state law now requires "consistency" between a proposed subdivision and the applicable general or specific plan. To find a development proposal "consistent", the local government must have officially adopted a general or specific plan and the proposed land use must be "compatible with the objectives, policies, general land uses and programs specified in such a plan."[1]

a. Subdivision Map Act

The state statute which confers on cities and counties the power to regulate subdivisions is known as the Subdivision Map Act. In recent years, important changes have been made in the statutory scheme, and in September 1974, the Act was completely reorganized and moved from its former location in the Business and Professions Code to the Planning and Land Use title of the Government Code.[2] While some additions and changes were made in the statute, the basic approval procedures and regulatory powers remain unchanged. The revised Act was effective March 1, 1975.

The 1974 reenactment broadened the definition of "subdivision" to include the division of any improved or unimproved land for the purpose of sale, lease or financing immediately or in the future.[3] The Act requires local governments to adopt ordinances to "regulate and control" those subdivisions for which a subdivision map is required by state law.[4] Most developers must submit both tentative and final subdivision maps, since these maps are required when land is divided into five or more parcels. Even though a division of land may produce more than five parcels, tentative and final maps are not required where the resulting parcels are very large or do not require new streets or other improvements.[5] In such cases, however, "parcel maps" are required (although the local government may waive this requirement in individual cases).[6] Even where no map is required by state law (where the division is into less than five parcels), cities and counties may regulate the division of land as long as such ordinances are no more restrictive than their other subdivision regulations.

The local ordinances required by state law must specifically provide for proper grading and erosion control. All subdivision ordinances, however, may also regulate "design and improvement".[7] In recent years, the scope of subdivision regulations has been significantly broadened by expanding the meaning of these terms. Until 1971, "design" included matters relating to street alignment, grades and widths, rights-of-way for drainage and sanitary sewers, and land to be dedicated for recreational purposes. "Improvement" was defined as the streets and utilities necessary for the general use of lot owners. In 1971, these terms were broadened. "Design" now includes "such specific requirements in the plan and configuration of the entire subdivision as may be necessary or convenient to insure conformity to or implementation of applicable general or specific plans of a city or county."[8] The definition of "improvements" was similarly broadened.[9] In 1974, "design" was again expanded to encompass traffic access, lot size and configuration, all grading, all easements, and fire roads and fire breaks.[10]

The Subdivision Map Act applies to both general law and charter cities, since subdivisions are not "municipal affairs". Local government can impose regulations beyond those contained in the Map Act, but no local ordinance can impose conditions which are inconsistent with the Act.[11] Thus, the subdivision statute defines local governments' powers more precisely and provides more guidance than does the state zoning law, which expressly grants cities and counties broad discretion to enact or not to enact their own ordinances.

b. Procedure

The Subdivision Map Act outlines the administrative

procedures for gaining approval to divide up one existing tract of land. Time limits for each step in the process are specified by law, but these limits may be extended by the mutual consent of the local government and the subdivider.[12] Moreover, local ordinances may modify the procedures set forth in state law to the extent allowed by the Act.[13]

The developer first prepares in accordance with the local ordinance a tentative map which is submitted to an "advisory agency". The agency is any body selected by the city or county to investigate and report on the design and improvement of proposed subdivisions or to impose requirements upon and approve subdivision maps.[14] Generally this function is undertaken by the planning commission or planning department which examines the tentative map to ensure that it is "consistent with" the subdivision regulations and the general plan. Provisions are also made for review by local governments of tentative maps of proposed subdivisions in adjoining jurisdictions.

Because environmental factors must be considered in approving a subdivision, and because local governments often do not have the time and money to adequately evaluate the environmental impact, the Act provides for a review of proposed subdivisions by the state Office of Intergovernmental Management on the request of the local government.[15] State level review is mandatory for residential subdivisions of 50 or more parcels.[16] The Office of Intergovernmental Management acts as a clearinghouse and directs appropriate state agencies to review and comment on the environmental impact of the proposed subdivision.[17] The review must be completed within 30 days and cover the factors listed in the California Environmental Quality Act of 1970.[18]

Where the advisory agency is not itself authorized to approve or disapprove the tentative map—as in the case of the typical planning commission—it must make a written report to the city council or board of supervisors within 50 days.[19] The local legislature must then fix a meeting date within 30 days for its approval, conditional approval or disapproval of the tentative map.[20] If the advisory agency is authorized to approve the subdivision map, it must do so within 50 days of its initial submission. The statute provides the subdivider with the opportunity to appeal any action of the advisory agency, and the 1974 amendments allow an appeal to the local legislature for a public hearing by "any interested person adversely affected", if a local ordinance provides for this procedure.[21]

Within 12 months (or 18 months if extended by local ordinance) of approval or conditional approval of the tentative map, the developer prepares a final subdivision map in accordance with the tentative map.[22] If the tentative map expires without a special extension of time, a final map cannot be filed without first submitting another tentative map. The content of the final map is prescribed in detail by the statute and was modernized by the 1974 legislation.[23] The final map is submitted directly to the local legislature which must act on the proposal at its next regular meeting held ten days or more after submission. The city council or board of supervisors shall approve the map if it conforms to all applicable local subdivision ordinances and the Subdivision Map Act.[24] As provided by state law, these local ordinances may impose exactions upon the subdivider. Additionally, the Act itself provides that subdivision approval be withheld in certain circumstances.

c. Exactions

The power to regulate subdivision is exercised primarily in two ways: requiring the dedication of land in return for approving the tentative map and withholding approval of the map altogether. Within broad constitutional and statutory limits, cities and counties may attach many conditions to their approval in order to implement the policies and land use designations in the local general plan. Thus, local governments may exact from the developer land or fees which are used to internalize the costs of development otherwise imposed on the community as a whole.

The Subdivision Map Act expressly enables cities and counties by local ordinance to require the dedication of real property within the subdivision for streets, alleys, drainage, public utility easements and "other public easements".[25] Developers of subdivisions within elementary school districts may also be required to reserve land "to assure residents of the subdivision adequate public school service."[26] However, the school district is required to repay the subdivider the original cost of the land plus certain amounts for improvements and back taxes. This is still an advantage to the local government, since the original cost of the land may be considerably less than the present value. Moreover, this land can remain vacant for a number of years; a school need not be constructed immediately. If the land is not used for a school within ten years, however, the developer can repurchase the land for the original amount.

A recent statute enables a city or county to require "the dedication of land, the payment of fees in lieu thereof, or a combination of both, for park or recreational purposes as a condition" to map approval.[27] While there are several restrictions which the law places on the exercise of this power, four deserve mention. First, the park dedication ordinance must include definite standards for determining the proportion that subdivisions must dedicate. This requirement prevents local governments from treating subdividers unequally. Second, the local legislative body must have included a recreation element in its general plan. This helps to ensure that the dedication which has been exacted is consistent with a planning policy. Third, the land or fees must be used only for providing recreational facilities to serve the subdivision. Finally, the statute requires that the amount of land dedicated bear a "reasonable relationship" to the recreational needs created by the subdivision. While the last two provisions appear to limit the city's power, they have been broadly interpreted by the courts, including the California Supreme Court in *Associated Home Builders v. City of Walnut Creek.*[28]

While the above dedications may be required by the local government, the statute now requires dedication of one type of land. Recent amendments require "reasonable public access" to beaches or the shoreline of a lake or reservoir owned by the government before approval of the subdivision map.[29] Reasonable access is to be determined by the local government. Public use of rivers and streams is protected in the same way.[30]

In addition to the dedication of land, local governments can also require the payment of fees by the subdivider "for purposes of defraying the actual or estimated costs of constructing" planned drainage and sanitary sewer facilities.[31] Again, the state statute imposes several conditions on the exercise of this power. The ordinance must refer to a drainage or sewer plan adopted for a particular area, and in the case of a city this plan must be in conformity with county and special district plans of this type as determined by the county or special district.

d. Withholding Subdivision Approval

The Subdivision Map Act also gives local government the power to refuse subdivision proposals for a number of specific reasons. First, a city or county must withhold permission to subdivide unless a final map is recorded which complies with state statutes and local ordinances.[32] For example, if the developer refuses to dedicate the land for park and recreational purposes, which an ordinance requires, his proposal must be refused. A subdivision may also be rejected, of course, if it does not comply with the zoning ordinance. Second, subdivision

approval must be denied if the governing body makes any of the following findings: that the proposed subdivision map is inconsistent with the general and specific plans; that the site is not physically suitable for the type or density of the proposed development; or that the design of the subdivision is likely to cause "substantial environmental damage" or serious public health problems.[33] However, these findings may not result in disapproval if the final map is in "substantial compliance with" a previously approved tentative map.[34] Third, as mentioned above, no subdivision map may be approved unless the local legislative body finds that the proposed subdivision is "consistent with" the applicable general plan. These statutory provisions combine to give local governments great power to withhold approval of subdivision maps which conflict with their land use planning and growth management objectives.

Urban Renewal

As with the development of a major subdivision, the redevelopment of an urban area is an activity which can either promote, frustrate or actually militate against implementation of the local general plan. Until recently, the traditional, federally sponsored program of urban renewal involved all levels of government—funded through grants-in-aid by the federal government, legally controlled by the state and administered by the local government. Moreover, urban renewal is further complicated by the need to integrate planning, zoning, subdivision regulation, building codes and other land use controls to bring a major project to completion.

a. Community Redevelopment Law

To enable local governments to participate in the federal urban renewal program, the state Legislature provided for creation of a redevelopment agency in each community.[1] To activate the agency, the local legislative body must declare there is a need for a renewal agency.[2] After this declaration of need, which is subject to local referendum, the city council appoints five members to the agency board for staggered terms of up to three years.[3] In the alternative, the local legislature may declare itself to be the redevelopment agency and function with the same duties and powers.[4]

The territorial jurisdiction of a county agency is the unincorporated area of the county; a city agency operates within the city limits.[5] Cooperation among several communities can be increased by the joint exercise of their redevelopment powers to form a joint local agency.[6] The legislative body of a community may authorize the renewal agency of a contiguous community to operate within its boundaries.[7] The statute directs the renewal agency to "cooperate" with the local planning commission in formulating the redevelopment plan.[8]

The powers granted to the local agency are quite broad. It may acquire land by purchase, lease or eminent domain, relocate persons displaced, make site preparations, build some types of structures and sell the acquired land. A renewal agency is required to sell or lease all real property it owns in the project area subject to conditions that the new land uses conform to the redevelopment plan.[9] Other governmental bodies may assist the agency by dedicating land, supplying needed public services, and replanning, rezoning and making modifications to building regulations and ordinances.[10]

The recent interest in redevelopment in California is attributable in part to the use of tax increment financing. This technique allows all new (net) tax dollars realized after initiation of a project to be applied directly to the project; the negative tax resource impacts and losses for other agencies has generated considerable controversy about the procedure, allayed in part by in lieu payments.

Many steps for implementing an urban renewal project are also prescribed by state law. The local jurisdiction must have an adopted general plan to which the redevelopment plan must conform.[11] Any person or group may request the designation of a "survey area" by the local legislature or agency so as to determine the preliminary feasibility of a redevelopment project.[12] The planning commission then selects one or more "project areas" which are the blighted areas to be renewed. A preliminary plan for the project area is prepared by the planning commission, containing a general statement of the proposed land uses, densities and street layout; demonstrating conformity to the local general plan; and describing the project's impact on the surrounding neighborhood.[13]

State law provides in detail the contents of the next, more comprehensive redevelopment plan prepared by the redevelopment agency. This plan must provide for participation of landowners, describe the proposed method of financing, include diagrams of the type and size of buildings and open space areas, and contain a neighborhood impact element.[14] The local legislative body must hold a public hearing before it adopts the redevelopment plan. The ordinance of adoption must have the specified contents, such as a finding that the project area is a blighted area, that the project is feasible to carry out and that the redevelopment plan conforms to the local general plan.[15]

Recent additions to this implementation procedure include the preparation of an environmental impact report and circulation of that document,[16] and the formation of a project area committee (PAC) if a substantial number of low and moderate income families will be displaced by redevelopment.[17] The PAC is intended to provide input into the urban renewal process by those who are most directly affected. To this end, the local renewal agency must consult with the PAC and the planning commission in preparing the redevelopment plan.

The local legislature, by requiring the local agency to submit contracts for prior approval, may exercise continuing supervision of the renewal agency's activities.[18] Furthermore, the agency must also conduct a public hearing on a biennial basis to review the redevelopment plan and progress in its implementation.[19]

b. Special Housing and Renewal Law

Supplementary renewal legislation, enacted in 1968, enables residents of renewal areas to initiate and finance rehabilitation and thereby to reduce the need for land acquisition by the renewal agency.[20] The law enables the renewal area agency to act as agent for property owners and residents and encourages cooperative self-help efforts of persons within the renewal area.

The mechanism for achieving these goals is the "renewal area agency". Agency formation begins with submission of a petition, signed by at least 20 percent of the area residents, to the local legislative body. The proposal is studied by the planning commission with participation of the petitioners. Actual creation of the agency requires the approval of the local legislature. Two-thirds of the 15-member board of directors of the renewal area agency must be residents of the renewal area.[21]

The agency's first activities are to develop a preliminary plan and analyze the economic feasibility of rehabilitation. Innovative techniques and technology may be applied, and local building code provisions may be suspended by the local legislature to allow completion of the proposed construction.[22] The local planning commission reviews and approves the specific rehabilitation plans. The commission's recommendations are forwarded to the local legislature which may approve, disapprove or modify the proposal. Only after such approval, may the issuance of tax exempt bonds and implementation of the plan begin.

While the renewal area agency has considerable power, the planning commission and local legislature may control its exercise in many instances.[23] Importantly, the Special Housing and Renewal Act has not yet been successfully implemented in any community since its enactment.[24]

Housing Programs

State law provides three mechanisms for implementing the mandatory housing element of the local general plan. In each case, the creation of these agencies is a matter for local determination, since the state legislation merely enables cities and counties to undertake major housing programs.

a. Housing Authorities Law

The present form of this statute, intended to assist provision of safe and sanitary dwellings for low income persons, was enacted in 1951. Although the law creates a housing authority in every city and county, the authority is not truly in existence unless the local legislature declares there is a need for such an agency.[1] Three geographical areas of operation are specified. A city housing authority may act within the city and an area within five miles of its boundaries (except for the unincorporated area of a county which has a county housing authority or another city unless that city has consented.)[2] A county authority may operate throughout the county, except within those cities having their own housing authorities.[3]

A third type of housing authority was authorized in 1970. An "area" authority may be created by two or more cities or counties in any combination.[4] After declaring the need for an authority to function within its jurisdiction, each local legislature appoints two persons as commissioners of the authority. Its geographical area of operation is the combined areas of the participating cities and counties.[5]

A housing authority is a public non-profit corporation acting independently of the local government.[6] Its general powers include the construction, acquisition and operation of "housing projects", which are defined as undertakings financed in whole or in part by the federal or state governments to provide sanitary and safe dwellings in urban or rural areas.[7] A housing authority is subject to all planning, zoning and building ordinances and is to "take into consideration" the relationship of the housing project to a long-range plan applicable to the local area.[8]

All powers of the housing authority are vested in the commissioners[9] who are appointed by the local legislative body.[10] The city council or board of supervisors may declare itself to be the several commissioners of the authority, in which case that legislative body may create, as an advisory group, a housing commission of a size and composition determined by the local legislature.[11] In the operation of housing projects, a city or county may call upon residents and existing community organizations to form a community housing advisory committee.[12]

b. Housing Cooperation Law

State legislation provides that to aid in the implementation of the Housing Authorities Law a city, county, commission or state agency may offer several types of assistance.[13] These "state public bodies" may dedicate, sell or lease property to the authority; furnish many services and facilities including utilities and recreational areas; provide streets and roads; "plan or replan, zone or rezone any part of its territory"; and "make exceptions to building regulations and ordinances".[14]

c. Area Housing Councils

Because local or even area housing authorities may not be able to adequately provide for regional housing needs, the proper institution for housing planning and implementation in many situations may be an area housing council. Moreover, the enabling legislation tailored specifically to housing councils avoids reliance on inadequate statutory provisions pertaining to regional planning districts and joint powers agreements.

Cities and counties may combine to form an area housing council, which then develops an area housing plan for the respective member jurisdictions.[15] This plan is described only generally as consisting of "standards and plans for the improvement of housing and for provisions of adequate sites for housing".[16] No other powers or duties are specified. Member governments may adopt the area housing plan as the housing element of their general plans if it conforms to CIR guidelines for general plan elements.[17] Upon such adoption, a city is entitled to half of its proportionate share of the council's surcharge on local building permits. These funds are restricted to implementing the housing elements of the respective general plans. The commissioners of an area housing council are to consist of: the planning director of each member jurisdiction, the executive director of the housing authority of each jurisdiction and two commissioners appointed by the local legislatures "who shall be representative of the housing and construction industry".[18]

Growth Management

Subdivision regulation, many forms of zoning and urban renewal programs can all be important devices for implementing the general plan. However, some local governments have found that in addition to determining the eventual physical development of the communities, they must guide the timing and location of development. To accomplish this, traditional land use controls have been combined with effective planning programs to form innovative schemes for plan implementation.[1]

a. Temporary Moratoria on Development

One of the many adverse effects of uncontrolled growth is the overburdening of water, sewage and other public services. In reaction to such pressing problems, some communities have placed moratoria on further development until planning is completed, regulations are adopted, and public facilities are expanded. For example, a city ordinance could simply declare that no more building permits for residential construction would be issued until certain standards for the provision of public service are met. In one city, "satisfactory solutions" to the problem of inadequate facilities were stated to be: (1) no double sessions in the schools or overcrowded classrooms as determined by the California Education Code, (2) sewage treatment facilities must comply with standards set forth by the Regional Water Quality Control Board, and (3) no rationing of drinking water. Another city imposed a two-year moratorium on zoning changes to residential use if the property is within an overcrowded school district. In the alternative, the ordinance allows the school district to agree with the developer that he will provide temporary school buildings as needed.

b. Special Development Permits

The most recent and comprehensive implementation programs attempt to solve problems resulting from fragmented administration of zoning, building permits and subdivision regulations. Although not another form of zoning, these programs to guide the timing and sequence of development are sometimes referred to as "phased zoning". Such schemes do not supplant the local planning process but are used to implement the policies and land designations of the general plan. A new special permit is required for residential development, although these programs differ from each other in other respects, and are described below.

(1) Capital Improvement and Service Indicators

One type of "phased zoning" does not in fact rezone property. Rather, land zoned for residential use is not allowed to be subdivided until the landowner obtains a special permit from the city council. This permit is granted only if the landowner can show the availability of adequate public services such as sewers, drainage, park sites and roads. Adequacy of service is measured by accumulating points on a scale designated in the ordinance. For example, 50 percent drainage capacity could earn the developer one point but 100 percent capacity earns him five points. Similarly, the landowner could receive five points for direct access to a secondary or collector road, and no points if such a road were more than one mile away. A landowner instead of accumulating points could provide the needed services himself, an almost prohibitively expensive undertaking. Or, he could wait for the city to extend and improve public services over an 18-year period under its capital budget program. Thus, development in a restricted area would be phased as the city is willing and able to extend public services.

(2) Quota Systems

A similar system—also based upon accumulating points toward a special permit for subdivision development—adds a new administrative body and incorporates broader criteria which extend beyond the availability of public services. This regulatory system has two major elements. First, the housing element of the city's general plan sets a quota for the total number of residential units to be constructed in any one year. Second, a competition among rival subdivision plans is held once a year to decide which of the proposed projects are to fill the quota.

Subdivision applications are considered by a reviewing board composed of local government officials and citizens. The board rates each application on specific criteria in two general categories: (a) availability of public services; and (b) quality of design and contribution to public welfare. The first category includes such criteria as the capacity of water, sewer and school systems. The second category includes the provision of open space by the developer, low and moderate income housing, and architectural design quality. Each criterion is judged on a scale of points, and a specific number of points is required for approval. The board holds a public hearing on the application and submits the final ratings to the city council, starting with those projects receiving the most points. Thus, a yearly quota is imposed which acts as a development timing mechanism, rather than the capital improvements plan for the extension of services. Under this scheme, the city can encourage the desirable types of development by weighing points based on design, income level and environmental impact.

(3) Joint City-County Control

A third system of allocating an annual quota of housing units is based on previously adopted development plans and involves both city councils and boards of supervisors. By resolution of the local legislatures, a review board is established to implement the growth policies of the county and cities' general plans.

A resolution of the board of supervisors initiates definition of a review area that includes one or more cities. Public hearings are held, and thereafter each city and the county enact a development control ordinance and enter into a joint powers agreement. Once the agreement is formalized, no residential development, other than single family houses on previously approved lots, may be constructed without the approval of the review board. Each year, the city councils in each review area and the board of supervisors meet to determine how many units are to be approved in the following year based on planned growth rates.

The board is composed of some combination of local government officials and citizens and meets every six months to rate development proposals in accordance with criteria based on adopted planning policies. Points are earned for conformity with the county and city plans, such as environmental quality, availability of public utilities, design features and provision of low and moderate income housing units. If there are more projects than allowable units, those projects with the highest score are approved. For very large developments, an allocation of units over several years can be arranged.

(4) Mapping of Growth Sequence Zones

Some jurisdictions have begun to give consideration to the actual pre-stated mapping of growth zones in a manner akin to a zoning map. The problems are sizable, including the necessity for significant amounts of data upon which to base division into immediate urbanization, near-term urbanization, reserve, long-term reserve zones, etc., and the comprehensibility of a totally new set of zones. However, where the criteria for the mapping are sound and explicit and where the locational

information on the growth indicators (e.g., public services, hazards, socio-economic composition and natural resources) is abundant, this approach may have the best long-term potential for meeting the wide range of political, legal and procedural growth management demands.

Property Taxation

California law enables city and county governments to give tax advantages to landowners who devote their property to open space and agricultural uses. The purpose is to relieve a pressing tax burden that often drives landowners to develop their property by imposing lower taxes for publicly beneficial use of their land. Until 1968, the California Constitution required property tax assessors to value land at its "highest and best" use. The result was that a farmer living near a city paid taxes on the speculative value of his land as a subdivision rather than on its current value for agricultural use. The dynamics of the market increased the value of land near urban centers, forcing owners of undeveloped land either to sell or to devote their land to a more intensive use.

A state constitutional amendment was adopted in 1968 authorizing the Legislature to allow open space and agricultural lands to be assessed at their actual, rather than speculative, use if they were subject to an "enforceable restriction".[1] Such restrictions must limit the use of the land to recreation, enjoyment of scenic beauty, use of natural resources or production of food or fiber. In return for restrictions on the use of his land, the landowner benefits from a lower property tax. Assessors are required to value this land by considering only the uses legally available to the owner.[2]

The most commonly used form of tax incentive is the California Land Conservation Act, popularly known as the Williamson Act.[3] This statute enables cities and counties to form "agricultural, preserves" and to enter into contracts with owners of land with such preserves. Only agricultural, recreational and open space land is eligible for contractual restrictions, but areas such as salt ponds and wildlife habitats have also been brought within the Act.[4] Once land is contractually restricted, it qualifies for the special valuation for property tax purposes. Presumably, a "use value" assessment will result in a lower tax bill and thereby encourage landowners to enter into a contract.

Agricultural preserves may be created by the city or county having jurisdiction over the land in question. The local legislative body must hold a hearing and submit the proposal for a preserve to the planning department or planning commission. The city or county must have a general plan, and the planning agency must report to the local legislature whether the preserve would be consistent with the general plan.[5]

A preserve must contain at least 100 acres, unless "unique characteristics" necessitate a smaller preserve which also must be consistent with the general plan. Agricultural preserves may not contain land ineligible for a Williamson Act contract. Additionally, all land within a preserve and not under contract must be restricted by zoning or other controls within two years of the first contract. These land use restrictions need only prevent uses of non-contract land that are incompatible with contract land.[6]

The Williamson Act also protects agricultural preserves from condemnation for other uses. The purpose is to prevent public agencies from acquiring land under contract at lower prices.[7] The law also declares a policy to avoid locating public improvements or utilities in agricultural preserves whenever practicable.

All land within an agricultural preserve is not automatically placed under an "enforceable restriction". Each landowner, if he chooses to do so, may apply for a contract with the local government. The procedure for creating a contract is similar to that for establishing an agricultural preserve.

Contracts run for a period of at least ten years and are automatically renewed each year for an additional year. The contract must exclude all uses other than those specified in the Act and is binding on all purchasers from the owner. Contracts are enforceable in court by both the landowner and local government. Either the landowner or local government may decide not to renew the contract; the contract will then run for ten years from the last renewal date. But since renewal is automatic, the contract runs forever until one party takes the initiative and files notice of non-renewal.[8]

While non-renewal leaves the contract in effect for the remainder of its term, cancellation terminates it immediately. Only the landowner may request to cancel a Williamson Act contract. He must petition the local legislature, which may grant cancellation if it is consistent with the Act and in the public interest. Economic burden on the landowner is not a sufficient excuse for cancellation. The local governing body must hold a public hearing before cancelling the contract, and all owners of land in the preserve are to be notified. A protest of more than 50 percent of the landowners in the preserve blocks the cancellation. When a contract is cancelled,

the assessor will reassess the land (the assessed value being 25 percent of the full cash value), and the landowner is required to pay as deferred taxes 50 percent of the newly assessed value of the property. The governing body may waive this requirement.[9]

California Environmental Quality Act

As noted above, the local general plan too often lacks sufficient detail to guide the individual land use decisions which promote or hinder implementation of the plan. Very general policy statements and diagrams do not furnish the specific criteria needed to evaluate impacts of a proposed development or project. Partly in response to this shortcoming, the California Environmental Quality Act (CEQA) was adopted in 1970.[1] Although CEQA is a device which may help to implement the local plan, it typically constitutes one part of the process by which other implementation mechanisms are applied, e.g., subdivision approval procedures. CEQA also attempts to regulate those activities of state agencies and programs which may have significant environmental implications.

Following the lead of the National Environmental Policy Act of 1969 which applies to federal activities (including federal funding programs which assist state and local governments),[2] CEQA contains two basic components. First, the Act declares a legislative policy to "develop and maintain a high-quality environment now and in the future, and take all action necessary to protect, rehabilitate, and enhance the environmental quality of the state."[3] To ensure that environmental protection is the "guiding criterion in public decisions", state agencies "which regulate activities of private individuals, corporations, and public agencies . . . shall regulate such activities so that major consideration is given to preventing environmental damage."[4]

Second, CEQA establishes procedures for governmental decision-making which are incorporated into existing processes but which attempt also to generate and disseminate needed information about environmental consequences. This information is set out in an environmental impact report (EIR)—an informational document which is to be considered by the public agency—prior to its approval or disapproval of activities having a significant effect on the environment.[5] The statutory scheme is supplemented and made more precise by CEQA implementation guidelines prepared by the Office of Planning and Research and adopted by the Secretary of the Resources Agency.[6]

a. Coverage of CEQA

EIRs are prepared for individual "projects" by governmental units, broadly defined to include any state agency, board or commission, county, city, regional agency or "other political subdivision".[7] Those projects subject to EIRs are also broadly defined to encompass activities directly undertaken by an agency; activities funded wholly or partly by governmental agencies; and the issuance of permits, certificates or "other entitlement."[8] Thus, private activities and developments requiring governmental approval fall within CEQA's provisions. This definition, along with other important amendments to CEQA, was added by AB 889 in December 1972, following the California Supreme Court's decision in *Friends of Mammoth v. Board of Supervisors of Mono County.*[9]

However, an EIR is not required for every project. An environmental report need be prepared only if three additional conditions are met. First, the project must be one which will have a "significant effect" on the "environment". "Environment" is defined as those physical conditions—not social or economic factors—that will be affected by the proposed project.[10] "Significant effect" is to be determined for each individual project, since an activity in one location may have little impact, while in another area it could have seriously adverse consequences. The guidelines direct the state or local agency to consider those primary consequences which are directly related to the project as well as the secondary consequences which are associated with the primary impacts.[11] An example of a primary effect is the population growth which may result from construction of a new sewage treatment plant, while an associated secondary impact would be increased water and energy consumption patterns.

The guidelines state that a project which conflicts with environmental plans and goals adopted by the local community will usually have a significant effect.[12] Findings of significance are mandatory where:

(a) The impacts would potentially degrade the quality of the environment or curtail "the range of the environment".

(b) The impacts could achieve short-term, to the disadvantage of long-term, environmental goals. A short-term environmental impact occurs in a relatively brief, well-defined period of time while a long-term impact endures well into the future.

(c) The project impacts are individually limited but cumulatively considerable. A project may affect two or more separate resources where the impact on each resource is relatively small. If the total effect of the environmental impacts is significant, an EIR must be prepared.

(d) The environmental effects of a project will cause substantial adverse effects on human beings, either directly or indirectly.[13]

These criteria, any one of which is determinative, are too vague to be of much help to a government official: the standard is still a matter of judgment.

A second mandatory condition for EIR preparation is that the project must be "discretionary" and not a "ministerial" or emergency activity.[14] "Ministerial" projects are those whose approval or disapproval are not within the judgment of the agency. The guidelines state that, in the absence of a contrary provision in local ordinances, issuance of building permits, approval of final subdivision maps and approval of individual utility service connections are usually to be regarded as ministerial.[15] "Discretionary" projects are defined by CEQA to include the enactment and amendment of zoning ordinances, issuance of zoning variances, issuance of conditional use permits and approval of tentative subdivision maps.[16]

And third, the project must not be "categorically exempt". As authorized by CEQA, OPR has developed guidelines for determining which projects are exempt from EIR preparation, because they are considered never to have a significant effect on the environment. The guidelines set forth in some detail the categorically exempt activities in 12 classes, including existing facilities, replacement or reconstruction, new construction of small structures, minor alterations to land, information, collection, inspections and loans.[17] By statute, feasibility or planning studies for possible future actions (which the agency has not approved, adopted or funded) are exempt from the EIR requirement, but must nevertheless include a consideration of environmental factors.[18]

Thus, if the government activity is a "project", is determined to have a significant effect, is discretionary and is not categorically exempt, an EIR must be prepared.

b. Contents of an EIR

An impact report can be valuable to decision-makers only if it includes a complete and detailed, but understandable, description of all environmental consequences. CEQA provides that the report must include the following topics:

(1) The environmental impact of the proposed project.

(2) Any adverse environmental effects which cannot be avoided if the project is implemented.

(3) Mitigation measures proposed to minimize the impact of the project.

(4) Alternatives to the proposed project.

(5) The relationship between local short term uses of man's environment and the maintenance and enhancement of long term productivity.

(6) Any irreversible environmental changes of the proposed project should it be implemented.

(7) The growth inducing impact of the proposed project.[19]

The OPR guidelines further delineate the contents of an EIR.[20] A report must include maps of the project location and a statement of the project objectives. An EIR must describe the environment in the vicinity of the project, especially the regional setting, with reference to related projects (existing and planned) in order to examine the cumulative impact of such projects. Two important aspects of the OPR guidelines relate to project alternatives and growth inducing impacts. With regard to these, the guidelines provide as follows:

"Alternatives to the Proposed Action: Describe any known alternatives to the project or to the location of the project, which could feasibly attain the basic objectives of the project, and why they were rejected in favor of the ultimate choice. The specific alternative of "no project" must also always be evaluated, along with the impact. Attention should be paid to alternatives capable of substantially reducing or eliminating any environmentally adverse impacts, even if these alternatives substantially impede the attainment of the project objectives, and are most costly.

"The Growth-Inducing Impact of the Proposed Action: Discuss the ways in which the proposed project could foster economic or population growth, either directly or indirectly, in the surrounding environment. Included in this are projects which would remove obstacles to population growth (a major expansion of a waste water treatment plant might, for example, allow for more construction in service areas). Increases in the population may further tax existing community service facilities so consideration must be given to this impact. Also discuss the characteristics of some projects which may encourage and facilitate other activities that could signifi-

cantly affect the environment, either individually or cumulatively. It must not be assumed that growth in any area is necessarily beneficial, detrimental, or of little significance to the environment."[21]

The degree of specificity in an EIR "will correspond to the degree of specificity involved in the underlying activity".[22] Thus, an EIR on the adoption of a comprehensive zoning ordinance or local general plan should focus on secondary consequences and need not be as specific as an EIR for a public works project, for example. The guidelines further provide that a separate EIR is not required for adoption of a general plan or plan element if the plan addresses all the aspects required by CEQA and the guidelines.[23]

c. The EIR Process

The first step taken by a government body in preparing an environmental impact report is to determine whether CEQA applies to the proposed project. If the project could have a potentially significant effect, but the agency determines to the contrary, a short "negative declaration" is prepared.[24] This one-page document describes the project and the reasons supporting a finding of no significant impact.

If an EIR required by law is to be prepared, a full set of procedures are set in motion. The guidelines suggest that the EIR process should be combined "to the extent possible" with existing planning, review and project approval processes of the responsible agency.[25] A preliminary determination must be made where two or more agencies would carry out or approve a single project. The "lead agency" usually has the greatest responsibility and supervisory role over the project and is responsible for preparation of the EIR.[26] This decision is made on a case-by-case basis with OPR acting as arbiter in event of disputes. When two or more agencies are involved, consultation among the responsible agencies is required to ensure that all views are considered in completing a negative declaration or draft EIR.[27] These and other notices on the progress of an EIR are published in the "California EIR Monitor" published by the Resources Agency.

If a private party is carrying out the activity, the lead agency may require that party to submit necessary data and information. A draft EIR is prepared which must reflect the agency's independent judgment,[28] and the draft is circulated for comment to "any public agency which has jurisdiction by law with respect to the project".[29] If an EIR is prepared by a state body, a copy is to be filed with the local planning agency. The guidelines suggest that opportunity for public comment should also be provided. A notice of completion of the draft EIR is to be filed with the Secretary of the Resources Agency.

The state or local agency evaluates the comments received and prepares a final EIR. No specific provisions for public participation are set forth in the Act or in the guidelines. Time for review and comment by the public on draft and final EIRs should be "adequate", and a public hearing should be held when "it would facilitate the purposes and goals of CEQA".[30] OPR suggests that state and regional clearinghouses distribute EIRs to other governmental agencies.[31] Local agencies may contract for private preparation of the EIR.[32]

The local legislature or governing board of a state agency certifies that the final EIR has been prepared in compliance with the statute and guidelines and considered by the body or responsible officer. The local legislature or state agency, in light of the information contained in the EIR, then decides whether to approve the proposed project. CEQA does not seem to require an agency to disapprove a project merely because the EIR indicates long-term, adverse environmental impacts. However, this issue remains unresolved. After making a decision on the project, the lead agency submits a notice of determination, which is filed with the appropriate county clerk or Secretary of the Resources Agency.[33]

d. Planning Process Assessment

The most serious problem with the EIR requirement is that major expenditures of money, staff resources and citizen energy have been consumed in EIR writing, reviewing and litigating, and in general, using impact reports as weapons rather than aids. Most reports include dull, technical documentation of impacts which are inimical to meaningful public debate of environmental issues. Some reports are so thick that almost anyone can find something in them to support a position.

Hence, a major difficulty is that EIRs divert attention and resources when communities should be concerned about new and continuing problems such as transportation, housing and rational growth policy, as well as effective environmental quality programs. The EIR favors environmental and physical considerations and tends to ignore, or at least gives only short shrift to, social, economic, fiscal and governmental factors. This is ironic for a process which should provide a modified cost-benefit analysis. Another problem is the proliferation of new environmental commissions, a phenomenon

complicating an already complex planning decision-making system. In fact, the environmental impact report has taken on a life of its own, usually totally distinct from the planning process and all the more disconcerting since the analyses undertaken should be those normally included in a well formulated planning process.

Whatever the shortcomings of that planning process, this trend is not productive. The EIR is product-incarnate, since most of the effort is directed solely toward preparation of the report. Its function seems to be to provide public information and exposure, but it is not structured to provide a logical basis for decisions. A reading of CEQA and guidelines shows that compendious and extremely detailed data on particular proposals (but only generalizations about other alternatives) is not only welcomed but generally rewarded by governmental and judicial acceptance.

Thus, the environmental impact reporting process, as now mandated, is a simplistic approach to complex issues. In any project, there is never a single action involved but sets of actions. First are the environmental impacts from use of materials, their transport and methods and procedures of construction. Second are the results of the physical existence of the project itself. Third are the subsequent, secondary and indirect effects. Hence, the procedure should identify impacts at each appropriate scale and time for the information to be used when decisions are made at that juncture. There is also the problem of attempting to judge impacts without regard to the community's views about them. Citizen participation is needed before reports are done, rather than afterwards. The present method does not allow for assessment of cumulative impacts of multiple actions, the probability of impacts occurring or generally the nature of off-site impacts. An end-of-the-pipe, incremental perspective is adopted rather than a sequential and comprehensive viewpoint. Just as the general plan has been criticized for being a static snapshot of a future end-state, so too is the EIR a static documentation of two end-states or slices through time: the present, and when the project is completed.

Admittedly, CEQA has had beneficial effects, including provision of new opportunities for greater administrative discretion in the regulation of land uses. The additional information generated often implies or facilitates negotiation between a developer and the public. In some instances, especially where the environmental impact report is done by someone other than the developer, there has been the opportunity for major, beneficial design changes.

Local Agency Formation Commissions

a. Introduction

There is an obvious and direct relationship between emerging land use patterns and the provision of governmental services to an area. The nature of those services, or the inability to provide them, affects the probable land uses as well as influencing development of adjacent areas. Therefore, policies which create or alter local governmental entities that supply public services can have important implications for land use planning.

The rapid population increase in California following World War II generated pressures to provide needed governmental services. Competition frequently developed among cities to increase their territory by annexation of nearby unincorporated areas and resulted in contrived, illogical municipal boundaries and shapes. The demand for governmental services induced formation of special districts, with the net result that a jumbled, often irrational pattern of local government entities proliferated throughout the state at the expense of planned growth and efficient government. Developers bought less expensive land outside an incorporated city and then applied for annexation. The traditional view was that subdivisions would increase the tax base and more than offset the additional costs of required services. This process resulted in "leapfrog" development, uneconomical extension of public services, and premature or unnecessary destruction of open space.

Various types of special districts have come into existence either to fill a void where no other appropriate government entity existed or to overcome state constitutional limitations on the debt levels of cities and counties. Special districts are usually created to perform a small number of government functions in a restricted geographic area. Such special districts may be a rational approach for sparsely populated areas, at least for an interim period preceding incorporation or annexation. But, it has been argued, extensive utilization of special districts has resulted in duplication, waste and inefficiency. Special districts frequently pursue their own ends and provide short-sighted government; their functions are often not well coordinated with adjoining or overlapping districts; and the result is further fragmentation of local government responsibilities and operations.[1] In addition, special districts typically are unresponsive and undemocratic, because the decentralization of decision-making into numerous small, dispersed government entities yields low visibility, confusion and apathy on the part of residents.

b. Legislative History and Objectives

The Legislature in 1963 enacted the Knox-Nisbet Act creating Local Agency Formation Commissions (LAFCOs) to help reorder all inefficient proliferation of local government powers. LAFCOs currently operate under the statutory authority of the Knox-Nisbet Act[2] and District Reorganization Act of 1965.[3] The former gives LAFCOs control over the growth and development of cities while the latter confers powers to control the multiplication of special districts.

Special districts are defined as instruments of the state for the local performance of governmental or proprietary functions within limited boundaries but not to include cities, counties or school districts. This definition was expanded by statutory amendment to include county service areas but still does not include special assessment and improvement districts.[4]

c. Duties and Organization

Basically, LAFCOs review most of the important types of local governmental structural changes including city annexation, incorporations and disincorporations as well as special district formations, dissolutions, annexations or detachments of territory, consolidations and reorganizations. A LAFCO is an administrative body operating at the county level, which represents both the county and cities. It is comprised of five members: two county supervisors, two city officials and a public representative chosen by the other four members.[5]

The legislative rationale for LAFCOs is to discourage urban sprawl and to insure an orderly formation and development of cities and special districts which supply services to residents of the county and cities.[6] Implicit is the need for planning on which to base its allocative decisions. In this regard LAFCOs are required to initiate studies of existing cities and special districts so as to determine their maximum service areas and capabilities.[7]

(1) Spheres of Influence

In addition, each LAFCO is to determine the "sphere of influence" of each city and special district within its jurisdiction. The term "sphere of influence" means a plan describing the probable ultimate boundaries and service areas of the governmental entity.[8] The statute lists some of the factors that should be considered in developing a sphere of influence:

(a) The maximum possible service area of the agency;

(b) The range of services the agency is providing or could provide;

(c) Projected future population growth of the area;

(d) Type of development occurring or planned for the area;

(e) Future service needs of the area;

(f) The level and adequacy of present services in the area; and,

(g) The interdependence and interaction between the service area and the area surrounding it.

Once developed, the spheres of influence are to be used as a prime factor in making regular decisions regarding proposals which are submitted.

(2) The Knox-Nisbet Act

Under the Knox-Nisbet Act[9] a LAFCO is given the power to review and approve or disapprove proposals for: incorporation of cities; formation of special districts; annexation of territory by local agencies (but it cannot impose conditions which would directly regulate land use or subdivision); exclusion of territory from a city; disincorporation of a city; consolidation of two or more cities; and development of new communities.

A commission has broad powers to deny or condition proposals. Besides considering the sphere of influence of local agencies, the statute lists the following factors as relevant:

(a) Population, land area and use, topography, natural boundaries and projected growth in the area and adjacent areas over ten years;

(b) Need for organized community services, present adequacy of area services, probable future needs and the effect of the proposal;

(c) Effects on adjacent areas, mutual social and economic interests, and local government structure;

(d) The location of the proposed boundaries of the area affected relative to lines of assessment and ownership and to creation of isolated areas of service; and,

(e) Conformity with appropriate city or county general plans.[10]

Additionally, a commission may adopt its own standards for evaluating proposals.[11]

(3) The District Reorganization Act

The District Reorganization Act attempts to deal specifically with rationalizing the use of special districts. This Act enables a LAFCO to hold hearings and decide proposed organizational changes in special districts. The Act establishes procedures to be followed whenever a special district undergoes a change in organization,[12] which is defined to include annexation or detachment of land, merger of one district with another or consolidation or dissolution of a district.[13]

The initiative for organizational change must arise with a petition by landowner-voters, a petition by voters, or a resolution by a county, city or district legislative body. For example, after the commission has conducted hearings and recommended in favor of dissolution, the board of supervisors must then make one or more findings before dissolution of a special district can actually occur: (a) that there has been non-use of corporate powers; (b) that dissolution of the district would be in the best interest of landowners or present and future inhabitants; or (c) that the district is a resident voter district and is uninhabited. If the finding is based on (a) or (c), then dissolution may be ordered without voter approval. However, if the decision for dissolution is based on (b), then dissolution is subject to confirmation by the voters. This is considered a serious obstacle to the dissolution of inefficient special districts.

Under both the Knox-Nisbet and the District Reorganization Acts, no power is given to a LAFCO on its own to initiate proceedings for formation, reorganization, incorporation or dissolution of special districts. A LAFCO, in effect, must passively wait for proposals to be submitted. Some feel that LAFCOs should be able to initiate proposals for dissolution based on the best interests of present or future inhabitants[14] and thereby eliminate inefficient special districts.

d. Planning Process Assessment

The effectiveness of a LAFCO necessarily turns upon the quality of its planning functions. The commissions are authorized to initiate studies of cities and special districts, to define spheres of influence, and to adopt standards and procedures for evaluating submitted proposals. Thus, a LAFCO has considerable latitude and flexibility as to how proposals are evaluated. For instance, a commission would certainly appear justified in denying a proposal due to adverse environmental factors. LAFCOs have been used to preserve open spaces. Without commission approval no city or special district can be created to provide public services, and hence, extensive private development becomes nearly impossible.

The bulk of a LAFCO's work concerns the urban fringe areas around existing cities. During the interim period preceding annexation by a city, an unincorporated fringe is often served by county service areas. These may be useful transition entities for providing needed services during the interim period. A 1967 amendment extended the jurisdiction of a LAFCO to include such county service areas.[15]

Sometimes a developer may be able to receive needed services from existing special districts outside a city so that there is no need to request annexation. A potentially significant amendment was passed in 1970 allowing a LAFCO to influence such a situation. It gave LAFCOs some control over existing special districts by increasing their membership from five to seven, the two additional members being selected by a special district selection committee.[16] This option allows a LAFCO to control provision of new or different functions or services by existing special districts.

LAFCOs can be powerful instruments of "regional home rule", because they are better equipped to deal with areawide problems than a city or county acting alone. Since commission membership is restricted to local politicians, a LAFCO is sensitive to local conditions and political realities. Arguably, a state commission would be improper for the normal business of a LAFCO, which relates to minor incremental changes in existing conditions and requires a detailed knowledge of the local community. However, it has been urged that for broad regional issues of greater complexity, there is need for a higher level review board with a larger and more sophisticated staff, broader policy perspectives and less ties to local politics. Such a review board could more effectively deal with larger issues particularly where proposals cross county lines, and could also mediate conflict between two or more concerned commissions.

LAFCO decisions do not appear to be appealable to any other administrative body. The decisions are generally final, because courts are hesitant to overturn the judgement of "quasi-political" bodies without a clear showing of abuse of discretion or unreasonableness. It is argued that a city can increase the respect for its growth management decisions by adopting a long range general policy for providing utilities in conjunction with the spheres of influence developed by a LAFCO.[17] This could be done by extending services to an "urban ser-

vice" area immediately outside the current developed area while holding back services from an outer "urban reserve" area. LAFCO participation would help ensure consideration of area needs, and the courts would probably uphold such a plan for phasing governmental services. A municipal determination made in conjunction with a LAFCO for allocating urban services could be more readily found to be in the best interests of the environment and the region in terms of costs and sound land use policy.

Airport Land Use Commissions

Counties with a population less than four million persons may create an Airport Land Use Commission to study and recommend uses and restrictions on land surrounding public airports so as to ensure safe air navigation and to promote air commerce. These counties must have at least one public airport which is served by an air carrier certified by the state Public Utilities Commission or the federal Civil Aeronautics Board.[1] Counties with a population of more than four million persons, such as Los Angeles, are to designate the county planning commission as the responsible agency.

Airport Land Use Commissions are intended to foster compatible zoning and land uses near existing airports and are to require that new construction in these areas conforms to standards promulgated by the state Division of Aeronautics.[2] To this end, 1967 legislation authorized the Commissions to study and make recommendations concerning (a) the need for height restrictions on buildings near airports, and (b) land uses surrounding airports.[3] The findings of the Commissions, however, were not binding but "advisory only to the involved jurisdictions."[4]

Legislation was passed in 1970, and amended in 1973, which provided the Commissions with some land use planning authority. Commissions are to formulate comprehensive land use plans for areas surrounding public airports to "provide for the orderly growth" of the airports and surrounding areas as well as to "safeguard the general welfare of nearby inhabitants and the public in general."[5] The plan should be long-range in nature, covering at least the next 20 years, and be consistent with the state Airport Plan. The Commissions may develop height restrictions, specify uses of land surrounding airports and determine building standards, including soundproofing, adjacent to airports. Public agencies operating airports subject to the jurisdiction of a Commission must file relevant changes in their respective development plans with the Commissions for their approval. Inconsistent plans are referred back to the initiating public agency for reconsideration. Decisions of a Commission or of a county planning commission acting as a commission, can be overruled by the initiating public agency by a four-fifths vote.

SUMMARY CHART OF PLANNING AGENCIES

The following chart presents a summary description of the functions and organization of the major agencies involved in state, regional and local planning in California. This is intended primarily to serve as a ready reference source; for full information on the agencies and related laws, the reader is directed to the full study (*Land and the Environment: Planning in California Today*).

A. STATE PLANNING

B. REGIONAL PLANNING

C. LOCAL PLANNING

A. STATE PLANNING

1. STATE COMPREHENSIVE PLANNING

OFFICE OF PLANNING AND RESEARCH

Functions: To "coordinate" the research, development and operations of a statewide environmental monitoring system that relates growth to environmental quality and state planning objectives; to guide the preparation of environmental impact reports by state and local agencies under the California Environmental Quality Act; to assist in formulating long range goals and policies for various factors affecting state development and environmental quality, including state agency functional plans; to "regularly evaluate" plans and programs of state agencies and make recommendations when needed; and to "coordinate" with state, regional and local agencies the development of objectives, criteria and procedures for evaluating public and private impacts on the environment.

Organization: Director of Office appointed by and responsible to the Governor.

Planning Process Observations: Lacks direct operating or regulatory powers over land use and state/regional/local projects and programs; increasingly irrelevant role in state land use planning with emergence of such de facto land use planning agencies as the state Department of Transportation and the Energy Resources Conservation and Development Commission; functions primarily as research staff for the Governor and Cabinet; lacks strong political backing to make full commitment to state land use planning; and has inadequate budget to fulfill its mandate to produce a comprehensive state development plan.

COUNCIL ON INTERGOVERNMENTAL RELATIONS

Functions: To establish criteria and act as state clearinghouse for local and regional agency applications for federal urban planning grants; to develop guidelines for the preparation and content of mandatory elements required for city and county general plans; to assist state and local agencies in dealing with growth and development problems through planning advisory services and direct technical assistance; and to maintain and improve regional cooperation and intergovernmental coordination and communication.

Organization: Governing body includes 22 members, appointed to four-year terms by the Governor, representing cities, counties special districts, school districts, state and regional officials and the public; administratively placed within the Office of Planning and Research.

Planning Process Observations: Insignificant statutory or political mandate in state, regional and local land use planning; guidelines promulgated by CIR for mandatory general plan elements judged inadequate, complex and sometimes unbalanced; lacks review power to ensure compliance of local general plans with established guidlelines.

2. STATE DEVELOPMENT PLANNING

DEPARTMENT OF TRANSPORTATION

Functions: To prepare the California Transportation Plan for achieving a coordinated and balanced statewide transportation system; to perform multi-modal transportation planning in cooperation with local and regional transportation planning agencies; and to finance, design and construct the state's highway and freeway systems.

Organization: Director appointed by the Governor and statutorily located under the Secretary of Business and Transportation. The State Transportation Board consists of seven members appointed by the Governor subject to Senate confirmation, to serve four-year terms on the Board.

Planning Process Observations: Absent a comprehensive statewide land use policy and planning process, Caltrans functions as the de facto state planning agency; may lack statutory authority to resolve transportation planning conflicts at the regional and local levels; preparation of state Transportation Plan dependent on inputs and plans of substate transportation planning agencies and on long-range land use assumptions of local general plans which, as practical matter, have highly variable quality and potential conflicts.

DEPARTMENT OF HOUSING AND COMMUNITY DEVELOPMENT

Functions: To establish policies and promulgate housing regulations and minimum standards pursuant to various housing related laws; to develop guidelines for preparation of housing elements of local general plans and for relocation of households displaced by public works projects; to "assist" local governments and private enterprise on community development matters; to administer and enforce minimum housing standards; to maintain a statistical and research service; to make recommendations to the Governor for changes in state and federal housing laws; to "encourage" planning and other activities intended to increase housing supply and quality; to prepare the California Statewide Housing Element; to "coordinate" federal-state relationships in housing and to encourage full utilization of federal programs which assist "the residents of this state, the private housing industry and local government, in satisfying the California's housing needs".

Organization: Governing body is a nine member, policy setting Commission appointed by the Governor; director appointed by and responsible to the Governor.

Planning Process Observations: Has low visibility, with nominal powers and budget, but nevertheless instructed by the Legislature to accomplish a broad mandate for preparing a statewide housing element; lack of adequate political support both by the Legislature and particularly by the former Administration; frequent internal reorganization within the Department; statutory emphasis on federal programs rather than establishment of state programs other than those for code enforcement and technical assistance; and over-reliance on private market ability to meet housing needs of low- and moderate-income groups.

STATE DEVELOPMENT PLANNING (contd.)

PUBLIC WORKS BOARD

Functions: To review state construction projects funded by the Legislature and to approve their construction and timing on the basis of immediate needs of state agencies, cost considerations and the need for developing public works to relieve unemployment; to approve land acquisition by all state agencies except the Department of Transportation, Department of Water Resources, Reclamation Board, University of California and Community colleges; and to approve sales of surplus state property authorized by the Legislature.

Organization: Governing body is comprised of three voting members and four non-voting members: the voting members are the directors of the Department of General Services, Finance and Transportation; non-voting members are two senators appointed by the Senate Rules Committee and two assemblymen appointed by Assembly Speaker.

Planning Process Observations: Has notable influence on planning decisions of other state agencies, including land acquisitions for the state park system; does not make policy but can veto or effect modification of projects proposed by the Legislature and other state agencies; generally low visibility.

3. STATE ENVIRONMENTAL PLANNING

AIR RESOURCES BOARD

Functions: To set ambient air quality standards on a basinwide scale for each air basin in the state, in consideration of the public welfare including health, illness, sensory irritation, aesthetic values, interference with visibility and "effects on the economy"; to maintain statewide networks of air quality surveillance and air pollution inventory; to develop test procedures to measure compliance with state stationary emission standards and those of substate air pollution control districts; to adopt and approve motor vehicle emission systems and standards, and stationary and other non-vehicular sources for each air basin; to promulgate rules and regulations pursuant to requirements of the Clean Air Act Amendments of 1970; and to review local rules and regulations to determine whether to override substate control programs.

Organization: Governing body consists of five members appointed by and serving at the pleasure of the Governor; administratively located in the Resources Agency.

Planning Process Observations: The State Implementation Plan, which is required under federal law, was rejected by Environmental Protection Agency as "not acceptable" due to: inadequate state level review and regulation procedures; lack of a comprehensive, long range planning

STATE ENVIRONMENTAL PLANNING (contd.)

approach; and no direct short-term relationship between land use controls and air quality. As statutorily established, the Board consists of members who serve part time only and "at the pleasure" of the Governor, both of which may account for the Board's lack of aggressive action in the past.

STATE WATER RESOURCES CONTROL BOARD

Functions: To formulate state water quality policies; to review actions of the nine regional (substate) water control boards; to provide administrative and policy guidance to the regional boards; to coordinate and review all water quality investigations and plans of state agencies; to administer state and federal grant programs for water quality control and sewage treatment plants; to regulate surface water conditions and water rights to achieve water quality goals; to enforce discharge requirements through regional boards by cease and desist orders, and through clean-up and other remedial orders; and to administer federal and state programs for treatment plants through review and certification powers.

Organization: Governing body of five members is appointed by the Governor subject to Senate approval, with four members having to meet stipulated technical qualifications; chief executive officer appointed by the Board; located in Resources Agency.

SOLID WASTE MANAGEMENT BOARD

Functions: Initiates statewide solid waste management policy; coordinates research and development program and related information and research activities; provides guidelines and necessary technical assistance for the preparation of substate solid waste plans by counties or regional agencies; reviews substate plans for compliance with State Policy for Solid Waste Management.

Organization: Located within Resources Agency; seven voting members; five appointed by Governor, subject to Senate confirmation: one is to be a city councilman of a city of more than 250,000 persons, another to be a supervisor of a county of more than 500,000 persons, two to represent solid waste industries of northern and southern California, a fifth to represent public with specialized education and experience in environmental quality and pollution control; two others to be registered civil engineers with specialized knowledge of natural resources conservation and resources recovery, appointed by Assembly speaker and Senate Rules Committee; directors of Health and Agriculture and Chief of Division of Mines and Geology ex officio, non-voting.

Planning Process Observations: No clear authority in relation to local solid waste management programs; operating meaning of overall state policy not clear in relation to substate plans; uncertain relationship to solid waste disposal activities of other state agencies.

v

A. STATE PLANNING

STATE ENVIRONMENTAL PLANNING (contd.)

COASTAL ZONE CONSERVATION COMMISSION

Functions: To prepare the Coastal Zone Conservation Plan and to administer the interim permit system; to adopt regulations to carry out the Coastal Zone Conservation Act; and to pursue judicial remedies through the state Attorney General's Office.

Organization: The Commission structure is two-tiered: a state commission and six regional (substate) commissions. The state Commission consists of 12 members, six from the regional commissions and six representing the public at large, two each appointed by the Governor, Senate Rules Committee and Speaker of the Assembly. The regional commissions' membership is split evenly between local governments and the public. Four of the regional commissions have 12 members, one has 14 and one 16. All supervisors are appointed by their own boards of supervisors, all city councilmen by the local city selection committee (except for Los Angeles and San Diego), and public representatives are appointed by the Governor, Senate Rules Committee and Speaker of the Assembly.

Planning Process Observations: The planning efforts of CZCC highlight the difficulty of critical area planning in the absence of state planning policy. CZCC has been forced to deal with such broad issues as energy, transportation and recreation due to state policy vacuum. Its permit authority, which has pervasive and direct impacts, has highlighted issues of regulation, compensation, intergovernmental coordination of regulatory policy, and the relationship between state and substate agencies. Program has been underbudgeted, but planning progress appears sufficient to meet statutory deadlines, notwithstanding the complex process mandated.

4. STATE ENERGY PLANNING

ENERGY RESOURCES CONSERVATION AND DEVELOPMENT COMMISSION

Functions: To collect and continually evaluate utility consumption trends and forecasts of energy supply and demand; to analyze social, economic and environmental consequences of past trends and future forecasts, and to use these analyses as a basis for planning the siting and design of electric power generating and related facilities; to promulgate and adopt standards for power plant siting, design, and safety, superseding standards of all agencies except air and water quality and areas of federal preemption; to act as the repository of nearly exclusive power to certify all new electric generating sites and related facilities; to conduct research and development programs; and to develop emergency plans for periods of energy shortage.

Organization: Part of the Resources Agency; governing body of five members appointed by the

STATE ENERGY PLANNING (contd.)

Governor with approval of Senate, and two non-voting members appointed by Secretary of Resources Agency and President of PUC.

Planning Process
Observations: Commission activities not yet fully assessable.

PUBLIC UTILITIES COMMISSION

Functions: To regulate the services and rates of certain privately owned utilities and transportation companies; to license the operation of plants, equipment, apparatus or facilities of public utilities; to certify that the construction of a new plant or expansion of an existing facility is for public convenience and necessity; to review and approve power plant siting; and to establish standards and criteria for these decision making processes.

Organization: Governing body includes five members appointed by the Governor subject to Senate confirmation; an independent state agency.

Planning Process
Observations: PUC decisions have long-term effects on local environments and state development patterns. Hence, Commission decision-making also fulfilling a de facto planning function; inadequate comprehensive planning to evaluate long-term implications of decisions; Commission action frequently overturns staff recommendations; and influence on power plant siting subsumed by new Energy Commission.

5. STATE NATURAL RESOURCES PLANNING

STATE LANDS COMMISSION

Functions: Has exclusive responsibility for administering ungranted and unpatented public lands owned by the state or under its control; has statutory power to sell, lease or dispose of any land under its jurisdiction if the transaction is "in the public interest"; reviews and approves use permit applications relating to state lands; may exchange state tidelands and submerged lands for publicly or privately owned lands in the interest of the state for specified purposes.

Organization: Governing body includes three ex-officio members: Lieutenant Governor, state Controller and Director of Finance; an independent agency.

Planning Process
Observations: May significantly influence land use planning and growth patterns in some areas; Commission actions not guided by adequate comprehensive planning activity; no statutory or administratve requirements for planning support.

STATE NATURAL RESOURCES PLANNING (contd.)

DEPARTMENT OF WATER RESOURCES

Functions: Conservation, development and transportation of state's water resources; overseas California Water Plan; conducts investigations and hearings on availability of water supplies for export from the watersheds of origin and reports to Legislature; planning for public recreation uses and fish and wildlife preservation as part of its general project development activities for water facilities; undertakes studies for construction of projects needed for ground water protection, advising localities on latter.

Organization: Located in Resources Agency; controlled by director appointed by Governor; regulatory power shared with California Water Commission with nine members appointed by Governor with Senate approval.

Planning Process Observations: Does much land use projection and planning in state as part of California Water Plan implementation; planning generally regarded as being of high quality; water resources development and conservation decisions have potentially far-reaching growth impacts.

DEPARTMENT OF PARKS AND RECREATION

Functions: Charged with administering, developing, planning and operating park and recreation facilities in the state; may acquire or lease property; to maintain comprehensive plan for development of outdoor reaction pursuant to the federal Land and Water Conservation Act; to coordinate state and local agencies in planning, developing and maintaining outdoor recreation; charged with designing, constructing, operating, managing and maintaining recreational facilities at State Water Projects; to develop trail systems; and to undertake landscape analysis.

Organization: An executive department within the Resources Agency, operating under a nine-member Parks and Recreation Commission appointed by the Governor subject to Senate approval.

Planning Process Observations: As lead agency in developing and maintaining state recreation plans, it is directly involved in a single-purpose statewide planning process. Plans prepared by the Department become official policy when adopted by Commission, and approved by Secretary of Resources and Governor. As a conduit for federal funds, it can have a limited impact on local decisions.

DEPARTMENT OF FISH AND GAME

Functions: To regulate the taking or possession of birds, mammals, fish, amphibians and reptiles except for commercial purposes; to promulgate rules and regulations relating to the state's fish and wildlife; to develop criteria for determining whether a species or subspecies is endangered and to make a biennial inventory of threatened species; to

STATE NATURAL RESOURCES PLANNING (contd.)

manage, control and protect spawning areas on state lands; to conduct research programs and coordinate water quality activities as they affect fish and wildlife; to establish ecological reserves and acquire property for conservation purposes; and to prepare and implement a state Fish and Wildlife Plan.

Organization: Governed by five-member Commission and Wildlife Conservation Board responsible for fish and game policies and wildlife conservation property acquisition decisions; director appointed by Governor and responsible to the Secretary of Resources Agency.

Planning Process Observations: Has limited planning function, with minimal influence on state's land use planning decisions; effects most direct when dealing with areas involving endangered or rare species including habitats; has limited funding and cannot be expected to initiate land use planning decisions.

B. REGIONAL PLANNING

JOINT EXERCISE OF POWERS ACT

COUNCILS OF GOVERNMENT

General Functions: California's COGs are typically formed under the Joint Exercise of Powers Act on a voluntary basis, with a few formed under the Area Planning Law; their formation has been a response to (a) problems of overlapping service areas and fragmented local authority, or (b) federal legislative requirements and incentives. Statutorily, COGs formed under Joint Powers Agreement can have wide range of powers and responsibilities as determined by the participating local governments. Most non-metropolitan COGs are "single county" associations formed in response to federal legislation and have three basic functions: (a) A-95 clearinghouse review; (b) areawide planning; and (c) provision of technical assistance to member jurisdictions. Metropolitan COGs perform the same basic functions, but with larger staff and budget, and more cooperation from members. The following are three major metropolitan COGs:

(1) Southern California Association of Governments.

As an established and increasingly active COG, SCAG has ongoing programs of technical assistance to communities of under 50,000 population; has reviewed and commented on numerous projects involving hundreds of millions of dollars in grant requests through its A-95 and EIR review processes; has prepared and adopted the airport element of the regional transportation plan; is preparing the regional transportation plans; and has undertaken major steps toward growth management with completion and adoption of revised growth forecasts comprising three "spatial allocation" alternatives.

(2) Association of Bay Area Governments.

As a COG that covers an area with numerous single purpose agencies, ABAG has placed heavy emphasis an interagency cooperation, thus muting, although not overcoming, the fragmentation of planning in the Bay Area. Has completed 18 studies of areawide needs and problems, including a comprehensive regional plan (Regional Plan, 1970-1990) and other plan elements. Currently studying a regional growth policy and will pursue goal of reaching agreement with member local governments and single purpose agencies on overall growth projections, specific growth rates and distributions for parts of region.

(3) Comprehensive Planning Organzation

Although a single-county COG, CPO covers nearly 1.5 million people in its jurisdiction which includes San Diego County and 13 local cities. Governed by a 14-member Board of Directors and executive committee appointed by the Board. Has recently completed an open space plan and working on a regional transportation plan. With a staff of more than 40 persons, and a budget exceeding $2 million, one of the most active California COGs. Like other single-county COGs, it has suffered problems of planning coordination with the county and major central city, but recent efforts have improved such coordination.

JOINT EXERCISE OF POWERS ACT (contd.)

Planning Process Assessment: Without statutorily defined purposes and functions, a COG's ability to perform and enforce regional comprehensive planning in the short run depends almost entirely on willingness of local governments to cooperate; lack taxing powers and depend on federal grants and voluntary contributions from member governments; have no direct legal authority to regulate land use; and the A-95 review process may not be effective in influencing long-term land use because of structural and operational shortcomings. Composition of COGs emphasizes local government representation and until recently has given little consideration to citizen participation in regional decision-making.

Organization: Large metropolitan COGs typically have a general assembly composed of representatives from each member city and county and an executive committee that meets more frequently. The executive committee in practice makes most operational policy decisions, while the general assembly is responsible for broader COG policies, for reviewing policy decisions of the executive committee, and for reviewing and adopting budgets. Policy committees are formed to review and take action on particular issues. A sizeable professional staff is provided to support these committees. Smaller, non-metropolitan COGs take various organizational forms as determined by single-county needs and preferences.

STATUTORY REGIONAL PLANNING

METROPOLITAN TRANSPORTATION COMMISSION (S.F. BAY AREA)

Functions: Established by state legislation, MTC has specific planning, finance and other powers. It was required to develop a regional transportation plan which was to: (a) include state and federal highways, transbay bridges, and mass transit systems and interface with multi-modal systems; (b) estimate regional transportation needs for a ten-year period; (c) schedule transportation priorities according to these needs; (d) develop a financial program which includes proposals for financing construction and operating costs for each segment of the regional transportation system, consideration of potential revenue sources and recommendations of appropriate legislation; and (e) study the role of regional harbors and airports relative to surface transportation and the regional transportation plan. Also, to review and approve applications for federal and state funds by local governments and transportation districts for their "compatibility" with the regional plan; and to provide "all available assistance" to public transit systems to ensure adequate feeder service to multi-county systems.

Planning Process Assessment: MTC has broken with the Bay Area's heritage of single purpose transportation planning agencies and attempted to relate its planning efforts to ABAG data and policies. It recently completed the Regional Transportation Control Plan which deals with broad land use and environmental quality issues. However, the agency retains a single element

STATUTORY REGIONAL PLANNING (contd.)

focus and is unlikely to coordinate fully with regional planning counterparts absent of some form of regional consolidation.

Organization: Governed by a 19-member board representing the member counties and includes three non-voting members representing the state Secretary of Business and Transportation and the federal Departments of Transportation and Housing and Urban Development.

SAN FRANCISCO BAY CONSERVATION AND DEVELOPMENT COMMISSION

Functions: BCDC is a regulatory and planning agency with the primary function of balancing conservation and development needs in San Francisco Bay and a shoreline zone. Administers a permit system pursuant to policies, standards and criteria articulated in the adopted Bay Plan, a planning document prepared and continually reviewed by the Commission. Enforcement provisions are both criminal and civil, with appeal and final resolution in the state court system.

Planning Process Assessment: BCDC has achieved recognition as one of the most effective natural resource planning agencies in the nation. Since adoption of the Bay Plan, the Commission has programs for plan evaluation and revision for special area planning, to detail the original plan. The continuing permit function has prodded local government to give greater planning consideration to water-oriented issues. Federal agencies have cooperated fully with BCDC through memoranda of understanding.

Organization: Governing body is comprised of 27 members representing federal agencies (U.S. Army Corps of Engineers and Environmental Protection Agency), state agencies (Resources, and Business and Transportation Agencies, Department of Finance and State Lands Commission) the San Francisco Bay Regional Water Quality Control Board, counties and cities in the region, and the public at large.

TAHOE REGIONAL PLANNING AGENCY

Functions: Primarily a regulatory agency, the TRPA is authorized to adopt ordinances, rules, regulations and policies necessary to implement interim and regional plans adopted by Agency. Each regulation is to establish a minimum standard applicable to the whole basin, but a city or county may adopt more stringent standards as necessary. Functional areas to which the standards must apply are prescribed by the enabling legislation of California and Nevada. Public construction projects and certain specified business and recreational establishments are exempted from TRPA regulations. Agency may ensure compliance with the regional plan, ordinances, rules, regulations and policies; court action may be instituted to compel local jurisdictions to enforce the TRPA ordinances.

Planning Process Assessment: TRPA suffers from the basic infirmities of an interstate Compact which is unable to respond to changing conditions. Compact requires the dual-majority approval or

STATUTORY REGIONAL PLANNING (contd.)

rejection of proposals and does not include power or budget for acquisition. Many ordinances to implement the plan delegate enforcement to local government. California has attempted to guard its portion of the Lake by creating another agency (California Tahoe Regional Planning Agency); the Lake remains a single body of water whose planning needs to be unified and implemented.

Organization: Governed by a ten-member board, with major representation by local governments in the region. California representatives include two county appointees, one city representative, a gubernatorial appointee and Secretary of Resources Agency; Nevada representatives include three county representatives, one gubernatorial appointee, and Director of Department of Conservation and Natural Resources. A majority vote of each state's delegation (i.e., a dual majority) is required to approve any matter.

CALIFORNIA-TAHOE REGIONAL PLANNING AGENCY

Functions: Essentially California's supplement to TRPA, CTRPA has powers parallel to TRPA, including preparation and maintenance of a regional general plan and promulgation of necessary ordinances, regulations and policies to implement the adopted plan. Additionally, all California public works projects must be reviewed and approved by CTRPA for compliance with its adopted regional plan before submission to TRPA.

Organization: Governing body consists of one member appointed by El Dorado and Placer Counties, one appointed by the City of South Lake Tahoe, one appointed by the Governor subject to Senate confirmation and the Secretary of the Resources Agency.

MISCELLANEOUS ENABLING LAWS

AREA PLANNING LAW

Enables counties and cities to undertake joint planning activities. Systems for organization, functions and financing must be accepted by participants. No implementing power involved.

REGIONAL PLANNING DISTRICT LAW

Operative in regional areas designated by a State Planning Advisory Committee, but requires approval of 2/3 of counties and 2/3 of cities. Precluded where joint powers agreement has conventional functions. The Law has never been activated.

DISTRICT PLANNING LAW

The planning district must include two or more counties. Representatives from supervisors and councils have four-year terms. Basic function is to prepare a "comprehensive long-term general plan". The law has never been used.

LOCAL PLANNING INSTITUTIONS AND PERFORMANCE

LOCAL PLANNING COMMISSION

Functions: To develop and maintain a general plan; to develop specific plans as needed; to review periodically the local capital improvement program; to hold public hearings on the zoning ordinance, amendments or variances and to make recommendations to the legislative body on these matters; to serve as the board of zoning or zoning administrator where such offices were not established; and to perform such other functions as the legislative body may provide, including reviewing and certifying compliance of subdivision maps with local zoning provisions, general plans and specific plans where applicable.

Organization: Composed of citizens appointed by elected officials. Method of appointment and term of office are governed by local ordinance, but state law provides that commissions of counties and general law cities have five to nine members. A professional body, the planning department, is usually included in the structure.

Planning Process Assessment: The local planning process has serious deficiencies in such areas as environmental planning, citizen participation and intergovernmental coordination. The preparation, adoption and revision of general plans may be highly ineffectual, even chaotic, and qualitatively uncertain. Many shortcomings can be traced to inadequate state legislation which fails to provide sufficient guidance, incentives or penalties for effective planning. As to citizen participation, the law requires two hearings for adopting general plans or revisions, but no specific or regularized procedures are established. There is no statutory mechanism for effective intergovernmental integration of plans. Referral to other jurisdictions is often a mere formality, the failure of which does not affect a plan's validity, and there is no mechanism to resolve interlocal conflicts. There is no requirement for regional review of local plans. Because no state standards prescribe commission membership, planning commissions appointed by city councils or county boards may be inexpert, uninvolved or biased toward irrelevant aims. Commissions have difficulty recommending proposals that benefit the region but burden the local jurisdictions or that contravene implied governing body policy. There is little statutory direction of the planning process which, left to local interpretation, has led to deficiencies in data collection, inventories of existing conditions and lack of direction in early stages of plan development. Conversely, adaptation for local character is absent.

Another statutory omission is the absence of methods for enforcing planning requirements. No real penalties have been imposed on those jurisdictions failing to comply with statutory deadlines.

PLANNING RELATIONSHIPS WITH OTHER LOCAL AGENCIES.

a. City Council/Board of Supervisors: Planning Commission

In some cities or counties, the planning commission handles day-to-day administration of land use ordinances, thus relieving the local legislature. Regardless of the arrangement, city council or board approval is required to enact implementing ordinances, including

LOCAL PLANNING INSTITUTIONS (contd.)

zoning ordinance revisions and adoption or revision of a general plan or its elements; or to approve or disapprove a subdivision map.

b. Redevelopment Agency: Planning Commission

A redevelopment or renewal agency is generally independent of the commission. It is, however, to "cooperate" with the commission in formulating redevelopment plans. In many cities and counties the legislative body acts as the agency. To implement a redevelopment project, the local government must have an adopted general plan to which the redevelopment plan must conform. Upon designation of a "survey area" by the city council or agency, the commission is to determine the feasibility of a redevelopment project. The commission selects one or more "project areas" within the survey area based on findings of "blight" as defined by the Community Redevelopment Law. The planning department prepares the preliminary plan, to be adopted by the commission and then the agency. Based upon the preliminary plan, the agency prepares a redevelopment plan, the contents of which are specified by state law. In preparing the redevelopment plan, the agency must "consult with" the commission and project area committee.

The redevelopment plan is reviewed by the commission and project area committee which reports and make recommendations to the legislative body. The redevelopment plan is then submitted to the legislative body for approval. If the commission recommends against the redevelopment plan, a two-thirds majority of the legislative body is needed for approval.

c. Housing Authority: Planning Commission

The general powers of a housing authority include construction, acquisition and operation of "housing projects", defined as undertakings financed in whole or part by federal or state funds to provide safe and sanitary dwellings. A housing authority is subject to local planning, zoning and building ordinances and must "take into consideration" the relationship of a housing project to any long-range plan.

LOCAL AGENCY FORMATION COMMISSIONS

Functions: To control creation and expansion of cities and special districts which supply services; and to initiate studies of existing cities and special districts to determine maximum service areas and capabilities. County service areas are within a LAFCO's jurisdiction. To determine the "sphere of influence" of cities and special districts so as to establish a basis for making regular decisions regarding proposals submitted.

Organization: A LAFCO is an administrative body operating at the county level and represents the county and its cities. It is composed of five members: two county supervisors; two city councilmen; and a public representative.

LOCAL PLANNING INSTITUTIONS (contd.)

Planning Process Assessment: The effectiveness of a LAFCO depends on the quality of its planning. LAFCO decisions are final and can be instruments of "area home rule" by dealing with countywide jurisdictional problems. Membership is restricted to local government representatives; it is highly sensitive to local conditions and politics.

AIRPORT LAND USE COMMISSIONS

Functions: To foster compatible land uses near existing airports; to require that new construction in such areas conform to state standards; to formulate land use plans for areas surrounding public airports; to develop height restrictions, specify land uses and determine building standards to implement the plan; and to approve airport development plans.

Planning Process Assessment: Commission decisions may be overruled by the governing body of the initiating public agency by a four-fifths vote.

Organization: For counties with less than four million population, governing board is a seven-member commission composed of county, city, airports and public representatives. For counties with population over four million (only Los Angeles County now) the planning commission acts as Airport Land Use Commission.

Chapter Three

CALIFORNIA PLANNING

MAJOR FINDINGS AND OPTIONS FOR CHANGE

This report has examined land use planning in California from three principal perspectives: an overview of its background and major operative factors—governmental, economic, social, environmental; the statutes and institutions which shape (or fail to shape) the planning process at state/substate, regional and local levels; and in some instances, a critical assessment of the performance of these statutes and institutions.

While the preceding sections are essentially descriptive, analytical and evaluative, this concluding section summarizes and in addition outlines options and alternative models for change at the state, regional and local levels. The section is organized into two parts. The first part presents the summary findings of the report which also may be construed as criteria for change—the basic and sometimes pervasive problems that require searching attention. That is followed by a comprehensive statement of alternative institutional and planning process models—the options for change.

It was never the purpose of this study either to bolster the viewpoint of one interest group or another, or to set forth specific proposals for reform of the planning law, institutions or processes. The latter is left to the involved interest groups and ultimately to the public, Legislature and Governor. Hopefully, the findings, options for change and related information of this final section will stimulate more informed debate.

A. MAJOR FINDINGS

State Planning Process

State Comprehensive Planning

The state has yet to devise a qualitatively adequate and politically acceptable statewide policy or plan which effectively integrates land use, environmental and development objectives, as well as the now largely autonomous planning processes of the state's transportation, air quality, water quality and finance agencies.

The state has no comprehensive or environmental planning process, but simply a collection of functional planning processes ranging from the state to the local levels, each more or less independent of each other.

Established in 1970 to succeed the former State Office of Planning, the Office of Planning and Research has yet to reach its potential for statewide environmental and land use policy planning. In fact, OPR's performance to date may be characterized as the artful avoidance of the legislative command to develop a statewide land use policy by generating, instead, various reports and interagency "coordination" schemes.

One factor contributing to OPR's disappointing performance is its ambiguous statutory mandate as to developing a state land use policy, planning and implementation program. The legislation also conferred comparatively weak planning powers on OPR to evaluate, to assist, to coordinate, etc. Nonetheless, as part of the Governor's Office, OPR could have enjoyed a compelling political mandate surmounting some of the statutory defects rather than focusing on interagency coordination and "staff" reports.

A second contributing factor is the lesson learned from the two previous Administrations: the state planning agency and process, if they are to survive changes in administrations as well as succeed at the outset, must be semi-independent politically and yet remain responsive to the policies of the Governor and Legislature. Thus, the state planning agency and process—especially if they are actively to undertake statewide land use and environmental quality policy planning—must be structurally independent of, but not distant from, the Governor and Legislature. Such semi-independence is further necessitated by the tempestuous politics of land development and conservation, the traditional "home rule" ideology of California local government, the accommodationist land use development ethic, and related economic expectations.

The Council on Intergovernmental Relations is constituted as an advisory agency whose chief function—

the articulation of guidelines for local preparation of general plan elements could be readily performed administratively by a state planning agency. Thus, CIR lingers on as a statutory dinosaur.

State Development Planning

Created in 1972, as the successor to the Department of Public Works, Caltrans may be viewed as an experiment as to whether:

(a) The former highway agency can stimulate planning and development for multi-modal systems, especially when its principal finance and implementation powers are limited to highway and freeway development.

(b) The so-called "bottom up" planning process, despite its political advantages, is qualitatively feasible of developing a statewide plan.

(c) The department, on its own initiative, can recognize, revise and/or delete proposed freeways where such projects do not affirmatively support air quality and orderly growth policies, particularly in the five critical air basins.

In the absence of a comprehensive, enforceable state policy which effectively integrates the planning, budgetary and related decision-making processes of the environmental, public works and functional agencies, the State Transportation Plan will become California's de facto land use plan. Because it must be based upon 41 substate transportation plans which, in turn, incorporate the land use, development and growth assumptions of local general plans throughout the state, the State Transportation Plan also runs the danger of being no better than the state's local planning process.

Caltrans and the substate transportation planning agencies will become the state's de facto land use planning organizations—a role Caltrans avowedly does not want but is able to assume due to its extensive organization of planners throughout the state. Caltrans, however, has acknowledged both the need for a state land use policy as well as the de facto land use implications of its State Transportation Plan.

The State Transportation Board apparently is unable statutorily to centralize state level policy-making and thus to resolve adequately conflicts regarding transportation planning and multi-modal balance of programs within Caltrans.

Caltrans is not empowered to implement regional mass transit systems upon the request of, and in association with, local and regional authorities—thereby perpetuating the Department's automobile/highway bias and exacerbating the transportation and air quality problems of the major metropolitan areas.

State Environmental Planning

In contrast to the State Water Resources Control Board the Air Resources Board is a classic example that land use politics and effective air quality planning do not mix well, particularly as to:

(a) The ARB board (as distinguished from the SWRCB and State Transportation Board) which exclusively serves "at the pleasure" of the Governor and is composed of part-time members with no requisite qualifications.

(b) The single-county Air Pollution Control Districts, composed ex officio of local county supervisors, which often have displayed little initiative for implementing those statewide air quality programs which involve land use and transportation constraints.

(c) State level development of air quality controls and plans—without federal pressure from the Environmental Protection Agency—which are capable of meeting national ambient air standards in the critical air basins by regulating land use and transportation development.

Air quality planning exemplifies the emergence of indirect land use controls which are potentially able to alter long-term land use development patterns, but are seemingly incapable (especially in the short-run) of achieving national ambient air standards in the state's five critical air basins. State water quality and transportation planning, similarly, are best viewed as having long-range land use and development implications. Accordingly, the issue becomes: should the state's land use and development patterns, particularly in the major metropolitan areas, be increasingly shaped by the air quality, water quality and transportation agencies, their programs and planning processes?

The "coordinating councils" of the single-county APCDs have not worked well, in part because of governing board membership problems. In the metropolitan areas (critical air basins), they do not function as regional air quality agencies nor are their regulatory functions integrated with the comprehensive regional planning programs of Councils of Governments.

Although ARB pioneered vehicle exhaust controls, it has lagged significantly in attempting to clear the air and preserve the health of the vast majority of the state's populations inhabiting the metropolitan areas. It has preferred instead to react, sometimes negatively, to federal initiatives for the urban areas. For example, ARB has yet to develop a State Implementation Plan with sufficient land use and transportation controls to be acceptable to EPA for attaining and maintaining ambient air standards in the critical, metropolitan air basins.

SWRCB is generally credited with developing an excellent statewide water quality program, serving as a model for subsequent federal legislation. Although the program tends to be narrowly single-purpose, focusing on "hardware" strategies and tending to overlook broader land use, air quality and regional planning relationships, it provides an institutional and planning model exemplifying that state government can, in fact, devise a successful state/substate environmental program.

State Energy Planning

The 1974 statute establishing the Energy Resources and Conservation Commission provides another example of how state government, if it wants to, can (a) overcome the fragmented responses of single purpose agencies for the planning, regulation and allocation of a resource which significantly affects land development and conservation patterns; and (b) develop a single, more comprehensive agency which integrates, rather than "coordinates", governmental decision-making regarding a vital resource.

Not only is the Commission the first state agency of its kind in the nation, it suggests another institutional model for the planning, regulation and "one stop" issuance of permits for resource development in critical areas of statewide significance, such as the coastal zone, bay and wet lands, endangered agricultural lands, and mountain and desert areas. Nevertheless, the Commission still must anticipate relating more clearly to a comprehensive state planning process, even though such a process does not yet exist.

Regional Planning Process

Critical Area Planning

Three statutory "critical area" agencies have arisen on an ad hoc basis in California, which focus primarily on balancing development and conservation of areas with unique environmental amenities. Curiously, each agency is water-oriented and makes tradeoffs associated with the planning, regulation and allocation of water-related resources at the regional or state level: bay (San Francisco Bay Conservation and Development Commission), lake (Tahoe Regional Planning Agency) and ocean (Coastal Zone Conservation Commission). Moreover, each agency is empowered to integrate regional/local planning with the issuance of development permits but cannot affirmatively initiate regionally desirable development.

Metropolitan and Regional Planning

The state statutes enable, but do not require, comprehensive interlocal and regional planning, and thereby rely wholly upon local and/or federal initiative for any kind of movement toward addressing regional problems of local and statewide interest. The state's hesitation to support comprehensive regional planning is no longer defensible as, for example, transportation, housing, air quality and water quality problems multiply in the metropolitan areas, and federally supported Councils of Governments struggle to address them.

The planning law does not adequately consider (a) the universal disuse of the permissive District Planning, Regional Planning District and Area Planning Laws, or (b) the inability of the Joint Exercise of Powers Act to enable different roles and powers for metropolitan and non-metropolitan COGs. The JEPA makes no provision for requiring (a) citizen representation on COG governing bodies and other planning-related agencies based on a joint powers agreement; (b) planning jurisdiction extending beyond the boundaries of the member local governments; and (c) taxation of area residents to meet new regional needs or to reduce interjurisdictional fiscal disparities. Thus, the California COGs, all of which are based upon the JEPA, are merely legal extensions of their member local governments, too closely tied to the governmental interests of the participants, and in need of greater organizational and financial independence.

Most of the state's COGs are single-county, in non-metropolitan areas and formed in reaction to federal legislative requirements. While the non-metropolitan COGs undertake areawide planning, A-95 grant application reviews and technical assistance, a recent study of seven associations noted substantial decision-making, role definition, planning and organizational deficiencies. These same problems are apparent in the three major metropolitan COGs in the San Diego, Los Angeles and San Francisco regions but in various, less critical degrees.

The state has avoided any definition of regional planning roles for COGs, especially in the metropolitan areas, thereby abdicating responsibility for regional planning to the federal government and to federally related state/substate programs for transportation, air quality, water quality and other public works. The growth policy planning of the three metropolitan COGs merits state statutory recognition, interagency and financial support so as to officially and comprehensively address major land use/environmental quality problems in the San Diego, Los Angeles and San Francisco regions—problems created in part by the failure of state government to devise comprehensive policies and integrated programs.

The federal government—chiefly through the Environmental Protection Agency, Department of Housing and Urban Development, and Department of Transportation—has pursued, in effect, non-statutory approaches for stimulating evolution of the three major metropolitan COGs—Comprehensive Planning Organization (San Diego), Southern California Association of Governments (Los Angeles) and Association of Bay Area Governments (San Francisco). Despite inherent and ultimately limiting organizational weaknesses, these COGs are rapidly moving toward being able to guide land use development patterns through the exercise of federally delegated powers relating to transportation, air quality, water quality, housing, grant-in-aid and environmental impact reviews. Thus, their emerging ability to influence land uses is not grounded in state delegated powers (except for regional transportation planning in the Los Angeles and San Diego Region).

Local Planning Process

The status and authority of the local general plan have been elevated recently by statutory requirements for additional plan elements and "consistency" with the zoning ordinance and subdivision map approvals. While these are salutary steps, they raise serious questions concerning the adequacy of the legislative conception of the local planning process, including the following issues:

(a) Proliferating general plan elements and the "consistency" requirements are no substitute for qualitatively sufficient local plans, which can be effectively implemented to guide local land use, to improve environmental quality and to manage growth.

(b) The legislative conception of the general plan as "a pattern and guide" for "physical" development is simplistic, obsolete and fails to provide for the expression of state and regional policies, the realities of the contemporary planning process, environmental quality needs and constraints, and social and economic needs.

It may be that the inadequate statutory conception of the local general plan, particularly the bias toward "physical" planning, may be as responsible for critical land use and environmental problems at the regional and state levels as the absence of explicit state policies and planning.

The general tendency of state government to avoid land use, environmental quality and growth policy decisions has functionally shifted responsibility for statewide and regional problems onto local governments, which in many cases have not had the perspective, resources, motivation, expertise or legal powers to address them. Proliferating general plan elements relating to environmental planning, for example, not only shift the burden (administrative and financial) onto ill-equipped local governments, but also (a) create the illusion that environmental quality issues are being adequately addressed statewide, and (b) thereby facilitate further state temporizing on critical land use, environmental and growth policy issues.

There is need to rethink the entire institutional structure and process of local planning as to the roles, responsibilities and reviewability of the local planning staff, planning commission, city council or board of supervisors, and surrounding jurisdictions. For example, planning commissions, although intended to incorporate independent citizen involvement in the planning process, in practice have tended:

(a) To over-represent special interests with important stakes in land use and development.

(b) To over-attend to zoning and permits and many essentially administrative matters, thereby minimizing attention to basic policy issues regarding alternate land development patterns, community growth issues, and environmental amenities and constraints.

(c) To deter adequate citizen access and participation in planning decisions, in part because of the vague statutory language pertaining to "consult with" citizens and organized groups.

(d) To become, in some cases, politically impotent "buffers" for the local legislatures which not only appoint the planning commissioners, but can overturn their decisions; and/or to become "rubber stamps" for

the local planning staff and thereby fail to stimulate independent insight, leadership and debate in a community forum.

The planning law assumes an "island" theory of local planning—the general plan is a wholly autonomous and insular document, developed by a wholly autonomous and insular local government. Thus, the general plan can be statutorily isolated from a compelling integration with related intra- and intergovernmental decision-making. For example, the general plan is seen in part as a "basis for" local capital budgeting and as something "referred to" other local governments for their comments, which are then to be "considered." Accordingly, there is need for effectively integrating the general plan and planning process with:

(a) Intragovernmental finance and administrative processes and decision-making.

(b) Implementation devices such as zoning and subdivision map approvals going beyond the ambiguous requirement that the general plan and zoning are to be "consistent with" one another.

(c) Regional growth policy, housing and transportation plans, including regional review in the metropolitan areas for local compliance with state and regional policies and state statutory requirements.

(d) State/substate planning processes, particularly for air quality, water quality and coastal resources.

The blanket treatment of local government, without differentiation in a single statute, for different types, levels (city and county), sizes and character reflects a simplistic conception of complex land use needs and problems. Clearly, there should be markedly different planning requirements for a metropolitan city than for a rural county. Interestingly, this indiscriminate, all-encompassing character does not extend to another type of government, the often "invisible" special district, which remains aloof from most planning requirements and may proceed to extend its services and facilities without any real planning of its own or adherence to others' plans.

Curiously, the planning law manages to combine technical, legalistic procedures (e.g., referrals) for relatively unimportant matters with platitudes or conspicuous omissions in treating crucial needs (e.g., subjurisdiction plans). The markedly inferior quality of the local planning law is further indicated in part by omissions (a) of a statement of purpose, definitions, relationships to related local laws and (b) generally of enforcement mechanisms and functions. Its selective inattention to important matters suggests an implicit legislative policy of critical ommissions, thereby maintaining the historical subordination of the planning process to local land use, governmental, political and economic expectations.

Although the planning process has been traditionally impeded by the fragmentation of local governments, a plethora of special districts and interlocal competition for revenue-generating development, it is not clear whether Local Agency Formation Commissions have successfully mitigated these problems, or are themselves a source of additional interlocal problems. Thus, the performance of many LAFCOs raises serious questions as to:

(a) their reluctance or refusal to undertake long-range jurisdictional growth planning to provide a basis for their decision-making regarding incorporations, annexations, special district formation and definition of urban spheres of influence;

(b) the composition of their boards, particularly whether equal representation of county and city interests facilitates adequate resolution of city-county planning conflicts and jurisdictional policy;

(c) the reviewability of LAFCO decisions so as to ensure more rigorous compliance with the statutes as well as with areawide (regional) plans and growth policies.

General Findings

The proliferation of single purpose agencies, special districts, ad hoc commissions and general plan elements functionally serves to fragment attention and responsibility as to basic questions concerning the state's land use, environmental quality and growth distribution problems. Such fragmentation is symptomatic of a governmental decision-making process which thrives on disjointed incrementalism, temporizing "solutions" to problems that don't go away, and avoidance of fundamental questions as to California's alternative futures.

In the absence of an explicit and effective state planning process and policy, it was inevitable that substantial land use and environmental quality policy vacuums would develop. It was also inevitable that de facto substitutes would emerge to fill some of the vacuums through "backdoor" land use planning by single purpose agencies. Thus, it now makes more sense to ask not whether the state should initiate comprehensive land use

policy planning, but when and how the existing de facto plans and processes are to be rationalized, integrated and made to serve statewide policies—rather than the needs of various departments, programs and special interest groups.

California's planning law, processes and institutions stand in need of serious, intensive and immediate examination as to their assumptions, equity, effectiveness, intergovernmental relationships, responsiveness and form.

The predominant concern for most proposals for state level planning law reform has been to rationalize and improve state inputs—policies, plans, programs and budget decision-making—while wholly neglecting consideration of results and outputs, the "bottom lines" of state actions. While state programs should be more sensitive to land use and environmental quality concerns, whether they succeed in fact will be due in large part to effective legislative oversight and systematic monitoring of programmatic impacts at the local level. Unfortunately, state government thus far appears to have developed little capacity to do either. As a result, the danger continues that local governments will continue to bear the brunt of state programmatic failures, omissions and misdirection—and at the expense of limited local land, air and water resources. The "bottom up" planning process, in which substate agencies prepare components of a statewide plan, has proven generally to be qualitatively uncertain, giving way to pressures for "top down" planning by a state agency. Thus, the "bottom up" process, while politically attractive to the Legislature, is an unreliable mechanism for state policy and has been supplemented administratively by SWRCB, ARB and CZCC.

"Coordination" strategies have not proven to be effective methods for integrating local governments, state agencies and functional programs so as to realize common goals. As practiced at the state and substate levels, it can be a singular failure which, nonetheless, serves well the political purpose of creating the illusion of a coherent planning process. In most instances, it appears that either (a) the more powerful party (agency, government) prevails so that nothing significant is changed by interagency coordination, or (b) a smokescreen is generated, no significant decisions are made, and the institutional status quo is preserved. Unfortunately, the "need" for better "coordination" has become an article of faith for many planners and legislators.

The composition of most commissions, boards and

policy committees is overwhelmingly weighted in favor of other government officials, or the groups to be regulated, with only nominal provision for citizen representation or special competence and qualifications.

The time has arrived for careful study and analysis of whether the operative language of the planning law—such legal terms of art as "consistent with", "based on," "take into consideration," etc.—are so functionally ambiguous as to pervasively thwart the policies and purposes of the legislation.

Single-county agencies with de facto land use planning and/or regulatory powers—the APCDs, "regional" transportation planning agencies, single-county COGs—have compiled a notably uneven record of performance statewide and thus have not yet proven to be dependable planning entities. Moreover, the state government, when it wants to assure effective planning and implementation of a land use-related program, has avoided delegation of powers to single-county organizations.

Federal "forcing" legislation and programs, despite some conspicuous shortfalls in the air quality field, have been generally successful. The federal presence has assumed much of the programmatic leadership and stimulated closure of inter-governmental planning voids (but perhaps opening of wounds). This should have been the province of a state government concerned with developing air quality, water quality and transportation planning at state/substate levels and comprehensive regional planning by the regional COGs.

A substantial portion of the state's land use and environmental planning problems is attributable to a political penchant for avoiding difficult decisions and, thus, avoiding responsibility for land use, environmental, intergovernmental and other growth-related conflicts. The symptoms are pervasive: a body of planning law developed through piecemeal accretion and riddled with omissions, platitudes, ambiguity and ornamental detail; the "buck-passing" of land use issues by one state agency to another state or federal agency, by state government to local governments, and by one local government to neighboring local governments.

Moreover, legal and governmental processes tend to overshadow the worst features of private economic decision-making as to land development, shifting the burden of improper land uses onto the community, the costs of misallocating one resource onto the other resources, and the responsibility from one generation to future generations. *Thus, the "name of the game" in California has been to externalize land use responsibility and costs as much as possible. A new set of rules is long overdue.*

B. OPTIONS FOR CHANGE

Various models should be considered in formulating options to recast the existing planning process in California into one which is meaningful, effective and responsive to need. Clearly, there is no single amalgamation of model elements which can meet the variety of needs found in the many categories of choice. Hence, it is necessary to review the options and models within each category and to measure the component elements against the issues now confronting California. The categories include: (1) planning scope and functions; (2) organizational arrangements; (3) powers and responsibilities; and (4) planning process. By selecting the most appropriate models after an assessment of existing institutional constraints and responsibilities, improved planning processes can be formulated for California.

1. Options For State Planning

a. Planning Scope and Functions

Scope

The traditional purposes and foci of state planning have been undergoing rapid modification in recent years. In the 1960's there was a conceptual acknowledgment of the need for planning of many governmental services and programs. This was state planning in a broad sense—covering education, social welfare, resource development and conservation, economic development and public facilities. Generally, this was viewed at an interdepartmental level, with emphasis on orchestration of related programs, and identifying and rectifying agency gaps, overlaps and conflicts. There also was recognition of a need for planning of governmental financial programs, including the important functions of capital budgeting and revenue planning. This broad view of state planning was exemplified by the California Development Plan Program developed by the state Office of Planning from 1962-1966. The breadth of that effort was not matched by an equivalent achievement or depth of commitment.

The broader scope now has given way, even in California, to the more urgently felt need for planning for the physical, natural and economic environments, particularly for land use, public facilities, and employment.

Thus, the alternative substantive scopes of state planning, generally in order of present acceptance in California probably would include: physical development and growth, conservation of natural resources, economic development, resource development, fiscal matters, urban development, social welfare and human resources development, governmental organization and public services.

To capitalize on the present acceptance of a statewide interest in physical development and growth as well as conservation of natural resources, together defined loosely as environmental planning, intensive consideration logically could be given first to such environmental policy. In terms of planning for the environment there are several approaches, including planning for certain geographic areas, specific aspects of the environment or certain kinds of activities wherever located.

The geographic definition is broadly understood. The ALI Model Land Development Code endorsed the concept of state regulation of areas of critical state concern in its Article 7. It deals not only with geographic areas but also with certain kinds of development proposals and developments of regional impact. Other specific geographic alternatives for the application of state planning include special consideration for specific substate regions (which may not be solely environmental) within which the state takes greater authority, including metropolitan regions covering several counties, natural environmental regions, such as coastline areas, substate geographic regions which do not have adequate political leadership or identity, or regions in depressed economic condition.

Scope alternatives by specific elements or activities are less well understood. The key determinants typically are those aspects considered to be of "state concern" or "statewide concern." In the Vermont planning legislation, for instance, the purpose indicated is to protect "transcending state interests."

Functions

Another potential area of decision relates to state planning functions. At the lowest level, state planning can involve mere provision of planning services to local government for assistance, even on purely local problems. For instance, the California Council on Intergovernmental Relations provides services to local government in the form of guidelines interpreting the state planning law. It also has administered disbursal of federal urban planning assistance funds, attempted to encourage areawide perspectives for problems, and sought to stimulate planning activity, although its efforts have been minimal in impact.

The stimulus and coordination of regional planning has been a continuing function of many state planning agencies. States also have sought to promote understanding of regional planning in general, including conferences, citizen information programs, publications and educational seminars.

One of the most important functions of state planning is intergovernmental liaison. Many state planning agencies serve as clearinghouses for local government, regional agencies, state operating agencies and the federal government. Of course, the main arena for action is horizontal—at the state level itself, with efforts made to inform state operating and development agencies about proposed programs and reciprocal impacts.

The most central, traditional function of state planning agencies is formulation of policies, plans and planning programs; coordination of programs adopted by other agencies and levels of government with such state policies; and advising the legislative and executive branches of the planning implications of their actions and proposals.

As an example, the California Office of Planning and Research recently developed a statewide coordination procedure (essentially mandated by state law four years ago), calling for submission of planning documents, promulgation to all involved agencies, and written explanation for non-adherence to OPR recommendations. No significant new powers are involved, however.

Among other planning functions occasionally specified in state planning laws, in addition to preparation and maintenance of a state development or conservation plan, are the following: assistance in preparation of the annual or long-range capital improvement program or budget; coordination of basic research on opportunities and problems; provision of a central clearinghouse and repository for public research, studies, plans and projects; encouragement of regional planning; provision of staff advice to the governor and/or legislature on matters relating to growth, natural resource conservation and development, etc.; stimulation of public interest in state and regional planning; assistance in formulating regional plans in coordination with statewide interests; formulation of an annual development program; assistance in preparation of the annual budget; formulation and maintenance of functional plans for specific aspects of physical growth, conservation or development; review and making of recommendations on state laws to be modified to conform to state development policy; provision of planning assistance to all levels; and involvement in environmental impact assessment procedures.

b. Organizational Arrangements

Key issues with regard to state planning are the basic structure and organizational relationships of the state planning agency. An initial concern is whether state planning is to be an executive or legislative function. A related structural issue is whether there should be more than one "lead" agency with separate state planning functions. A final issue is whether there should be a central comprehensive planning agency with authority over the separate functional forms of planning for land use, environmental protection, transportation, energy, natural resources, etc.

A further consideration is whether actual decision-making should be made by staff, citizen commissions or elected representatives. There is no common pattern yet discernible. The following titles of lead agencies in eleven states strongly active in state planning may be instructive: Arizona Office of Environmental Planning; Arkansas State Planning Office; Colorado Land Use Commission and Office of Coordinator of Environmental Problems; Florida Division of State Planning, Administration Commission, Land and Water Adjudicatory Commission, and Board of Environmental Protection; Hawaii Land Use Planning Commission; Massachusetts Resource Management Policy Council and Housing Appeals Committee; Minnesota Environmental Quality Council and State Planning Office; Nebraska Land Use Commission and State Planning Office;

Oregon Land Conservation and Development Department and Commission; and Vermont State Planning Office and Environmental Board.

There are four major organizational models. The first is that of a state planning council which, once appointed by the governor, retains semi-autonomous authority to plan and implement plans, with assistance from the executive and legislative branches. This approach is akin to a strong planning commission concept at the local level. The Vermont Environmental Board is a good example; it is composed of nine part-time members appointed to staggered four-year terms (except the chairman who serves for only two years).

The second model is the planning agency as an arm of the chief executive. This is best exemplified by the Minnesota Environmental Quality Council with its potential for directly influencing executive vetoes. In Florida, the Administration Commission which designates areas of critical state concern is essentially the executive branch—the governor and six cabinet members. However in Florida, the agency which prepares the state plan is actually the Division of State Planning, located in the Department of Administration, along with such counterpart divisions as budget, personnel and retirement. This insulates it to some extent from the executive, but also reduces the role of the state plan vis-a-vis administratively formulated decision criteria. In Arizona and Colorado, the lead agencies are located in departments of community affairs and economic development, respectively, also providing insulation (and remoteness) from the chief executive. The executive approach exists in Arkansas and Maine where the state planning agencies are located in the governor's office.

The third model is a legislative model. The Oregon arrangement, although hard to characterize, may be the best illustration. Although state planning was fostered by the executive at the outset, all actions of the Land Conservation and Development Commission must be confirmed by a Joint Legislative Committee on Land Use, a legislative agency akin to a final decision-making body. The Land Conservation and Development Commission is actually part of the Department of Land Conservation and Development, with the latter providing the director and staff. The Department makes recommendations for the review of activities and inclusion of new activities or areas of critical state concern to the Joint Legislative Committee and the Legislature, but it also serves under the governor, and members of the commission are appointed by the governor. This gives it strong relationships with both branches.

A fourth model has judicial characteristics. For instance, appeals are taken from decisions of local government to the Florida Adjudicatory Commission, which is the governor and his elected cabinet sitting in review of local development decisions. The Massachusetts Housing Appeals Committee also has review authority. This model can only be ancillary to the others, but is a highly specialized response, with an aura of objectivity, equity and due process.

Organizational Relationships

Various devices are used to establish strong organizational relationships among the lead planning agency, legislative and executive agencies and programs, and regional and local agencies. In many instances, the lead agency coordinates the planning process in the state and by participating in environmental impact review can assume a major new coordinative role.

The state planning agency often staffs an interagency coordinating committee responsible for joint policy recommendations or decision-making activities. Examples occur in Maine, where the state planning director provides services to a land use subcommittee of the cabinet, and in Minnesota, where the state planning director heads the Environmental Quality Council. The Council reviews development projects by state agencies and the impact reports on them, and makes recommendations to the governor, including his possible veto. As noted above, the location of the lead agency in the governor's office enables it to coordinate activities of other agencies and can more strongly put the power of the governor behind recommendations; conversely it may assume strong political or even partisan attributes.

c. Powers and Responsibilities

Three types of powers now exist to carry out state planning: regulation, acquisition and development.

Regulation

The key power for carrying out a state plan is regulation. Four regulation models exist: (1) direct state land use control; (2) state regulation only in areas of critical concern or other legislatively designated geographic areas; (3) state regulation of distinct planning elements or functions; and (4) state delegation of regulation to regional or other entities.

The first model is direct state land use control. This is exemplified by the first state land use planning effort—the Hawaii Land Use Law. The law provides for a state Land Use Commission appointed by the governor and confirmed by the senate. The Commission is authorized to classify all public and private lands of the state into one of four classifications: urban, rural, agricultural or conservation. There is a mandated comprehensive review every five years. The details of allowed uses in the urban, rural and agricultural districts are administered by the four county governments, and of the conservation district by the state Department of Land and Natural Resources. Hawaii has had the longest experience with a state land use law, which has been in effect for about 11 years and the Land Use Commission which has functioned for about nine years. At the time of the last mandated five-year review, in 1969, it was noted that the state commission was markedly stricter than the counties in disapproving petitions for rezoning. Other findings were: scatteration diminished, speculative subdivision had reduced, and the conservation lands generally had been protected. Yet, on the debit side, there was concern about continuing conversion of agricultural lands, especially some of the most highly productive lands. Speculation in lands also had increased, causing land and housing prices to rise while some lands had been withheld from use. Most important was the discernible lack of consistency between state and county decisions; the counties were applying state criteria generally and loosely. Similarly, there has been a notable gap between state zoning and state real property tax assessment practices.

A remedial proposal has been put before the Hawaii Legislature. The new bill picks up the "areas of critical state concern" concept to give to the state more direct control over these areas, to include areas proposed for new towns, urban renewal, or in which major governmental or quasi-public development has been proposed, such as airports, highway facilities and public housing.

A second example of the first model, direct regulation, is the 1970 Vermont Environmental Control Law. The Vermont law provides criteria for regulation of specific types of uses throughout the state. It is administered by the state Environmental Board and nine district commissions. The specific land uses controlled by the law include commercial and industrial developments involving more than ten acres of land, or housing projects with ten or more units. Any development, regardless of acreage or units, above 2500 feet elevation also is covered. The method of control is by permit from one of the district commissions, based on criteria set forth in a state land use plan developed by the state Environmental

Board. The decisions of the district commission are subject only to appeal to the state Environmental Board. Criteria established by the Board take precedence over local land use controls.

The second model is state regulation only in areas of critical state concern or other designated areas. This is exemplified by the Florida system, patterned after the American Law Institute's Model Land Development Code. The Florida Environmental Land and Water Management Act of 1972 was the product of recommendations by the Governor's Task Force on Resource Management. It focuses on critical state concern areas, but also deals with major developments elsewhere. Under this process, the state land planning agency recommends designation of areas (up to an ultimate maximum of five percent of the state) and land development regulations.

The governor and the cabinet comprise both the Administration Commission and a State Land and Water Commission. The former actually designates the critical areas, specifies standards, and adopts the land development regulations. The latter decides appeals from critical area decisions of local government. Finally, the local government holds hearings and makes initial decisions on development proposals in the critical areas. Under the critical state concern power, the state must approve local land use regulations within the critical areas. In case local regulations do not meet with state approval or do not exist, the law provides that the Administration Commission may establish its own regulations. The critical areas are those in which development would have a significant impact upon environmental, historical, natural or archaeological resources of regional or statewide importance; areas significantly affected by, or having a significant effect upon, an existing or proposed major public facility; or areas of major public investment or proposed major development potential, which may include a proposed site for a new community designated in the state land development plan.

The second part of the Florida law is the "development of regional impact" (DRI) process. This is a technique for state participation in land development (as opposed to primarily conservation) regulation. Again, the procedure starts with the state land planning agency recommending the DRI regulations. The Administration Commission and the state Land and Water Use Commission then adopts the regulations and decides appeals from DRI decisions of local governments. Local government holds hearings and makes initial decisions on DRI proposals, after considering a "regional impact statement" and adopted state plans. The regional planning agency has a major role here, because it prepares the regional impact statements for the DRIs. The DRI procedure can be applied anywhere in the state if the proposed development would have a regional impact. This is distinct from critical area permits, applicable only in specified areas.

Delaware, in its Coastal Zone Act, also regulates new industrial development within a zone along the entire Delaware Bay coast, 100 miles in length, and along its 25-mile Atlantic coast. It has prohibited new oil refineries outright. The Michigan Shoreway Protection and Management Act requires its state Department of Natural Resources to identify environmental areas and recommend land use regulations to local governments. Local governments with shoreland covered by the Act are then given three years in which to zone in these high-risk or environmentally sensitive areas under the supervision of the state Water Resources Commission.

One of the most pertinent substate regulatory programs is reflected in the California Coastal Zone Conservation Act. The Commission, and its six substate coastal commissions, have four years in which to prepare a plan for the coastal zone. During that period, it has permit authority within a 1000-yard inland boundary, although its plan is for the entire area between the shoreline and the first coastal range, which can extend up to five miles inland. The issuance of interim permits is based upon the general criteria included in the legislation (enacted by initiative). At the end of the four-year period, when the plan is completed in 1976, the Legislature will determine future implementing powers (see Chapter Two).

The Adirondack Park Agency in New York State was created in 1971 to develop a plan for 3.7 million acres of the 6 million acre park. (The remainder is administered directly by the state.) The land use and development plan was designed to meet the objectives of preserving the natural resources and open space character of the park and to provide ample land and opportunity for continued urban and recreational development. It divides the park into areas and establishes regulations to control the intensity of land use and development in each area, including the type, character and extent of development. With adoption of the plan in 1973, the state legislature gave the agency the authority necessary to implement the plan.

The third model is regulation based on functional or activity distinctions. The Massachusetts Zoning Appeals Law is the only known example of a state's present use of direct regulatory power to overcome local exclusionary zoning practices with respect to low and moderate-income housing. (New York State's Urban Development

Corporation originally had the power but later lost it.) Any qualified developer seeking to build low or moderate-income housing requests a permit. If the permit is denied, the developer can appeal the local decision directly to the state Housing Appeals Committee created by the law. If the Committee determines the local decision was not reasonable or is inconsistent with "local needs," it is authorized to direct the zoning commission to issue the permit. "Local needs" is considered a function of regional need for low and moderate-income housing. In effect, if a local permit denial would aggravate a low or moderate-income housing shortage within the region, the denial would likely be found inconsistent with "local needs."

The Maine Site Location Law, enacted in 1970, requires large commercial or industrial developments to obtain permits from the state Environmental Improvement Commission. Also covered by the law are residential subdivisions larger than 20 acres and other residential developments that would require effluent discharge permits from the state. There is no overall state planning process to provide a basis for regulation, and reliance is placed only on generalized criteria.

In Oregon, the Land Conservation and Development Commission is charged with planning by requiring local adherence to statewide goals. The following activities may be designated by the Land Conservation and Development Commission as regulatable activities of statewide significance: planning and siting of public transportation facilities, public sewage systems, water supply systems, disposal sites and public schools. Other activities and areas of critical state concern may be added by the legislature as within the regulatory purview. One year after adoption of the statewide goals, the counties assume an overview responsibility in determining local ordinance conformance to goals. Appeals may be made by local governments and "substantially affected" groups and individuals.

The fourth model is the delegation of regulatory power to regional or substate entities. In a few states, the power to regulate development has been delegated to regional entities. The Twin Cities Metropolitan Council of St. Paul and Minneapolis, Minnesota, reviews and approves the development plans of all independent boards, commissions and agencies which have an areawide effect. Approval criteria are set forth in an adopted Metropolitan Development Guide. These major infrastructure decisions, even though they do not directly control local governments, necessarily have a major effect on metropolitan growth. However, under new legislation just signed, the Council is required to adopt guidelines indicating what public proposals are considered to be of metropolitan significance, to be submitted to the 1975 Legislature for its approval. The previous legislation also allowed the Council to require that municipalities and counties submit to the Council their private development approvals for review; any proposed matter with a substantial effect on metropolitan development could be suspended for 60 days. New legislation now grants the Council the ability to suspend for up to one year any project it determines to be of "metropolitan significance." This will become effective after July 1, 1975, if the legislature approves the proposed indicia of "metropolitan significance."

The San Francisco Bay Conservation and Development Commission was created in 1970, after its temporary predecessor had prepared a plan for the Bay. The BCDC has control over all dredging and filling of the Bay, all development or change of salt ponds, and for development within 100 feet of the Bay shoreline. The Commission is composed of representatives of local government, involved state agencies and regional agencies (see Chapter Two).

Another regional entity is the Tahoe Regional Planning Agency (covering portions of California and Nevada) led by a ten member commission with five each from California and Nevada. The Agency was given authority to approve new development in the Lake Tahoe Basin. Its plan has now been adopted and permits are being issued, based upon the plan, and it is adopting various zoning-type ordinances, (e.g., a shoreline ordinance). A major controversy involves the compact requirement for a dual majority (from each state) to reject a development. California has responded by creating its own Tahoe agency (see Chapter Two).

Acquisition and Development

Three models exist for exercise of the powers of acquisition and development for plan implementation.

The first model involves the acquisition of land and its banking for future use. This is best exemplified by the program of the Puerto Rico Land Administration, a public corporation with power to acquire land to be kept in reserve to facilitate state development of social and economic programs. Its program was launched in 1962.

The second model involves a more extensive power—the authority in a state agency (although not necessarily a state planning agency) to acquire land and develop or redevelop it, or dispose of it to other private entities for development. This is best exemplified by the New York State Urban Development Corporation with its statewide jurisdiction. It previously had more significant authority to redevelop for industrial or commercial development, or to provide housing, and was authorized to acquire land by purchase and lease or dispose of it to private entities. It also could borrow funds and utilize them for such purposes. The most important power it had previously was to prevent local zoning and building regulations from prohibiting projects. However, the "override" power with respect to residential projects proved so controversial that it was eliminated in 1973. The law now specifically requires that all but the largest cities of the state's local government bodies must approve any projects which UDC proposes.

The Hackensack Meadowlands Development Commission in New Jersey was created in 1968. Its jurisdiction extends over 14 northern New Jersey municipalities. The Commission is authorized to acquire and develop land, issue bonds, adopt a master plan, undertake redevelopment, and establish regulations for local enforcement. (Municipalities must revise any of their regulations inconsistent with the code adopted by the Commission.)

The third model is the use of legislation to empower other non-state agencies to engage in large scale development. Louisiana provides a good example with its New Community Development Act, drafted in response to the federal new town legislation. The Act's purpose is to promote growth of undeveloped areas by enabling local governments to create their own new community development corporations to undertake a broad range of acquisition and development activities, or recognize other quasi-public development corporations to exercise the same powers.

d. Planning Process

Process Attributes

The state planning process itself is as important as the other factors discussed above. This was recognized explicitly, for instance, in the Minnesota planning legislation, reflecting a strong process orientation by identifying as one of its objectives, "the provision of a framework within which the state can work to solve problems to be confronted in years to come." Basically, the state planning process involves identifying issues, problems and opportunities, indicating goals and objectives, developing information, formulating alternatives,

adopting plans and programs, implementing those programs, monitoring success, and ensuring enforcement.

Coordination

Other agencies, including local, regional and federal agencies as well as each pertinent state agency, should be allowed participation in preparation of the comprehensive plan. For instance, there should be close coordination with other forms of planning, including such functions as power plant siting, public land management, coastal zone management, housing, air and water quality management and transportation. Certain paramount principles should be respected in devising the state planning process—public involvement, a decision-making orientation, continuity of public accessibility and agency accountability. The following is a discussion of several other process aspects deserving special attention.

Citizen Involvement

Citizen input can be ensured by authority to call workshops, to undertake special public involvement and information surveys and studies, to report annually to the public on progress, and to engage in periodic revision of the plan after widespread public hearings.

Mechanisms to involve citizens formally are even more crucial. Three models exist for this purpose. (1) Use of special citizen advisory commissions, such as in Oregon and Colorado; (2) holding of widespread hearings, as is done in Arizona, Arkansas and Vermont; and (3) creation of substate commissions or entities more accessible to the public, as in Minnesota, Maine and on the California coast.

Planning Instruments

The instruments of state planning are important as the embodiment of policy and indicators of progress. The state development or conservation plan should embody state policy regarding physical growth and development, as well as the other foci noted in scope, above. It takes into account programs, projects and proposals as well as principal findings of fact and delineation in explicit terms of present and future growth potential and development and conservation problems and opportunities. It should set forth the major goals, objectives and policies in an understandable form. It should have a reasonably long-term plan horizon, but state annual and five-year development programs and budgets should be included.

Initiating Strategies

Clearly defined initiating strategies are important to set the stage for progress. In California the state planning issue has already been raised cogently. However, there may be interim steps necessary before a full-blown state planning program is launched.

Throughout the country there have been various initiating efforts made by existing state agencies, governors, legislatures, courts and private interest groups. For instance, the legislation enacted in Vermont was developed after the work of a citizens organization called the Natural Resources Council. The programs launched in Nebraska, Arizona and Colorado were initiated by state legislatures. In Colorado, the 1967 state Planning Act established the Office of State Planning in the governor's office, requiring development of a state plan. Yet in 1970, the Colorado Land Use Commission was formed with responsibility for developing a state land use plan and a program of implementation by December, 1973, indicating a need for "lay" initiation. Nevertheless, one of the most important leadership roles is that played by the governors, which have been prominent in Oregon, Florida and Massachusetts. In Oregon, the Land Conservation and Development Commission Law was essentially lobbied by the governor's office, although an important part also was played by the Joint Legislative Committee on Land Use. Similarly, the Florida Task Force, created by the governor, initiated most of the state planning activites which ensued.

Hence, the possible initiating models are: (1) citizen task forces; (2) formal land use study commissions; or (3) legislative or executive committees. These entities ordinarily devise the long-term systems and structures for state planning, occasionally also including initial goals and policies, and can pinpoint problems and imperatives.

Financing and Federal Influence

Financing of state planning normally comes from three sources: federal grants, general state funds and funds derived from special state programs, such as bond issue funding or legislative appropriations. When national land use legislation is passed, this may become the major source of financing for state planning, with state partial matching involved.

The latest federal bill, "The Land Use Policy and Planning Assistance Act of 1974," was defeated by the House of Representatives in June, 1974. It proposed annual state grants of $100 million over eight years, with a 75 percent federal share, which could have been passed on to local governments. The bill emphasized procedures for a continuous inventory and guiding of major land use decisions having regional and/or statewide impact. A state would be free to establish the process it wishes, although responsibility would be vested in a state designated agency and an intergovernmental advisory council. A state was encouraged to develop a balanced growth process to guide large-scale development of regional and statewide benefit, to control incompatible development around key facilities, and to conserve significant critical environmental areas. Options for land use controls would include: (1) direct state planning regulation; (2) local regulation and state review; or (3) a combination of both. Because the focus would be on major regional or statewide activities impacting land uses, all land use decisions would remain in the hands of local government outside of the areas specified.

New legislation (in several different forms) has now been drafted providing land use planning grants by the federal Department of the Interior aimed at encouraging states to establish means of resolving major land resource use decisions which impact more than one local government. The bills require creation of state agencies, the use of comprehensive inventories, and designation of significant areas of various kinds. They allow alternative means for implementation involving state and local governments, and provide for an average of from $60 million to $100 million per year over six to eight years. Most importantly, there is no substantive federal review proposed but a process review only, with federal actions mandated to be consistent with approved state programs.

2. Options for Regional Planning

a. Planning Scope and Functions

Scope

Regional planning is a tool for developing rational policies, plans and programs to anticipate and solve areawide problems. When applied to a metropolitan area—characterized by a dominant center, present or anticipated urbanization, and functional inter-dependence—it may also be called metropolitan planning. Regional planning aims to provide a basis for coordinating public and private decisions at a scale larger than individual local jurisdictions.

Like state planning, a broad range of models are available. Regional planning may be pursued in one form or another by a federal, interstate or state agency operating on a subarea basis, or by a regional, joint local or even a private agency. Most desirably, it is at least partially an intergovernmental process with different levels involved.

One of the most difficult aspects is the identification of the "planning region". Planning regions may vary with different planning issues, objectives and phases. (For instance, the federal government has designated "human resource" regions as large as Appalachia.) But such variation may be subordinated to practical or political needs.

There are hundreds of regional planning agencies in the United States. Their character, scope and functions vary widely. They range from voluntary private groups such as the New York Regional Plan Association to the Minneapolis-St. Paul Metropolitan Council, which can control the location and timing of certain public capital investments through its power over comprehensive plans of independent agencies. The Tahoe Regional Planning Agency has power to enact regulations to effectuate the adopted regional plan. The Adirondack Park Agency is empowered to review local land use programs and to approve applications for developments of major parkwide and regional impact. Other significant experiences in regional planning include those of the Toronto Metro Federation, which has been highly effective in its operating functions but somewhat less successful in areawide planning, and Dade County, Florida, which has the power to plan and regulate in municipal areas. However, models for regional planning agencies effective elsewhere in the country are disturbingly scarce.

The distinct, often unrelated planning in California regions highlight the major issues and exemplify the basically pluralistic setting in which a regional planning agency must operate. Each of the disparate regional agencies engaged in planning reflects some unique orientation. The conflicts, only now emerging, include those between conservation and economic development, between local autonomy and equality of opportunity and between mobility and environmental quality.

Clearly, regional planning has been primarily concerned with the form of physical development which would efficiently accommodate growth in the region. There is increasing concern for metropolitan disparities, particularly in the distribution of tax resources. Local

and regional plans are criticized for not dealing with issues of opportunity. For instance, plans which have included residential policies have been criticized recently for not posing and facing up to such questions as "housing for whom?" and "where are the jobs?"

One implication of such criticism is that metropolitan regional planning should give greater recognition to social problems and goals. The range of issues involved here may be illustrated in terms of current concerns for the future shape of regions. Should a policy of unlimited (albeit planned) or limited regional growth (i.e., with some ceiling on population) be adopted? Should regional planning aim at building new communities as a major alternative to central area urban renewal? Should regional planning formulate explicit policies about increasing the supply of low rent housing and about relocation of the people who live in neighborhoods slated for renewal? Are social as well as environmental and efficiency goals applicable in regional planning?

With respect to planning scope, then, at least three alternative models are pertinent: (a) regional physical development planning to clearly reflect social goals; (b) social planning strengthened and applied at the regional level; or (c) regional physical, environmental, economic and social planning integrated to the maximum extent possible. Although some form of regional planning is being performed in the country, social and economic planning are generally considered as emerging, experimental fields. Will emphasis on them retard planning for other needs? Can regional planning without them be meaningful? Such questions must be answered.

Functions

Three basic functional models exist for regional planning:

(1) Regional planning can retain its present, largely advisory responsibilities and role, preparing comprehensive plans and processes for these purposes. This could include existing research and information functions, technical assistance, provision for interagency or intergovernmental cooperation, and review-and-comment authority. However, approval and implementation of policies and programs would be largely the responsibilities of special-purpose agencies and local governments.

(2) Regional planning could move further in its coordinative role, stressing processes and plans for this purpose. In addition to some of the functions previously mentioned, a regional planning agency could prepare,

or sponsor the preparation by interrelated groups of agencies (and local governments), of development plans, programs, and capital budgets to be approved and carried out largely by the participating units, other than the planning agency. The agency could move in this direction by being given authority to set and enforce general regional development priorities, criteria and standards.

(3) Regional planning could be geared directly to regional decision-making, and prepare comprehensive plans, programs and other measures to be regionally approved and implemented. This assumes a policy-making regional government performing comprehensive planning functions, or one authorized to enforce and implement the planning agency's proposals. The essential point to be made at this juncture is that there should be sufficient authority to orient planning directly to developmental, regulatory and operating programs. These should be undertaken primarily in pursuance of distinctly regional objectives.

b. Organizational Arrangements

The organizational arrangements achieved will depend on the relative strength of the role desired for regional planning and decision-making. It may be assumed that the stronger this is, the more comprehensive and integrated the decision-making framework and the planning organization will be—and, further, the more central the planning function will be in internal arrangements.

Relationships with local government would range from the COG situation, in which local governments constitute the regional agency performing the comprehensive planning function, to a more independent regional agency. In the latter case, a clearer hierarchical pattern regarding planning and implementation could be set. In addition, the regional agency could supply aid, technical assistance and information to local governments, and cooperate with them in selected areas and undertakings.

The role of federal and state agencies would range from the current situation, with the threat of active state intervention often materializing, to the delegation of financial (e.g., block grants) and certain functional powers to the regional organization (per A-95 review). The state will be obliged to coordinate their programs and integrate their organizational structures at their own levels for a more streamlined connection with the regional organization. (This may as well be said for local governments, where school districts, independent commis-

sions, etc., need to be pulled closer to the general government.) The state also should be required to submit any of its regionally relevant proposals to the regional agency for information, comment or approval, and may undertake intergovernmental programs with it.

Regional organization, then, may range from (1) a loose overall structure, approximating the existing COGs (2) an "umbrella" structure with functional agencies coordinated under a regional "legislature", to (3) an integrated regional government with functional agencies serving as administrative divisions. At the regional level, the organization for planning would vary with the basic form.

Four alternative sub-models, for example, should be considered under a regional "umbrella" structure:

(1) Regional planning could be performed by one of several, mostly functional agencies, operating under an "umbrella" legislature but otherwise equal in status. Other agencies could be responsible for development, regulatory or operating functions.

(2) Functional planning could be performed at the higher of a two-tier arrangement, by groups of interrelated functional agencies (e.g., transportation) which would otherwise retain their identity at the operating level (e.g., BART and RTD). A separate development control unit would also exist at the planning level, but not for "regional planning" as such.

(3) A regional planning agency could exist midway between the regional legislature and the functional agencies; planning would be in a strong position to screen all proposed and adopted policies.

(4) A regional planning and development agency could exist midway as above, thus closely orienting planning to development responsibilities.

Other combinations are conceivable. There may be occasional task forces. A regional planning commission would probably be precluded by the pre-eminence of the governing body in current proposals. Leadership by planners or by a "manager/coordinator/administrator" may be required to maintain a broad-gauged yet effective planning program.

c. Powers and Responsibilities

Regional planning could remain mainly advisory. On the other hand, it could be associated with a range of powers, particularly in relation to local governments. In this regard, three basic models exist:

(1) Require local governments to adhere strictly to the regional plan.

(2) Require local conformance with "regional matters" on local proposals for development or changes in regulations. The regional agency would rely on the submission and/or review of local proposals to ascertain conformance and make more or less binding recommendations, perhaps utilizing "cease and desist" orders.

(3) Assuming no statutory compulsion for local conformance, permit regional and local appeals to a higher authority, which would pass declaratory judgments when its jurisdiction was invoked.

The first alternative places the plan in the strongest position, and removes the ambiguity of "regional matters." The most authoritative provision would make the regional plan supersede a local plan in case of conflict.

The second approach stresses the regulatory process, which increases the discretion of the regional agency, but also entails additional administrative burdens and need for developing rules and criteria to make the regulatory process manageable. In areas where diverse conditions exist, and general rules are inapplicable, a clear interpretation of what is considered "regional" will be hard to formulate.

In any case, the regional plan has to be adopted by the regional agency. Preliminary consultation with local governments may also be provided for. Specific provisions could enforce careful local consideration without adoption (e.g., public hearings) particularly when departure (e.g., by extraordinary local vote) from the regional plan is contemplated.

Aside from regulatory relationships with local and other jurisdictions, certain powers may be secured to facilitate implementation of plans. A regional planning agency (or its policy-making agency) with a relatively broad range of responsibilities should be able to influence the location, timing and extent of development by private and other public agencies, as well as secure sites for its own facilities and operations. Authority to acquire, reserve and dispose of land gives it the greatest latitude in controlling development, including land prices.

The extensive acquisition of land is both costly and, in some cases, legally, politically or fiscally indefensible. For this reason alternatives to outright purchase should be among the powers to implement plans. These could build in flexibility in dealing with special situations. Among these powers are acquisition of less-than-fee interests and options. Carrying out plans dealing with large-scale developments, such as airports, and broad conservation programs, may demand use of a broad arsenal of devices, many analogous to those used locally. Consideration might be given to investing a regional decision-making agency with the following powers for limited and specific purposes: "regional renewal" (assembling land for development purposes); broad classification regulation (within which localities continue to exercise local zoning authority); transferable development rights regulation; and fiscal devices, such as preferential assessment, mitigation of metropolitan disparities, development charges and required dedication of lands.

d. Planning Process

Process Attributes

Broadly conceived, regional planning is not just the work of professional planners or even the making of plans. It involves sophisticated forms of data collection, dissemination, projection and analysis; posing of alternatives and assessing costs and benefits; plan implementation, and interagency coordination. At the outset and at many points in the process, regional planning demands goal and policy formulation. Although it may involve similar methodology, regional planning differs from local planning in scale, scope and process. An important and continuing function is the identification and investigation of common areawide interests and issues and the resolution of interlocal conflicts. Regional planning should consider population, the economy, fiscal matters, land uses and activities, natural resources, ecology, physical design, social services and other regional phenomena. It must also consider ties to other regions.

Citizen Involvement

Regional planning must be made politically pertinent. This may require such techniques as surveys of citizen attitudes, hearings, advisory groups and even field offices. Because of the geographic size of the region, especially where local ties are limited, this can be a vexing problem. The potential of regional planning as a political tool through its information-gathering function must be conveyed to public officials and political parties.

Planning Instruments

Regional planning programs have resulted in the preparation of inventories of needs, planning studies and comprehensive plans. Some of them are moving into the preparation and implementation of programs to fulfill the development and operating responsibilities of many special-purpose regional agencies. As far as comprehensive regional planning is concerned, however, a "shelf" of planning instruments should be considered. Among the important ones that might be included are:

(1) A long-range, comprehensive development plan, perhaps for a 20-year period, adopted and reviewed regularly.

(2) A development program geared to the comprehensive plan, perhaps for five-year periods, with a capital improvement budget adopted and revised regularly.

(3) Functional development plans, programs and project designs for certain special functions or groups of functions (e.g., transportation), or special areas.

(4) Annual or biennial development programs with capital and operating budgets.

(5) Regulatory policies, standards and ordinances, including zoning-type classification or administrative review criteria and more precise variants.

The inclusiveness and detail of planning instruments depend on the strength of the role assumed for regional planning. In addition to those listed, the regional planning agency might prepare annual or biennial "budgets" of local and regional requests for federal block grants and revenue sharing funds, in conjunction with its present A-95 review role. The performance of data gathering, analysis and information functions, and use of cost/benefit and other analytical capabilities should also be considered.

The regional plan, if it is to be adopted and applied, should be comprehensive, and should have valid, meaningful and precise statements of goals, policies, criteria and standards so that it can be the basis for more precise plans and defensible implementing measures. In addition, of course, the plan should present the major development alternatives considered and recommended, with a summary of the consequences foreseen and analyses of costs and benefits.

The most useful concept of a plan for a region may well be quite different from the conventional local general plan. Instead of the typical land use, transportation,

conservation and public facility designations, the plan might include a more generalized sketch showing an "end direction" of spatial arrangements and relative concentration of persons and activity. It has been argued that "internal" urban land use and zoning-type map designations should be eliminated from the regional plan as a purely local idiom. Instead, plans should present regionally determined and allocated tragets (population, resources, housing, jobs, etc.). In any case, plan presentation should be such that the achievement of the underlying goals may be measured. Further, the plan must be closely related to the powers available for its implementation.

More specifically, what should be the elements or substantive scope of the plan? Existing California legislation for regional, area and district planning require elements which are classifiable largely under physical development. A wider range of functions may be considered in terms of emerging definitions of "regional problems." These might include: mass transportation; resource conservation and development; solid waste disposal; air pollution; airports; water quality control; housing and urban renewal; public health; social welfare; sewage disposal; education; governmental boundaries; and economic improvement.

The comprehensive development plan must be tied closely to the shorter-range development programs. The latter may include a delineation of basic program structure; statements of conditions, policies, and program targets; administrative and legal requirements, and a discussion of costs of implementation. An analysis of program elements would be useful for information and communication purposes, organizational analyses, cost/benefit analyses, budgeting and other phases of management. Capital improvement budgets should express priorities and phasing of land acquisition, reservation and disposition, and the development of facilities and major services; investment and cost analyses; fiscal as well as program policies and targets; sources and allocation of funds, etc.

Financial resources to support regional planning could be substantial. It may be anticipated that federal assistance, particularly "701" grants, will decline as the main support of regional planning. Local tax resources may have to be considered along with other possible sources: state assistance; bonds—general obligation, revenue and tax increment; service charges for technical assistance; real estate transfer taxes and development charges; in-lieu fees; and other operating revenues.

3. Options for Local Planning

a. Planning Scope and Functions

Scope

Just as the scope of state and regional planning was broadened somewhat to encompass social and economic issues in the last decade, and environmental factors in this decade, so too has the scope of local planning changed. The best measure of this, of course, is the change in the central feature of the California local planning process, the general plan.

At present there are nine required elements for the general plan in California. Of the nine, four elements (open space, conservation, noise and scenic highways) may be subsumed under the heading of "environmental quality," another four (land use, circulation, seismic safety and safety) could be placed under the heading of "physical-functional", while only one (housing) can be placed in a separate non-environmental, non-physical category.

The scope of local planning could be defined under the following options: (1) It should be broad enough to encompass the functions and responsibilities of the government which the planning function now serves. (When the government acts purely in a planning capacity, it may assume one scope for its plan, but must assume others when acting as a regulator, developer, facilitator, or manager.) (2) It should be as broad as the decisions which government must make regarding its present *and future;* or (3) It should be limited sharply by powers now available for implementation of its planning policy.

Scope alternatives also can be viewed using the conventional distinctions of governmental activity, to include any or all of the following, either with regard to present programs or future aspects: physical-locational aspects, economic development, social concerns and development, environmental quality, fiscal matters, public services and utilities, and natural resource management.

Most planning instruments consider these factors in goals statements. But, these aspects are often viewed only as forces or constraints on proposals, and the current conventional wisdom still remains an inordinate emphasis on physical-locational aspects of development as the elements of plans.

Functions

At least six distinct options for the local planning function can be identified, as follows:

(1) Long-range goal and policy making—This approach emphasizes the importance of achieving consensus on goals and of setting policies to be adhered to. The policy sphere has several different sub-functions, including policy determination, communication and implementation.

(2) Middle-range programming and assessment of alternatives—This functional approach emphasizes the more immediate and detailed specification of alternatives, and the assessment of relative benefits and costs involved, resulting in more refined programs of action and decisions. This view also emphasizes feedback and post-audit review of plans.

(3) General intelligence and present and future simulation—This approach, popular in the recent past, focuses on the formulation of models which accurately replicate the elements of housing, public facilities, transportation, and so forth. It suggests that the planning function can be most helpful by compiling and conveying up-to-date data and information. Implicit in this approach is that there is only limited modification of ongoing forces possible.

(4) Coordination and administrative facilitation—The emphasis of this functional approach is upon ameliorating of interagency conflicts, with the planning function providing a clearinghouse of program information.

(5) Limited governmental "line" function—In this option, the planning function has distinct and intensive duties revolving around regular procedures and specific planning-oriented duties, such as zoning administration, permits, subdivision approvals, design review, comments on referrals, etc.

(6) Incremental decision function—This functional scope is based on a belief that urban and natural systems are so complex and dynamic that only a few decisions and programs can be resolved at a time. The objective is to bring to bear the most pertinent information available on the particular issue addressed.

Clearly, these functional roles are not mutually exclusive, but embracing one or more of them serves to demarcate the more specific planning functions subsequently to be pursued.

b. Organizational Arrangements

The major options regarding organization of the local planning function revolve around a limited set of issues:

Should there be a planning commission? To whom should it report and serve? Should there be a departmental staff? To what extent does it have real decision-making authority? How responsive and/or politically autonomous should it be?

The answers to these and other questions lead to a set of more or less defined organizational options:

(1) Planning Oriented to the Management or Executive Function—This is the organizational counterpart of planning as an administrative function, above. Here the planning staff serves the executive directly but may also assist a planning commission or the governing body. In this instance, the director typically is hired by the chief executive or manager. Plans are often oriented to current operations, and planning becomes a staff and not a line function. The chief executive transmits planning policy recommendations to the governing body.

(2) Planning Oriented to the Legislative Function—In this view, planning is essentially a legislative, policy-oriented function. The governing body makes all final decisions, but the plan initially formulated by the planning commission becomes the key determining factor in legislative decisions. Hence, a planning commission in effect acts as a "committee" of the legislative body and may even have some representation from it.

(3) Semi-independent Planning Entity—This approach is based on the historic 1928 Standard City Planning Enabling Act (it dictated a commission including the mayor, an administrative official, a councilman and six lay members serving for staggered, six year terms). The master plan was proposed to be adopted by a two-thirds vote of the commission only, and the vote of the planning commission could be overridden only by a two-thirds vote of the governing body. This approach viewed planning as non-political and largely separated from the legislative and executive functions but with some minor relationships to them.

(4) Independent Planning Function—This approach sets the planning agency totally apart from other branches of government and makes it almost a "fourth power", having parity with the legislative, executive and judicial branches of government. Members of the planning agency may be appointed or directly elected.

(5) Community Development Agency—This organizational form is increasingly prevalent in larger cities. It was early described in a New York City proposal in the 1960's to create a Housing, Planning and Development Agency, and the new federal Housing and Community Development Act now encourages such consolidations among public housing and urban renewal agencies.

(6) Planning Totally as Staff Function with Planning Committees or Task Forces—This approach may be pursued in conjunction with the central management or other approaches. It essentially permits input from the general public by creation of groups with specified or "self-destruct" life spans and frequently includes citizens expert in fields related to planning.

c. Powers and Responsibilities

The selection of scope, function and organizational arrangements necessarily will have direct implications for the powers and responsibilities to be exercised and pursued. There are five major categories within which the powers to implement local planning policy can be classified: regulation, acquisition, direct development, administrative devices and indirect influences.

Under regulation, the workhorse remains zoning, or the mapping of zones in advance, with largely rigid controls. Deviation from zoning ordinances and maps is secured occasionally by a range of discretionary review approaches, such as planned unit development procedures, floating zones, design review, impact zoning review, environmental impact report findings, etc. The zoning ordinance and map have been subject to recent innovations leading to increased flexibility by use of special zones, combining zones, incentive approaches, floor-area, open space and livability ratios, and use classification systems (see Chapter Two).

Another direction for modifying the specific confines of zoning is by approaches which impose very specific planning-based controls typically in specific areas or to specific elements, in a system outside the scope of the zoning ordinance. These involve performance standards, specific plans or precise plans with regulatory effect, official plan lines, etc.

Until recently, subdivision regulation has been viewed as a largely perfunctory appraisal of internal facilities and design. However, new powers under California law now allow rejection of subdivisions on a variety of grounds, including prematurity. Certain exactions also may be made in the form of in lieu payments to offset costs of public provision of improvements for facilities required.

The power of acquisition may be used by purchase or condemnation. Interests which may be acquired for a variety of plan implementation purposes, include both fee and less-than-fee interests. The latter may be called development rights, easements, rights-of-way, etc.

Devices for gradual acquisition of interests are sale and leaseback, options to acquire, installment purchases, etc. A related power is the power to acquire by condemnation and to dispose to others for direct development in accordance with a plan, as in urban renewal.

Direct development at the local level has typically been pursued by local public works agencies in the form of community facilities, public utilities, streets, etc. Administrative devices are used so that such developments are related effectively to the planning process by power to require referrals of such proposals to planning agencies for review and comment. They are also built administratively into the planning process by capital improvement programming approaches which require public works agencies to submit their proposals for consolidation into middle-range capital programs in order to guide improvement and taxing decisions.

Various indirect financial influences may be used to implement local plans, including taxing policy, such as tax increment financing within redevelopment areas, bonding to finance planning and governmental actions, creation of assessment districts, etc.

In terms of framing options for *exercise* of the above powers and responsibilities, three general directions pursued by state and local governments can be identified;

(1) Strict Construction and Limitation of Powers— Under this option, the police power and other powers are applied narrowly and conservatively, as they may impinge upon private property and the deployment of administrative personnel. Under this option, planning implementation typically is modeled upon cumulative agency experience and strict adherence to state guidelines our attorney generals' opinions.

(2) Liberal Construction and Flexible Interpretation— Here, attitudes toward legislation and constitutional limitations are more liberal. Under this approach, powers are construed broadly, and innovations not explicitly prescribed may be attempted, but usually in a systematic and discrete form.

(3) Consolidated Exercise of Powers—This option involves attempts broadly to consolidate and coordinate the liberal exercise of plan implementation powers and to focus them in a concerted manner on particular issues or areas.

d. Planning Process

Process Attributes

There are many ingredients of a sound planning process. Community support is essential. Major interest groups must recognize the need for a plan and be involved in its formulation to assure acceptance and success. Direct involvement in the planning program by these groups will strengthen and are necessary to ensure a responsive program. The establishment of advisory committees provides advice and information as well as a sounding board for political feasibility and community acceptance.

Adequate administrative organization, understanding, cooperation and support of the planning program by other agencies is as important as citizen participation. Technical advisory committees of agency representatives should be considered. One of the most difficult aspects of plan formulation is the reconciliation of institutionalized biases of different agencies or professional groups.

The first step in the planning process is a detailed program of study. A program should set forth phases, completion dates and manpower allocations. Tentative planning boundaries should be established subject to later adjustment. Some factors to be considered are geographical features, man-made facilities, census tracts and traditional neighborhood delineations. The total study area should be sufficiently large to include all contiguous areas with significant relationships and effects.

Early establishment of initial goals and policies is imperative. The preliminary formulation should be undertaken concurrently with initial data collection. Tentative goals and policies will provide direction to the survey program. Moreover, goals and policies should remain flexible and subject to reconsideration as a result of study findings. But they should provide the most significant and binding commitments of the community, should focus on real issues, needs and problems, and be specific enough to permit interim decision-making within their context. Publication of the goals and policies at an early stage in the planning program will focus community attention upon the program content. The goals should place the community in a regional context, in proper relationship to other communities and the larger region.

Systematic data collection and analysis are the foundation of an intellectually sound planning program. Decisions eventually reached may be arrived at within a political context of compromise. Hence, the "facts" should speak for themselves, and have continuing usefulness. A thorough anatomy of the study area must be undertaken. Analysis and projection of such data is crucial.

Formulation of preliminary plan alternatives is at the heart of the planning process. Subsequently, and perhaps the most difficult part of the process, is the testing of alternatives to ascertain which most closely conforms to the goals and policies. This process may be partly intuitive, partly based on common sense or an understanding of market forces, partly based on cost-benefit analyses, and partly on a recognition of what is possible. Preliminary plan alternatives should be reviewed by the technical and lay advisory bodies. The review process should be aimed at making a selection and necessary technical adjustments and reaching a consensus, so that preliminary and final plans and implementation programs may be formulated.

Planning Instruments

There are several options for preparing the instruments which constitute a comprehensive community-wide plan:

(1) The General and Element Plan Approach—The presently mandated general plan is a two-dimensional, locationally specific depiction of a hypothetical end-state of a community within, typically, the following 15–20 years. The advantages of this form of instrument is the easy identification of sites and the possible correlation with zoning maps. The disadvantage is the static, simplistic and narrowly defined character of the instrument, focusing on the general plan map. It may be conveyed in element or area form.

(2) The Policy Plan Approach—There has been considerable recent interest in an approach which would concentrate on verbal and schematic depictions of ongoing community policy. The policy plan is better capable of incorporating such disparate but essential elements as goals, policies, criteria, programs, management standards, etc. Its scope can be broader, without the potential conflict with a central map, but if care is not taken, it can lapse into platitudes.

(3) The Development or Conservation Program—The general plan may be too specific to be flexible but too vague to convey accurately specific programmatic elements. Programming has evolved from efforts to formulate priorities for action, but has assumed importance in its own right as an appropriate form for a local planning instrument. It is action-oriented, setting forth specific steps to be taken at key junctures, with criteria for making necessary decisions. Programming received considerable impetus from federal requirements for community renewal programs, model cities programs and now community development programs.

Financing

The local planning function has for a long time benefited from direct federal funding, as well as from planning funds related to other federal programs. At present, the Comprehensive Planning Assistance Program ("701") has been severely limited by cutbacks and deferrals, notwithstanding the newly required planning activities for all grantees under the Housing and Community Development Act of 1974: (e.g., planning for land use, housing, environment, citizen involvement and equal opportunity).

The federal government also has broadened the scope of activities and recipients of comprehensive planning assistance, which has in many instances channeled such funds away from local land use planning. Countering this trend is the federal requirement that all recipients have a land use element by August, 1977.

In summary, it appears that local governments may have to fall back on their own financial resources to assure a sound planning process. The portions of community development revenue sharing which can be applied to comprehensive planning is not likely to be significant enough to offset even a small portion of the rising costs of such planning likely to be required in the near future.

FOOTNOTES

Chapter Two

CALIFORNIA PLANNING: LAW AND PERFORMANCE

A. State Planning Laws and Agencies

State Comprehensive Planning

Office of Planning and Research

1. Gov't Code §65035.
2. *Id.*
3. Gov't Code §65037.
4. Gov't Code §65035.
5. *Id.*
6. Gov't Code §65040.
7. Gov't Code §§65040, 65035; see also, Alan R. Perry, ''The Local General Plan in California,'' 9 San Diego L.R. 1, 9, (1971).
8. Gov't Code §65040.
9. Office of Planning and Research, ''A Statewide Information and Review Process,'' at 3, (June 24, 1974).
10. California State Department of Transportation, ''Caltrans' Response to General and Specific Interrogatories of the Senate Local Government Subcommittee on Land Use Planning,'' at 10, 6 (general), (July 18, 1974).
11. *Id.*, at 8 (general), 5 (specific).
12. California State Legislative Analyst, *Resources Conservation Board,* at 36, (February, 1974).
13. *Id.*, at 40.
14. Gov't Code §65041, also §65040.1.
15. Statutes 1970, Chapter 1534, p. 3101; attached to Gov't Code §65041.
16. Legislative Analyst, *supra,* at 11.
17. William C. Kahrl, ''A New State Planning Halt,'' *Cry California,* (winter 1970/1971), at 3.

Council on Intergovernmental Relations

1. Gov't Code §34207.
2. Gov't Code §3417.
3. Gov't Code §34219.
4. Gov't Code §34216.
5. Gov't Code §§34217.2, 34217.3.
6. California Council on Intergovernmental Relations, ''Recommendations for a State Policy on Sub-State Districting and Areawide Planning Organizations,'' (February 7, 1973).
7. Legislative Analyst, *Resources Conservation Board,* at 9, 36, (February, 1974).

State Development Planning

Department of Transportation

1. Statement by G.W. Fairman, Chief, California Plan Process Section, California Department of Transportation, quoted in League of Women Voters of California, *Air Quality/Transportation Action Kit,* at 25, (August, 1974).
2. Gov't Code §§14000, 14008.
3. See generally, ''Local and Regional Planners Gain the Upper Hand as State Reorganizes to Meet Future Transit Needs,'' in *California Journal,* (March, 1973).
4. Streets and Highways Code §100.2.
5. Gov't Code §13990.6.
6. *Id.*
7. Gov't Code §§13990, 14040.9.
8. Gov't Code §1400.5 (a),(b).
9. Gov't Code §14000 (b),(c),(d).
10. Gov't Code §14040.
11. Gov't Code §14040.2.
12. Gov't Code §14040.4
13. Gov't Code §14040.7.
14. Gov't Code §14040.8.
15. Gov't Code §13991 (b).
16. Gov't Code §13991.
17. Gov't Code §14042.
18. Gov't Code §14041.5.
19. Department of Transportation, *California Transportation Plan: Progress Report, April, 1974,* (June 6, 1974).
20. *Id.*, at 1.

21. *Id.* at 3, 4.
22. Streets and Highways Code §29532.
23. Gov't Code §65080.
24. Gov't Code §§14041 *et seq.*, 65081 *et seq.*
25. Gov't Code §§14041.5 (e),(f), 65081 (c),(d).
26. Gov't Code §§14041.7 *et seq.*, 65081.5 *et seq.*
27. See generally, California State Transportation Board, *Regional Transportation Plans: Guidelines,* (April, 1973).
28. *Id.,* at ii.
29. *Id.,* at 83.
30. Gov't Code §14000 (b).
31. Gov't Code §14000 (c).
32. 42 U.S.C. §1857 c-5 (c).
33. 38 Federal Register 31678, (November 16, 1973).
34. "Logically, transportation strategies should be basic to air quality, transportation and land use planning. A decision to expand freeway capacity requires a complementary decision to increase population densities in an area and probably precludes providing high quality bus service or rapid transit. A decision governed by considerations of land use, air pollution control, and sound environmental planning that population in an urban area should be centered along a rapid transportation corridor, is, in all probability, simultaneously a decision that a competing freeway will not be constructed. The decision to add on and off access to a freeway may not be a major decision with respect to a freeway system but it is a major decision with respect to land use, pollution control and logical patterns of local planning and action in the vicinity of the ramp. Finally, a decision to preserve an area in open space alters drastically the method of providing transportation facilities to the area." Legislative Analyst, *Resources Conservation Board,* at 32, (February, 1974).
35. *Id.,* at 29 and 33.
36. Department of Transportation, "Caltrans' Response to General and Specific Interrogatories of the Senate Local Government Subcommittee on Land Use Planning," at 1, (July 18, 1974).
37. *Id.,* at 6.
38. *Id.*
39. *Id.,* at 10.
40. *Id.,* at 5.
41. Legislative Analyst, *supra,* at 33.

Department of Housing and Community Development

1. Statutes 1954, Chapter 1222.
2. Health & Safety Code §3700 *et seq.*

State Environmental Quality Planning

California Air Quality Program

1. D. Mandelker and S. Rothschild, "The Role of Land-Use Controls in Combating Air Pollution Under the Clean Air Act of 1970," 3 Ecology L.Q. 235.
2. 42 U.S.C. §§1857–1858a, amending the Air Quality Act of 1967, 42 U.S.C. §§1857–571 (supp. V, 1970).
3. 42 U.S.C. §1857 c-5 (a)(4).
4. 42 U.S.C. §1857 c-6.
5. Indirect sources are those which generate increased vehicular traffic and thus increased vehicular emissions.
6. Other enforcement mechanisms include State Implementation Plan provision for emissions controls on all sources. Air quality, moreover, is a factor to be considered in environmental impact reports for many development projects, e.g., highways.
7. 42 U.S.C. §1857 c-5(a)(2)(B).
8. J. Krier, *Environmental Law and Policy,* at 302 (1971).
9. 42 U.S.C. §§1857–1857.1 (1964).
10. Middleton, "Summary of the Air Quality Act of 1967," 10 Arizona L.R. 25–26, 29, quoted in Krier, *supra,* at 304.
11. Krier, *supra,* at 307.
12. Stevens, "Air Pollution and the Federal System: Responses to Felt Necessitites," 22 Hastings L.J. 661, 669–74 (1971).
13. *Id.,* at 670.
14. 42 U.S.C. §1857 c-4 (2).
15. 40 C.F.R. 51.11 (1)–(6).
16. National Air Pollution Control Administration, *Legal Authority Session,* Jan., 1970, quoted in Krier, *supra,* at 335.
17. 42 U.S.C. §1857 c-8.
18. *Id.*
19. 42 U.S.C. §1857 c-5 (a)(4).
20. 40 C.F.R. §51.18 (a).
21. 42 U.S.C. §1857 c-5 (c).
22. 40 C.F.R. §51.1 (n), quoted in Mandelker, *supra,* at 252.
23. U.S. Environmental Protection Agency, Region IX, "Land Use Seminar Reference Document," (unpublished, March, 1974), at 3.
24. 334 F. Supp. 253 (D.D.C. 1972), aff'd mem., _____ F. 2d _____ (19____); 4 ERC 1815 (D.C. Cir. 1972), aff'd by equally divided court sub mon., *Sierra Club,* 412 U.S. 541 (19730.
25. 38 Fred Reg. 18986 (1973).
26. 42 U.S.C. §1857 f-6a.
27. Stevens, *supra,* at 676.
28. Health & Safety Code §§24198–24214, 24220.
29. Health & Safety Code §39012.
30. Health & Safety Code §39000 *et seq.*
31. Health & Safety Code §39011.
32. Health & Safety Code §39012.
33. Health & Safety Code §39011.
34. Health & Safety Code §39012.
35. Health & Safety Code §39020–23.
36. Air Resources Board, *Annual Report: Air Pollution in California,* (1973).
37. *Id.,* p.4.
38. *Id.*
39. Health & Safety Code §§39012, 39051.
40. Health & Safety Code §39054.
41. Health & Safety Code §39052 (f).

42. Health & Safety Code §39054.
43. Health & Safety Code §39054.2; emphasis supplied.
44. Air Resources Board, *supra,* at 26.
45. *Id.*
46. See text at fn. 15–18.
47. League of Women Voters of California, *Air Quality/ Transportation Action Kit,* (August, 1974), at 2.
48. Legislative Analyst, *Resources Conservation Board* (February, 1974), at 24.
49. *Id.,* at 18–19.
50. League of Women Voters, *supra.*
51. California Air Resrouces Board, *A Report to the Legislature on Guidelines for Relating Air Pollution Control to Land Use and Transportation Planning in the State of California,* (August, 1973).
52. Bob Simmons, "State Lags in Clearing the Air," in *California Journal,* (October 1973), at 330.
53. *Id.*
54. League of Woman Voters, *supra.*
55. Simmons, *supra,* at 331.
56. Legislative Analyst, *supra,* at 17–18.
57. Legislative Analyst, *supra,* at 18; emphasis supplied.
58. Air Resources Board, Annual Report, *Air Pollution in California* (1973).
59. Legislative Analyst, *supra,* at 20.
60. Resources Agency, "State Responsibilities for Traffic Controls to Reduce Air Pollution." Statement attached to Memorandum from Ford B. Ford, Deputy Secretary, Resources Agency to Ed Thomas, Administrative Officer to the Cabinet, Governor's Office, November 5, 1973.
61. Legislative Analyst, *supra,* at 33.
62. *Id.,* at 1.

California Water Quality Program

Federal Background

1. Act of October 8, 1972, PL 95–50, 33 U.S.C.A. §1251 *et seq.*
2. 1973 Wisconsin L.R. 894.
3. 33 U.S.C. 1251.
4. S. Rep. No. 10, 89th Cong., 1st Sess. 9 (1965), quoted in 2 Fordham Urban L.J. 179, 193.
5. *Id.,* at 194.
6. 33 U.S.C. §1313.
7. 33 U.S.C. §1313 (b)(2).
8. 33 U.S.C. §1313 (c)(2).
9. 33 U.S.C. §1326 (c).
10. 33 U.S.C. §1362 (11).
11. 33 U.S.C. §1364 (14).
12. 33 U.S.C. §1311 (b)(1)(A).
13. 33 U.S.C. §1311 (b) (1) (B), (C).
14. 33 U.S.C. §1316 (a)(1).
15. 33 U.S.C. §1316 (b)(1)(A).
16. 33 U.S.C. §1313(e).
17. 33 U.S.C. §1342 (b).
18. 33 U.S.C. §1342 (c)(3).
19. 33 U.S.C. §1343 (d).
20. 33 U.S.C. §1343 (e).
21. U.S. Environmental Protection Agency, Region IX, "Land Use Seminar Reference Document," (unpublished, March, 1974), at 9.
22. FWPCA §303 (e)(1),(2).
23. EPA, "Water Quality Management Basin Plans: Policies and Procedures," 39 Federal Register 19634 (June 3, 1974).
24. *Id.*
25. Teknekron, Inc., "State Continuing Planning Process," (n.d.), at 2,3.
26. EPA, *supra,* at 17 *et seq.*
27. Teknekron, *supra,* at 3.
28. FWPCA §208(a), 33 USCA §1288 (a).
29. FWPCA §208 (b)(1(, 33 USCA §1288 (b)(1).
30. FWPCA §208 (a)(4), 33 USCA §1288 (a)(4).
31. 33 U.S.C. §1281 (c).

State Water Resources Control Board

1. Craig, "California Water Law in Perspective," West's Ann. Water Code, (1971), at LXXXIII.
2. Water Code §174.
3. Craig, *supra,* at LXXXIV.
4. Water Code §§13020 *et seq.*
5. Water Code §13301.
6. Water Code §§13301, 13331.
7. Craig, *supra,* at LXXXIV.
8. Water Code §§1243.5, 1257, 1258.
9. Water Code §§2100–2102.
10. Water Code §13000.
11. Water Code §13001.
12. Gov't Code §12850.
13. Water Code §175.
14. *Id.*
15. Water Code §182.
16. Water Code §186.
17. Water Code §13171.
18. Water Code §§13120–13124.
19. Water Code §13160.
20. Water Code §§13600–13608.
21. Water Code §13140.
22. Water Code §13162.
23. Water Code §13163.
24. Water Code §13169.
25. Water Code §1320.
26. Water Code §13201.
27. Water Code §13260.
28. Water Code §13360.
29. Water Code §§13300–13303.
30. Water Code §§13331, 13350.
31. Water Code §13304.
32. Water Code §13301.
33. Water Code §13225.

34. Water Code §§13143, 13144.
35. Water Code §13145.
36. Water Code §13146.
37. Water Code §13142.
38. Water Code §§13240, 13241.
39. Water Code §13242.
40. Water Code §13243.
41. Water Code §§13244, 13245.
42. Water Code §13240.
43. Water Code §13225.
44. Water Code §§13600, 13604.
45. Water Code §13400 *et seq.*

Solid Waste Management Board

1. Keppel, "Nixon Decision to Stay Out of 'the Garbage Business' Leaves New State Board with More Mandate Than Funds," in *California Journal,* May 1973, at 162, 163.
2. Keppel, *supra,* at 164.
3. Keppel, *supra,* at 163.
4. Keppel, *supra.*
5. *Id.*
6. *Id.*
7. "Jurisdictional Disputes Slow Efforts To Give the State an Effective Role in Solid Waste Management," in *California Journal,* October 1971, at 279, 284.
8. Gov't Code §66701.
9. Gov't Code §66730.
10. Gov't Code §66740.
11. Gov't Code §66751.
12. Gov't Code §66731.
13. See, *e.g.,* Keppel, *supra.*
14. Gov't Code §66770.
15. Gov't Code §66771.
16. Gov't Code §66770, Health and Safety Code §4520.
17. Gov't Code §66770, 66773.
18. Gov't Code §66783.
19. Gov't Code §66780.
20. Gov't Code §66717.
21. Gov't Code §66780.
22. *Id.*
23. Gov't Code §66719.
24. Gov't Code §66720.
25. Gov't Code §66780.
26. *Id.*
27. *Id.*
28. Gov't Code §66751.
29. Gov't Code §66781.
30. Gov't Code §66732(d).
31. *Id.*
32. Keppel, *supra,* at 164.
33. Gov't Code §66730.
34. Gov't Code §66732 (a), (f), (g).
35. Gov't Code §66785.
36. *Id.*
37. *Id.*

38. *Id.*
39. Gov't Code §§66790, 66791.

State Energy Planning

Energy Resources Conservation and Development Commission

1. Pub. Res. Code §25000 *et seq.*
2. Pub. Res. Code §2851 *et seq.*
3. See Generally Rand, *California's Electric Quandary,* (1973).
4. Pub. Res. Code §25222.
5. Pub. Res. Code §25216.
6. Pub. Res. Code §25216.3.
7. Pub. Res. Code §25309 (a).
8. Pub. Res. Code §25309 (b).

State Natural Resources Planning

Coastal Zone Conservation Commission

1. Mogulof, "Land Use Determination in the California Coastal Zone, Intergovernmental and Other Conflicts," (unpublished, 1974).
2. Pub. Res. Code §27001.
3. Pub. Res. Code §27100.
4. Pub. Res. Code §27001 (b).
5. Pub. Res. Code §27001 (c).
6. Pub. Res. Code §27001 (d).
7. Pub. Res. Code §27201.
8. *Id.*
9. *Id.*
10. Pub. Res. Code §27202 (a),(b),(c).
11. Pub. Res. Code §27202 (d).
12. Mogulof, *supra.*
13. *Pub. Res. Code* §27240.
14. Pub. Res. Code §27241.
15. Pub. Res. Code §27302.
16. Pub. Res. Code §27304.
17. Pub. Res. Code §27320.
18. Coastal Zone Conservation Commission, *Annual Report* (1973).
19. Pub. Res. Code §27400.
20. Pub. Res. Code §27104.
21. See the BCDC Report.
22. Pub. Res. Code §27400.
23. *Id.*
24. Pub. Res. Code §27400 (a),(b),(c),(e)
25. Pub. Res. Code §27402.
26. Pub. Res. Code §27403.
27. Pub. Res. Code §27404. The California Supreme Court in *San Diego Regional Commission v. See the Sea, Ltd.,* 9 Cal. 3d 888, 109 Cal Rptr. 377 (1973)., has effectively expanded the exemption clause. The Court construed the language of section 27400, "wishing to perform any de-

velopment'' to mean ''wishing to commence any development.'' The majority argued that the voters approving Proposition 20 did not intend to establish a development moratorium, and that to require a permit for developments begun before February 1, 1973, would have resulted in a moratorium because of procedural delays. Thus, the exemption provision of section 27404 is effectively expanded to include any project on which substantial work was performed prior to February 1, 1973.

Department of Water Resources

1. Craig, ''California Water Law in Perspective,'' West's Ann. Water Code, (1971) at LXXXVI; Water Code §123.
2. Water Code §120.
3. Water Code §125.
4. Water Code §152.
5. Water Code §§156,122.
6. Water Code §161.
7. Water Code §162.
8. Water Code §165.
9. Water Code §164.
10. Water Code §163.
11. Water Code §161.5.
12. Craig, *supra,* at LXXX.
13. Water Code §10000.
14. Water Code §10004.
15. Water Code §10005.
16. Water Code §10004.
17. Water Code §10005.
18. Craig, *supra.*
19. Water Code §232.
20. Water Code §§11900, 11901.
21. Water Code §11910.
22. *Id.*
23. Water Code §11910.5.
24. Water Code §11911.
25. Water Code §12922.1
26. Water Code §12923.
27. Water Code §12923.1
28. Water Code §8410.
29. Water Code §8402 (f).
30. Water Code §8411.

B. Regional Planning Laws and Agencies

1. Regional Planning Enabling Laws

1. Gov't Code §66100 *et seq.*
2. Gov't Code §65060.7.
3. Gov't Code §65060.8.
4. Gov't Code §65060.1.
5. Gov't Code §65060.2.
6. Gov't Code §65065.1.
7. Gov't Code §§65601, 65604, and 65650.

2. Joint Powers Agreements

1. Gov't Code §6500 *et seq.*
2. Gov't Code §6580 *et seq.*
3. 40 U.S.C. §461 (b), as amended (1970).
4. U.S. Department of Housing and Urban Development, Circulars MPD 6415. 2A and 6415.3.
5. 42 U.S.C. §4231 (1970).
6. Gov't Code §6500.
7. Gov't Code §6503.
8. Gov't Code §6508.1. Emphasis added.
9. M. Marks and S. Taber, ''Prospects for Regional Planning in California,'' 4 Pacific L.J. 117, 125 (1972).
10. Urban Management Consultants, ''State of California Selected COG Evaluation Report,'' (May 15, 1974).
11. Pub. Res. Code §21000 *et seq.*
12. Title 14, California Administrative Code, §§15085, 15086, 15161.
13. 46 U.S.C. §4321 *et seq.*
14. W. Brussat, ''Realizing the Potentials of A-95,'' in *Planning 1971,* American Society of Planning Officials, (1971).
15. Federal Highway Act, §134; Federal Mass Transportation Act, §9; and California State Legislature, SB 325 and AB 69.
16. Association of Bay Area Governments, Bylaws, as amended Feb. 21, 1974.
17. Pub. Res. Code §27201.
18. Barton-Aschman Associates, *Toward a Unified Planning Program for the San Francisco Bay Area,* prepared ABAG, (September, 1970).
19. AB 2040, sponsored by Assemblyman Knox.
20. ABAG, Issue Paper No. 4, ''Formulation of Regional Growth Policy,'' (October, 1973).
21. *Oakwood at Madison, Inc. v. Township of Madison,* 117 N.J. Super. 11, 283 A.2d 353 (1971); *Appeal of Girsch,* 437 Pa. 237, 263 A.2d 395 (1970); *Scott v. City of Indian Wells,* 6 Cal. 3d. 541, 492 P.2d 1137, 99 Cal. Rptr. 745 (1972); *Construction Industry Association v. City of Petaluma,* 375 F. Supp. 574, (N.D. Cal. 1974), appeal pending.
22. Urban Management Consultants, *supra.*
23. Erie, Kirlin, Rabinowitz, ''Propositions on the Performance of Metropolitan Institutions,'' in *Reform of Metropolitan Governments,* (1972), at 34.
24. *Id.,* at 35.
25. *Id.,* at 37–38.

3. Regional Statutory Agencies

Metropolitan Transportation Commission

1. ''Local and Regional Planners Gain the Upper Hand as State Reorganizes to Meet Future Transit Needs,'' in *California Journal,* (March, 1973), at 84.
2. Department of Transportation, ''California Transportation Plan: Progress Report,'' April, 1974, at 18.

3. Gov't Code §66521.
4. Gov't Code §66504.
5. Gov't Code §66507.
6. Gov't Code §66509.
7. Gov't Code §66512.
8. Gov't Code §66520.
9. Gov't Code §66514.
10. Gov't Code §66518.

San Francisco Bay Conservation and Development Commission

1. Gov't Code §66601.
2. Gov't Code §66605.1.
3. Gov't Code §66602.
4. Gov't Code §66602.1.
5. Gov't Code §66605.
6. 53 Op. Atty. Gen. 285, (1970).
7. Gov't Code §66605.
8. Gov't Code §66620.
9. Gov't Code §§66630, 66630.l.
10. Gov't Code §66652.
11. The criteria used by a regulatory body as the basis for regulatory decisions may be challenged for being to vague and arbitrary. When BCDC legislation was first enacted, the Commission was to approve a permit according to these criteria: "(1) necessary to the health, safety or welfare of the public in the entire bay area, of (2) of such a nature that it will not adversely affect the comprehensive plan being prepared." This second criterion appears broad, but both criteria were upheld by the California Supreme Court, in *People ex rel. San Francisco Bay Conservation and Dev. Com. V. Town of Emeryville, 72 Cal. Rptr. 790, 786–789* and *Candlestick Properties, Inc. v. SFBCDC, 89 Cal. Rptr. 897, 905–906* (1970). In *Emeryville,* the court stated, "the objective sought to be achieved by the McAteer-Petris Act is depicted with remarkably clarity," citing Government Code §§66600, 66601, 66603, 66604. The criteria have since become better defined with adoption of the San Francisco Bay Plan.
12. Gov't Code §66653.
13. Gov't Code §66632 (b).
14. Gov't Code §66632 (a).
15. Gov't Code §66639.
16. Gov't Code §66655.
17. Gov't Code §66632.2.
18. Gov't Code §66660.1.
19. Gov't Code §66606.

Tahoe Regional Planning Agency

1. The discussion of the TRPA's legislative history is adapted from Ayer, "Water Quality Control at Lake Tahoe: Dissertation on Grasshopper Soup," 58 Cal. L.Rev. 1273, 1320.
2. Tahoe Regional Planning Compact, Art. 1 (a), (b), (Gov't Code §§66800, 66801).

3. Art. 1 (c).
4. *Id.*
5. Art. II (a).
6. Art. II (g).
7. Art. V (a).
8. Art. V (b).
9. *Id.*
10. Art. V (c).
11. Art. V (d).
12. Art. VI (a).
13. *Id.*
14. *Id.*
15. *Id.*
16. Gov't Code §67020.
17. Gov't Code §67103.
18. *Id.*
19. Art. VI (e).
20. Art. VI (f).

C. Local Planning Laws and Agencies

Local Planning Institutions and Performance

1. Note, "Parochialism on the Bay: An Analysis of Land Use Planning in the San Francisco Bay Area", 55 Cal. L. Rev. 836, 839, (1967).
2. Gov't Code §65400.
3. U.S. Environmental Protection Agency, Promoting Environmental Quality Through Urban Planning and Controls, (February, 1974).
4. D. Heeter, *Toward a More Effective Land-Use Guidance System,* (1969).
5. Gov't Code §65110.
6. Gov't Code §65101.
7. Gov't Code §65150.
8. Gov't Code §65304.
9. A. Perry, "The Local 'General Plan' in California", 9 San Diego L. Rev. 1, 18, (1971).
10. Gov't Code §65304.
11. Gov't Code §§65305, 65306.
12. Gov't Code §65563.
13. Gov't Code §65302.
14. *Id.*
15. Gov't Code §34211.1
16. Gov't Code §65300.
17. Gov't Code §65301.
18. Gov't Code §65302.
19. California Constitution, Art. XI, §11.
20. Cal. Const. Art. IV, §25.
21. Cal. Const. Art. XI, §§6 and 8.
22. Gov't Code §65700.
23. Gov't Code §65302.

24. Association of Bay Area Governments, *How to Implement Open Space Plans for the San Francisco Bay Area,* (1973), vol. 1, at 3–4.
25. Gov't Code §65302.
26. Gov't Code §65562.
27. Gov't Code §65564.
28. Gov't Code §65303.
29. Gov't Code §65302.2.
30. San Diego County Counsel, "Memorandum re: A.B. 1301," (Oct. 1, 1973).
31. Opinion of Legislative Counsel, Senate Daily Journal, (Dec. 1, 1972).
32. Gov't. Code §§65566, 65567.
33. Council on Intergovernmental Relations, *Local Planning in California–A Survey* (April, 1973).
34. Gov't Code §34211.1.
35. Gov't Code §65450.
36. D. Hagman, *California Zoning Practice,* §2.27.
37. Gov't Code §65450.1.
38. Gov't Code §65552.
39. Gov't Code §65304.
40. Gov't Code §65858.
41. Gov't Code §65351.
42. Gov't Code §65352.
43. Gov't Code §65355.
44. Gov't. Code §§65356, 65356.1.
45. Gov't Code §65360.
46. Gov't Code §65400.
47. *Id.*
48. A Perry, *supra,* at 1, 21.
49. Gov't Code §65361.
50. U.S. Environmental Protection Agency, *supra,* at 64–106.
51. Note, "Parochialism on the Bay," *supra,* at 836, 843.
52. R. Cranston, "The Why, Where and How of Broadened Public Participation in the Administrative Process," 60 Georgetown L. J. 525 (1972).
53. Contra Costa Planning Department, Planning Commission Files, 1974–75.
54. Gov't Code §65305–6.
55. M. Clawson and P. Hall, *Planning and Urban Growth,* 281, (1973).
56. Note, "Parochialism on the Bay," *supra,* at 836, 846.
57. Town and Country Planning Act of 1947.
58. Gov't Code §65567.
59. D. Hagman, *supra,* at 53.
60. Council on Intergovernmental Relations, *Local Planning in California–A Survey,* (April, 1973).
61. Association of Bay Area Governments, *Zoning and Growth,* (1973).
62. D. Hagman, *supra,* at 51.
63. M. Kaplan, *Urban Planning in the 1960's: A Design for Irrelevancy,* (1973).
64. A Perry, *supra,* at 1, 27.
65. Gov't Code §65860.
66. Council on Intergovernmental Relations, *supra.*

Local Planning Implementation

Zoning

1. *Village of Euclid v. Ambler Realty Co.,* 272 U.S. 365, 47 Sup. Ct. 114, 716 L. Ed. 303, (1926); *Consolidated Rock Products v. City of Los Angeles,* 57 Cal. 2d 515, 20 Cal. Rptr. 638, (1962).
2. Cal. Const. Art XI; Gov't Code §65850 *et seq.*
3. Gov't Code §65803.
4. Gov't Code §65800.
5. Gov't Code §65850 (a).
6. D. Hagman, *Urban Planning and Land Development Control Law,* §54.
7. Gov't Code §65850 (c).
8. D. Hagman, *supra,* §63.
9. Stanford Environmental Law Society, *California Land Use Primer,* (revised ed. 1975).
10. Gov't Code §65853.
11. Gov't Code §65852.
12. Gov't Code §65804.
13. Gov't Code §65855.
14. Gov't Code §§65856, 65857.
15. Gov't Code §65906.
16. D. Hagman, *supra,* §106.
17. Gov't Code §§65900, 901, 903.
18. Gov't Code §§65904, 902.
19. Gov't Code §65860 (a).
20. Gov't Code §65860 (a), (as amended 1972).
21. Council on Intergovernmental Relations, *General Plan Guidelines,* at 11–13, (Sept. 20, 1973); endorsed in Op. Atty. Gen. No. CV72/114 (a), at 7, (Jan. 15, 1975).
22. Gov't Code §65860 (b).
23. Gov't Code §65567.
24. 56 Ops. Atty. Gen. 404, (1973).
25. Gov't Code §65860 (c).

Subdivision Regulation

1. Gov't. Code §66473.5.
2. Senate Bill 977.
3. Gov't. Code §66424.
4. Gov't. Code §66411.
5. Gov't. Code §66426 (a)–(d).
6. Gov't. Code §§66426, 66428, and 66444–66450.
7. Gov't. Code §66411.
8. Gov't. Code §66418 (9).
9. Gov't. Code §66419.
10. Gov't. Code §66418 (3)–(7).
11. Gov't. Code §66421.
12. Gov't. Code §66451.1.
13. Gov't. Code §66451.
14. Gov't. Code §66415.
15. Gov't. Code §66455.5.
16. Gov't. Code §66455.5; Bus. & Prof. Code §11000.5.
17. Gov't. Code §12037.

18. Pub. Res. Code §21000 *et seq.*
19. Gov't. Code §66452.1.
20. Gov't. Code §66452.2.
21. Gov't. Code §66452.5.
22. Gov't. Code §§66452.6, 66456.
23. Gov't. Code §§66433–66443.
24. Gov't. Code §66458.
25. Gov't. Code §66475.
26. Gov't. Code §66478.
27. Gov't. Code §66477.
28. 4 Cal. 3d 633, 94 Cal. Rptr. 630, (1971).
29. Gov't. Code §§66478.11, .12.
30. Gov't. Code §66478.4.
31. Gov't. Code §66483.
32. Gov't. Code §66473.
33. Gov't. Code §66474.
34. Gov't. Code §66474.1.

Urban Renewal

1. Health & Safety Code §33000 *et seq.*
2. Health & Safety Code §33101.
3. Health & Safety Code §§33110, 33112.
4. Health & Safety Code §33200.
5. Health & Safety Code §33120.
6. Health & Safety Code §33210.
7. Health & Safety Code §33213.
8. Health & Safety Code §33212.
9. Health & Safety Code §33432.
10. Health & Safety Code §33220.
11. Health & Safety Code §33331.
12. Health & Safety Code §§33311, 33312.
13. Health & Safety Code §§33324.
14. Health & Safety Code §§33330–33341.
15. Health & Safety Code §33367.
16. Pub. Res. Code §2100 *et seq.*.
17. Health & Safety Code §33385.
18. Health & Safety Code §33371.
19. Health & Safety Code §33348.5.
20. Health & Safety Code §§33703, 33708.
21. Health & Safety Code §§33704–706, 33709.
22. Health & Safety Code §33713.
23. Health & Safety Code §§33714–33728.
24. C. Chiu, *California Low and Moderate Income Housing Laws,* §8.3, (January, 1974).

Housing Programs

1. Health & Safety Code §34240.
2. Health & Safety Code §34208.
3. Health & Safety Code §34209.
4. Health & Safety Code §34246.
5. Health & Safety Code §§34240.1, 34247.
6. C. Chiu, *supra* §5.2.
7. Health & Safety Code §34212.

8. Health & Safety Code §34326.
9. Health & Safety Code §34275.
10. Health & Safety Code §§34270, 34271.
11. Health & Safety Code §§34290, 34291.
12. Health & Safety Code §34284, 34285.
13. Health & Safety Code §§34500–34521.
14. Health & Safety Code §§34510–34513.
15. Health & Safety Code §37860, 37870.
16. Health & Safety Code §37850.
17. Health & Safety Code §37872.
18. Health & Safety Code §37861.

Growth Management

1. Stanford Environmental Law Society, *supra,* at 102–112. It should be noted that the extent of government power to control local growth has not yet been determined. In this developing area of the law, many issues remain to be resolved, including application [extension] of the "right to travel" to land use regulations (see *Construction Industry Ass'n v. City of Petaluma,* 375 F. Supp. 574 (N.D. Cal. 1974), appeal pending), the nature of compelling governmental justifications, and the validity of procedures for the enactment of growth control measures (see *Builders Ass'n v. Superior Court (City of San Jose),* decided by California Supreme Court in late December 1974 for which a written opinion has not yet been published; and *Associated Home Builders v. City of Livermore,* 41 Cal. App. 3d 677 (1974), appeal pending).

Property Taxation

1. Cal. Const. Art. XXVIII.
2. Revenue & Tax Code §421–425.
3. Gov't. Code §51200–51295.
4. Gov't. Code §51201 (o).
5. Gov't. Code §§51230, 51234.
6. Gov't. Code §51230.
7. Gov't. Code §51292.
8. Gov't. Code §§51240–51253.
9. Gov't. Code §§51290–51285.

California Environmental Quality Act

1. Pub. Res. Code §21000 *et seq.*
2. 42 U.S.C. §4321 *et seq.*
3. Pub. Res. Code §21001.
4. Pub. Res. Code §§21001, 21000.
5. Pub. Res. Code §21061, 21062.
6. Pub. Res. Code §21083; 14 Cal. Admin. Code §§15110–16041 (as amended April 12, 1974).
7. Pub. Res. Code §21063.
8. Pub. Res. Code §21065.
9. 8 Cal. 3d 1, 104 Cal. Rptr. 16 (1972), modified 8 Cal. 3d 247, 104 Cal. Rptr. 761 (1972).

10. Pub. Res. Code §21060.5.
11. 14 Cal. Admin. Code §15081 (b).
12. 14 Cal. Admin. Code §15081 (c).
13. 14 Cal. Admin. Code §15082.
14. Pub. Res. Code §21080, 21085.
15. 14 Cal. Admin. Code §15073.
16. Pub. Res. Code §21080 (a).
17. 14 Cal. Admin. Code §§15100–15112.
18. Pub. Res. Code §21102.
19. Pub. Res. Code §21100.
20. 14 Cal. Admin. Code §§15140–15147.
21. 14 Cal. Admin. Code §15143 (d), (g).
22. 14 Cal. Admin. Code §15147.
23. 14 Cal. Admin. Code §15147 (c).
24. 14 Cal. Admin. Code §15083.
25. 14 Cal. Admin. Code §15086.
26. Pub. Res. Code §21067; 14 Cal. Admin. Code §§15064, 15065.
27. 14 Cal. Admin. Code §15066.
28. 14 Cal. Admin. Code §15085 (a).
29. Pub. Res. Code §§21104, 21153.
30. 14 Cal. Admin. Code §§15164, 15165, 15160.
31. 14 Cal. Admin. Code §15161.
32. 14 Cal. Admin. Code §15061.
33. 14 Cal. Admin. Code §15085.

Local Agency Formation Commissions

1. R. LeGates, "California Local Agency Formation Commis-
sion," Institute of Government Studies, University of California at Berkeley, (1970).
2. Gov't. Code §54773 *et seq.*
3. Gov't. Code §56000 *et seq.*
4. Gov't. Code §54775.
5. Gov't. Code §54780.
6. Gov't. Code §54774.
7. *Id.*
8. *Id.*
9. Gov't. Code §54790.
10. Gov't. Code §54796.
11. Gov't. Code §54790.
12. Gov't. Code §56001.
13. Gov't. Code §56028.
14. See, LeGates, *supra,* and "LAFCO and Special Districts Control" 23 Hast. L. J. 913, (1972).
15. Gov't. Code §54775.
16. Gov't. Code §§54850–54863, 54726 *supra.*
17. Stanford Environmental Law Society, *supra.*

Airport Land Use Commissions

1. Public Utilities Code §21670.
2. Public Utilities Code §21005.
3. Public Utilities Code 21674 (a), (b).
4. Public Utilities Code §§21674 (c), 21676.
5. Public Utilities Code §21675.

INDEX